BEING

HUMAN

Being Human: A Question of Survival. Revised Edition.
by Steve Carlsson
ISBN: 978-0-9943290-5-9
Copyright © Steve Carlsson 2016
stevecar144@iinet.net.au
Printed by CreateSpace (USA)
Page design by eText Press

BEING HUMAN

A Question of Survival

Revised Edition

Steve Carlsson

Acknowledgment

Many years ago, I stood in a country field in the mid-summer heat full of excitement at the prospect of learning to fly a hang glider. I arrived in a 1980's six-litre, gas-guzzling Jeep Cherokee and waited impatiently for the others to turn up. Eventually, an old yellow VW Beetle trundled onto the field and after pleasantries had been exchanged, I had quite the conversation with the driver, Ray S. This chance meeting of two very different people proved to be the start of a long-lasting friendship which over the years has changed my life and turned my outlook on the world inside out.

Before meeting Ray, who to this day remains and avid and unapologetic environmentalist, I was a 'petrol-head'. Perhaps you know the type. If it had an internal combustion engine and went fast, it was the focus of my attention. In other words, our backgrounds and opinions were worlds apart.

Even so, over the years, Ray who I now consider a wise elder, in his unrelenting and pragmatic way, encouraged an appreciation of the merits of having less rather than more. He always speaks of the importance of the natural world and of appreciating non-material pursuits. However, he does so with a level of patience, humility and steadfastness not often seen these days. Also, Ray is one of a small number of people I have met who does not judge, who does not have high expectations and who rarely, if ever, holds a grudge. These are impressive qualities to find in a person, and with a certain envy lurking I strive to be more like him.

However, despite Ray's help, it has been a long journey, from petrol head to environmental advocate. For a long time my ego resisted change. I based my persistent arguments on scepticism (about climate change and the dangers of our economic systems) in order to protect my addiction to the material world.

Eventually, however, with Ray's help I realised the sceptic's position (which would have us believe that people do not cause climate change and that the economy is all important) is flawed. Their arguments fail when pitted against unbiased peer-reviewed scientific evidence and simple common sense as to our future if we ruin our planet. Consequently, I have left the sceptics' arguments behind other than to ardently work to debunk them.

And so I need to say thanks Ray for your words of wisdom over the years, and thanks to my mother for listening to endless drafts and rewrites of this book. In particular, thanks to my wife Diana who has financially supported me through the years it has taken to put the words of a wise elder on paper.

Preface to the Revised Edition

The human spirit does not enjoy being held captive - by anything or anyone. In fact, we strive to be free of oppression in any form, so much so, that the foundation of our modern democracies is the notion of freedom. And yet, most of us are utterly constrained by, and completely at the mercy of an out-of-control economic leviathan – the global economy. This was the focus of the first edition of Being Human: A Question of Survival and remains so for the revised edition, albeit the language is far more positive and encouraging and more solutions to the problems it discusses are offered. What remains unchanged though, is the idea that we need to free ourselves from an era of wage slavery at the hands of our economic masters.

Did I say wage slavery? Yes indeed, because being forced to give up our time to earn enough to make debt repayments is tantamount to slavery. Forty years ago, I had a mate who was the epitome of the new age slave. In fact, he still is to this day. His life is dominated by the debt cycle with little hope of being able to repay what he owes.

To protect his identity, let's call him Max. Max had some odd beliefs. For instance he was convinced that if he was running out of fuel in his car, that going faster, and I mean absolutely flat out, was more likely to get him home or to a fuel station simply because he would get there quicker. He actually believed there was less chance of the tank running dry before he got home if he drove like a mad man. Looking back, I suspect he was actually trying to outrun his personal problems. Speeding in a car was little more than his way of expressing his anger at the financial entanglement he hated so much. The law, the safety of other road users, common sense, even his own health had no relevance to his life. He squeezed every last ounce of performance from that car's engine everywhere he went as he tried to escape life itself.

Why would someone live like this? Why did he put himself and others at so much risk?

It's simple really. He was as angry as hell but his ego would not let him talk about it and so he had no way to resolve the anger boiling inside him. He really was a self-styled Mad Max. From listening to him over the years I'm convinced he was frustrated at being constrained by the expectations of the economic world.

However, Max was no scholar and did not understand these expectations or how to avoid them. He left school at fifteen and worked as a kitchen hand. He was married with two kids by eighteen. The kid was now a father himself and living on a casual wage, barely making ends meet. Ouch, what a recipe for stress!

As a result, financial pressures weighed on his mind every day and angry driving became his outlet from the emotional strain he was under. So how did he end up like this? What happened to Max to send him down this path? Well, that's what this book is really about. It's about how the Max's in our world are created to be wage slaves or in other words how they become the 'meat in the economic grinder'.

Economic orthodoxy preaches that 'more is better'. More growth, more industry, more jobs, more debt and, as an added bonus more stress. However, all these things also mean less environment, less health and less happiness.

This was indeed Max's world - stress, anger and resentment

ruled his days. He never saw through the economic manipulation in his life. He never worked out how to 'play the game' and so ended up just making ends meet every week. That's the real reason why he was angry. That's why he sped everywhere he went. He resented his circumstances but didn't know how to speak up in a way that would make things better.

That's sad because he and the millions like him have the potential to be much more than mere wage slaves. However, our economic system loves people like Max. Why? Because they help it survive. The Max's of this world are its fuel and The Economy always keeps its tank well and truly topped up. That is, the Global Economy is the ultimate consumer, but it does not consume goods and services. The economy consumes people's lives. It consumes the environment and it consumes our freedom.

Not all of us are in Max's situation, but many are and as many have Max-like aspects to their lives.

This revised edition of Being Human: A Question of Survival is my attempt to explain how and why we might rethink the way we live so that we can enjoy real freedom instead of simply trying to survive the economic jungle.

I say, 'Let's stop being clones or even distant relatives of Mad Max and take back control of our destiny and enjoy some real freedom.'

Contents

Ten Paradoxes of the Economic Paradigm

The following paradoxes may paint a bleak and cynical picture of society, but they are intended as an indictment of the economic imperative and how it affects our lives, not of people per se. Also, addressing these ten conflicting 'causes and effects' would rid our world of much unhappiness and conflict which in itself is certainly more positive than bleak. However, the burning *question of survival* to answer is: 'Do we have what it takes to make a start?' The answer to that question comes in the chapters which follow.

1. Civilised people speak of 'the need to take the moral high ground' – but those same people have no intention of occupying it because that would require a fundamental change to how we do 'business'.

2. Human intent appears far nobler when seen from within.

3. We want to be happy and we work hard toward that goal, but, at the same time create discontent without much effort and then wallow in it.

4. Politicians are the butt of many jokes and rebukes, but we vote for them just the same.

5. Violence, in all its forms, is the cornerstone of civilisation.

6. We speak of 'tolerance and compassion' and then wreak havoc on anyone who disagrees with us.

7. Freedom underpins democracy, yet it requires a myriad of

laws backed by armed forces to coerce populations into accepting it is being delivered.

8. We love our kids so much that we send them to economic training camps, posing as education, for all the years they are too young to run away from us. When they are old enough, they become us.

9. We desperately want to be validated by others and so we are incredibly gregarious, yet we condone all manner of environmental vandalism as we build problem riddled cities to live in.

10. We strive to be alive and we strive to be healthy, but we seem unable to stop producing and consuming the junk products that poison us, our children, and our world.

Part One

Insight

Chapter One

Turning Point

Twenty something years ago during a debate about whether advances in technology can undo the damage done to our environment, a good friend and verbal sparring partner made the following comment. 'Our faith in economic activity to deliver a sustainable future is nothing more than an illusion.'

He went on to say, 'We live in denial about the impact technology is having on our world.' He also suggested, 'politicians and economists speak of sustainability and finding a balance between environmental protection and economic growth, but our natural world continues to be in a state of decline.' He then added, 'we go about our daily lives as if there will be some kind of fairy tale ending to the climate change we are causing.'

Those long ago comments inspired a great deal of debate because at the time I was a sceptic of human caused climate change, and predictably, my ego erupted at an apparent attack on my very economically centred lifestyle. However, over time and after much heated debate, it became obvious I was not a sceptic at all. I was actually in complete denial of the peer reviewed scientific evidence telling us to care for our planet or face dire consequences. The realisation that I had based my arguments on the blatantly misleading claims of a handful of fossil fuel industry funded sceptics sent my ego into overdrive. It did so because I had to admit to the damage I was doing and deal with the illusion I had been living under for so many years. That is, the illusion that my economic pursuits were more important than the health of our environment. It was quite a revelation and changing my views took several years.

In fact, to this day the struggle to avoid again being drawn into the world of economic rationalism requires constant vigilance. That's because, firstly, the man made things of this world are attractive, and secondly, because of how many years one is exposed to social conditioning telling us that unbridled consumption of resources is perfectly reasonable - It's not, not if we want a healthy biosphere for the future.

Regardless of the challenges my sparring partners' words carried with them, his fundamental argument was quite simple: What we are doing to our planet and each other in the name of economic growth, is not justifiable, it's not reasonable or healthy, and it's certainly not civilised. Nor is it founded on the moral high ground. It's not ethical or sustainable. Wow! That's quite a statement to digest. However, whether one accepts his argument or not, the difficulty with saying such things is that our economic growth model will feel important and relevant, and more often, completely essential to our lives, no matter how dire the threat it represents may be. In fact, many people laugh or scoff at the idea that we might be over doing economic activity. Instead, many will say more economic activity is needed in order to develop solutions to the environ-mental dangers we face, rather than seeing the need to slow down.

To begin exploring why economic activity has become so central to our lives, we need to critically examine two of its foundations.

Capitalism vs The Free Market Economy

A blend of capitalism and free market economics dominate modern Western societies. The result is an economic structure which raises troublesome questions. For instance, 'Is economic activity, which we tend to generically label as 'economics', really delivering improved human welfare, and, are our expectations about consuming the stuff of economic activity defensible and safe or are they quite dangerous?' Also, can we see the social justice and social equity espoused by defenders of modern Western democracies, actually being delivered? The answer has to be no if we consider the vast numbers of economically disadvantaged people in our world, let alone, the crime, suffering and exploitation we all know exists in far too greater volumes. This situation brings into question our values, attitudes and beliefs as a modern civilised people whose aim is peace and social stability. That is, why do we support such a problematic way of organising economic transactions?

The reason a challenge can be mounted against our civility is that capitalism allows for the ownership of the means of production. This in turn creates wealth and power hierarchies, in which, wealth is centralised because fairness in trade is biased toward the owners of the means of production. In simple terms, these hierarchies are a 'winners and losers' trading environment. Meaning one side of each trade *must be* less satisfied than the other for wealth to move upward: The obvious result being the creation of the haves and the have-nots.

Conversely, under an ideal free market economy buyers and sellers *agree* on prices thus both parties can be happy with the outcome of a transaction. Whilst this is a gross oversimplification of these nebulous concepts, it is useful as a launching point for a discussion of what amounts to a not so covert takeover of the foundation stones of modern Western societies.

Democracy, Freedom and Justice Operate for our Benefit

Despite rhetoric to the contrary, these three cornerstones of modern Western civilisation have been well and truly hijacked by the economic imperative. In fact, what we live with today are mere ghosts of their designers' intent. If that's true, and the entire premise of this book is to the affirmative, we need to understand what happened to democracy, freedom and justice.

The simple answer is that capitalism happened. Capitalism, which I use interchangeably with neoliberalism, has morphed democracy, freedom and justice into tools of the corporation: into tools of the economic machine. Meaning, today every aspect of democracy, freedom and justice revolves around 'money' in one way or another and this erodes, if not completely makes a mockery of, these three primary pillars of Western society.

The original intent of **democracy** was that governments would represent people's opinions. That's quite obvious, yes? Well...no. In fact, even that simple concept is hotly debated. For instance, some say the Founding Fathers created the US Constitution with benevolence and the benefit of the community at heart. Conversely, others point to Benjamin Franklin, Thomas Jefferson, George Washington and their cohort and see a group of businessmen more interested in protecting their wealth than founding a real democracy. They decided (in their own interest) that the people were not capable of managing the affairs of the nation and so took it upon themselves to divest the general population of that responsibility and right. In other words, they created a hierarchy which *only appears* to represent *the people's* opinion.

Similarly, any notion of **freedom** to 'do as we please' has been replaced by a quasi freedom which amounts to little more than endless participation in the economic system of wealth centralisation. Ironically, freedom is now delivered within a vast array of rules and regulations, usually backed up by monetary fines and even prison sentences! Even more insidiously, society has been addicted to affluence by a persistent mantra of money worship.

And as for **justice**, it is only available through wealth. For instance, engaging even an average lawyer to defend one's rights is too expensive for many people. And having access to the ear of politicians is equally problematic given the time constraints of employment and other responsibilities.

Regardless, it seems reasonable to accept that communities need a central organisational structure to guide, plan and administer the affairs of large numbers of people, just as children need parents to set their boundaries. But today's democratic governments do not represent the peoples' interests as per the original intent of democracy. Nor are governments as powerful as they once were.

Instead, these days many wealthy businesses have capital resources which allow influence far exceeding that of governments. The result is that governments have effectively lost control of social and business policy direction. Also, lost in this process, are the people's voices and the community driven policies we need to address social issues.

For instance, 'beneficial-to-business-policies' are often deployed regardless of the outcome of elections or how the people voted. It is saddening that the aspirations of inanimate corporate entities now effectively design social policy through their influence on governments. 'Mission statements' and 'KPI's' have come to surmount the will of the voting majority and the aspirations of elected politicians who supposedly 'govern' the corporations.

How did this come about? How have these business entities (which only exist because of corporate law) come to determine how real people live their lives?

The process started millions of years ago when our ancestors realised that having more was beneficial. In that distant past, it felt pleasant to be successful at gathering food etc, and importantly, the ability to have extra provided us with an advantage over the non-human world. And of course, *having enough* was essential to our survival.

In more recent times, we've been honing our business practices to ensure wealth generation, which is the modern day version of 'having more', never ceases. However, the environmental cost has been largely ignored. Thus, our genetic advantage, that is, our superior intellect which ensured we had enough as nomadic hunter gatherers, is now working against us as we over-consume.

In the past couple of hundred years, corporate entities have been able to accumulate so much wealth and power that they can effectively steer entire nations via their influence over governments and by influencing voters. Yes, *we* created the corporate leviathans to provide more of everything in our quest to be happier and more comfortable. But now we are fighting for survival as economic activity destroys our biosphere in the quest for ever greater profits.

And yet, to 'want more' underpins how we stay alive. It is our way of satisfying our hunger, thirst and our need for companionship. It also encapsulates how we are different to every other species that has ever lived on planet Earth. Wanting more than we really need truly is a uniquely human trait. Other creatures, such as squirrels store supplies to see them through a winter. We, on the other hand seem hell bent on consuming for no other reason than, we can.

Clearly, wanting enough is incredibly human, incredibly reasonable and absolutely necessary. But wanting vastly more than we need is the social, economic and cultural threat of our era. It's behind every form of conflict in our world. It always has been, and ultimately, it's the one thing we need to change about our way of life. However, we must ask the question: will accepting less be easier said than done? Absolutely it will, but it's not impossible and it *is* the new environmental imperative we need to come to grips with.

Fortunately, understanding how to curb our wants and become content with enough is also the path to personal freedom and greater happiness. It is where democracy was supposed to take us. And, it is what corporations could deliver if we 'retooled' them to meet the goal of raising human welfare. That is, the welfare of all humans, not just the few who through skill or plain luck sit atop the wealth pyramid.

I also suggest, the reasons for the many complaints about life I hear from day to day are not that we don't have enough, but rather, the reasons are that we have come to dislike the level of energy and effort needed to negotiate what we generically call 'the economy'. The economy is unpredictable, predatory, volatile and soulless. It represents everything we humans are supposedly evolving away from. In this sense, we are truly living under an illusion when we say corporate economic activity provides for our welfare.

Then, why do we support the economic machine so eagerly? Beyond all the obvious mechanical issues (such as earning an income to spend on necessities), it is because of our evolution. Our minds are primed to seek out the resources needed to keep us alive, but it is clear that we have far overstepped that mark. In other words, we have replaced a simple drive 'to survive', with the illogical economic imperative of 'more, more, more' for no other reason than that is what we are taught to do from the moment of our birth. And, it will be argued that our education system is little more than a training ground to this end.

Sure, seeking out resources is written into our DNA, but we allegedly have an intellect designed to deal with our leftover primal urges. The problem in my view is that we've modelled our economic systems on our primal wants rather than our intellectual needs. And it seems obvious our economic pursuits don't satisfy our yearning to be intellectually stimulated and socially connected, meaning we have the basis for amazing social and economic change should we accept the challenge.

Evidently also, we seem happy ignoring the reality that our resources are finite and will run out. Still, knowing that our addiction to having more isn't reasonable or sustainable seems to be losing the battle against our inner urge to accumulate.

Thus, it is how we manage our endless wants that has become the modern *question of survival* for humanity.

The first half of this book sets out my perspective on a host of issues, not the least of which is an attempt to expose and challenge the economic rationalist thinking that leads us to financial hardship. So much so that, even when we achieve economic success, there is too much stress and discontent associated with doing so.

The economic paradigm demands that we pursue more of everything even when the desire to work hard to repay our economic or environmental debt is long gone. And so, many people find themselves chasing more no matter how distasteful the journey becomes; no matter what the cost in terms of life energy, happiness or the environment.

The following chapters also look at how we try to utilise our outmoded primal survival impulses to 'get ahead' in an unemotional, technological world in which there are corporations with a deep and well-funded understanding of how to exploit our desires. The outcome is discontent, stress and financial entanglement.

This well planned and expertly executed exploitation sees us fall into the 'consumer trap', something our evolution has not prepared us for. To win the battle we need to deploy our intellect and have the courage to resist our primal emotions.

To assist in this struggle, in the latter chapters I set out an array of structural changes to our social fabric (suggested by imminently more qualified thinkers than I) aimed at making 'the economy' our servant again instead of it being the other way around.

I tackle some tough and personal questions: Questions about our ego, our wilfulness and our biological programming. Other environmental writers, have in my view, largely overlooked a somewhat simple concept when tackling the environment versus the economy debate, namely, the idea that we simply don't like being told what to do! Can our egos allow us to listen to the voice of reason? Can we win the battle against our primal human desires? Can intellect prevail?

I hope so for all our sakes.

In fact, I ask, 'What the heck is wrong with being told what to do?' It happens in every aspect of our lives. Every law we have created tells us what to do in one way or another. And yet we are quick to say, 'Don't tell me not to destroy the environment in the pursuit of economic wealth. I don't want to hear it.'

There it is, 'I want...' when the real issue is that we don't have the luxury of so much choice. Not if we are to protect our future prosperity (environmental or economic), our kid's futures or our very survival.

Chapter Two

What the Heck is Life all About?

I started to wrestle with the question, 'what the heck is life all about' many years ago. At that time, I'd just returned to work from several weeks of annual leave. The welcome back conversation with my boss was brief.

'How are you, Steve? All refreshed and ready to work?' he asked.

My answer was a genuine Freudian slip.

'Actually no,' I replied before I could stop myself. Oops! The cat was out of the bag. I mumbled something like, 'I don't think I can do this anymore.'

Three days later I was unemployed. I hadn't intended to resign on that day but there it was.

A few days before those life changing words, I was sitting on a beach trying to relax and forget about selling software. I needed to re-energise and find some enthusiasm for going back to work. Quite by chance, I met a traveller on that beach. We talked for a while and his story sounded familiar. He'd recently left his job for much the same reasons I was contemplating doing so. Like me he'd felt trapped; as if his life was under someone else's control. Maybe his story gave me the confidence to resign and maybe not; but either way I know now my resignation was inevitable.

Resigning with no prospect of a future income might seem reckless, but I had a plan of sorts. I'd scrimped and saved and paid out my housing finance. Yep, that was it. A one-line plan which read, become 'debt free' and quit. At best the plan was inadequate and yet the relief that came with it was amazing.

As I recall, for several weeks I wondered what I was going to do for a job. I remember sitting at a beach side cafe with a mate talking it over. He told me he'd recently paid two hundred and fifty dollars to have the gutters cleared of leaves on his second floor apartment. At the time, two hundred and fifty dollars was a lot of money for a few hours work. That story saw me purchase an extension ladder, place a 'handyman' advertisement in the local paper and within three weeks I had more work than I could handle.

That experience led me to ask, 'Why do we work at jobs we don't like?' And, 'Why do we fear not having money?' The answers seemed to relate to expectations more than anything else. If I'd set my sights on another sales job, a job I didn't want, I would have feared quitting again and work stress would have followed me around. Turning to more labour oriented work, something I enjoyed even though it lacked income security, took the fear away. Even so, it meant I had to alter my financial plans for the future because I no longer automatically qualified for bank finance.

With this in mind, I worked hard to make sure my expectations didn't slip back to what they were: excessive, expensive and ego-driven. Especially ego driven. It seems blatantly obvious to say our egos are stroked by earning money, or that our self-image is exploited by media exposure telling us to have ever higher expectations or for that matter any messages about possessions, status or affluence. The truth is, these messages are the life blood of the economy and our acceptance of economic propaganda is encouraged and nurtured by our education system throughout our formative years.

That is why, in my view, education is little more than a training ground for consumerism. And, it is that argument, and also the suggestion that we might work to protect our kids from such influences, which underpins much of what follows.

Looking at the effect of the media on society generally, it's pretty obvious that we take having ever more unnecessary products and services (not the necessities for staying alive) for granted. What we tend to deny or perhaps simply not think about though, is that this means we have to sacrifice so much of our life energy to earning the enormous amounts of money needed to pay for the stuff of this world. For instance, bringing running water to our homes seems reasonable despite the environmental and financial cost.

Understandably, few would question piped water. Nevertheless, when dams run dry because water is so easy and cheap to consume, we find solutions like desalination rather than reducing consumption. The extra cost pushes up our water bills and we complain about them but usually don't consider the real cause. The real cause is inculcation into an excessive way of life. In the present context, inculcation refers to the process of normalising our acceptance of over-consumption of all re-sources, not just water.

And it is critical to say, the impact of desalination on our environment does not even rate a mention in our media. Instead, the merits of such projects are highlighted and the infrastructure paraded as a great achievement.

This is my gripe: that we deny the reality of our circum-stances in favour of band-aid solutions destined to fail. The danger is that by the time we do see the trap it will be too late to turn back. Sadly, we blindly accept nothing but nothing can be allowed to slow our so-called progress. That is, the progress we label 'economic growth' which includes the building of desalination plants and a raft of other obscenely expensive infrastructure projects.

The great tragedy of our times is that supporters of economic growth deny the reality that resources are finite preferring to believe technology will find solutions to its own problems.

An all too common response to pointing an accusing finger at environmentally costly infrastructure is, '...as long as the world survives until I die, I don't care.' Comments like this confirm that we really have been brainwashed into accepting endless economic growth is good: that it represents progress. However, as the impossibility of infinite growth (because our planet *is* finite) becomes clearer, economic volatility caused by fear and trepidation has increased exponentially and will only get worse.

Rather than accepting the inevitability of having to slow down, we throw ever more of our dwindling resources into the economic fires. That's why, these days, I question our dependence on economic activity/money and ask: 'Is it really meeting our expectations? Is economic activity really raising the welfare of people?' The contradiction seems obvious if one simply looks at the vast array of problems in our world that can be explained by dubious economic activity. Of course, to reduce that activity is to challenge our biological drive to have more and our biology will be, to say the least, difficult to overcome. Given this, we need to ask, 'Is wanting more regardless of the costs inescapably a part of human nature? Are we doomed by our evolution on this front? The answer has to be, 'No, absolutely not because we have an intellect capable of seeing the right choices.'

However, too often where we could make intellectual choices we tend not to in favour of giving into our desires. Equally, it is also true that nature does not respect our human desires and can only sustainably satisfy our basic needs for food, water, shelter and a mate. It is our desire to extract (and transform) vastly more than the basics which is ruining the natural systems we rely on for life. Hence, we have a decision to make. Do we slow down and make our resources last, or use them hurriedly and risk the consequences? For too long we have been told the latter is sustainable. This is where our media and education systems are failing us.

Perhaps it's simply naive to expect advertisements telling us that 'happiness comes from wealth,' should be based on fact and be truthful, or that, trust and integrity are the fundamentals of our allegedly civilised society. And yet, a civilised society is what we are told our democratic governments have delivered. I suggest then, if we look around and find problems with the level of civility in our world, perhaps the kernel of those issues is right in front of us each time we consume the ideology of our economic imperative: That ideology being delivered by media content telling us lies about the safety, sustainability or benefits of having more of the unnecessary products and services we don't need, but certainly want. And of course, in order to have these items we have been convinced that we need money.

Sadly, one has to accept there are day-to-day reasons for acquiring at least some money, namely to have food water and shelter, but that belief only prevails because these things are now owned. Alternatively, instead of working to pay for the basics like water, we could make subsistence food, water and shelter free. In return, each person would provide an amount of labour per week to produce them. Then, the rest of our time, our personal time, could be devoted to working for luxuries should we choose to do so.

It may sound crazy (to make the basics free) but is it? Or perhaps, have we just forgotten that food, water and shelter are basic human rights and that we should have free access to them? We did once, so why not again?

Further, with our long ago non-money heritage in mind, I have to ask, 'Why do our societies cling to currencies as a means of exchange when we know how much trouble they bring?' After all, we put food on the cave floor for eons before we had money. What's more, we didn't need a mortgage to pay for the cave or a house until very recent times.

Taking another leap, we can ask, 'Why do our modern societies claim to provide justice, civility, democracy and social equity while the observable evidence demonstrates a massive lack of delivery. Given money is the likely cause, why do we persist with a monetary system which constantly undermines the key principles of modern Western societies? It seems there is a massive economic contradiction here, because the point of economic growth is to centralise wealth not to spread it around. One can't centralise wealth and increase the welfare of the entire population at the same time. These are mutually exclusive activities. Nevertheless, economic and political rhetoric suggests welfare for all is the goal of our communities.

Logically, there has to be an end point to wealth centralisation. That point comes when the use of labour is no longer required to produce goods, or at least when the need for labour is reduced to a tiny fraction of what it is today. In other words, if there is no labour to profit from wealth can no longer be centralised. The pity is that by the time that end point comes, all the wealth will have already been centralised and at that time capitalism will end.

In fact, this process has already started. Automation associated with the machine age is already reducing the need for labour and it will move to near zero in the short term. The final automation is artificial intelligence. When that technology is operational on a broad scale, the need for people in the workplace will approach zero.

Also, our population is ageing meaning the time will come when there are many more unemployed than working people. For instance, a recent media report stated that two and a half thousand journalists in Australia lost their jobs because Google and Facebook have automated the delivery of news content. Other examples include the effects of automation on: motor vehicle manufacturing, steel production, mining and agriculture. According to several futurists, as this trend continues across all industries, a subsistence income will have to be provided to avoid masses of people starving and economies collapsing. Yuval Noah Harari (in Homo Deus) and Paul Mason (in Postcapitalism) describe how this time is very near. Calum Chase (in The Economic Singularity) takes this concept further and discusses how negative taxation would provide a minimum wage. The idea of tax offices paying people rather than collecting taxes may seem fantastical today, but it is recognised by many futurists as the only workable means to ensure we all have at least a subsistence income in a largely automated world where people are no longer required to work.

However, that is all speculation for the time being, and returning to the here and now, many people still earn a living and a vast array of economic transactions take wealth from one person and transfer it to another. Those with the most money, make the most money and the rest squabble over the scraps. There is no equity or justice in such an economic model. If democracy and justice exist as described in text books and dictionaries, why do the poor have to beg for food? Why are so many people in prisons? Why is there so much suffering in our world? The least palatable answer is that economic activity operates purely in order to make profits-for-the-wealthy possible. This is the crux of the issue. We mostly work to prop up the wealth pyramid, not for the betterment of our state of mind or each other or the masses, but for the benefit of the pyramid itself, and it clearly and obviously favours those sitting at its zenith.

So overwhelmingly complete is social conditioning (inculcation) that by the time we reach adulthood, we need only the hint of an opportunity to rise to the top of the wealth pyramid to keep us working and aspiring, despite the reality that ninety-nine point nine per cent of us won't make it.

So overwhelmingly complete is the socialisation process, most of us don't even know it has already happened to us or is happening to our kids. We just accept that 'life's like that' and carry on working and striving regardless of the outcome.

By way of an explanation for this enduring process, we might have to accept as I hear so often, money is an expression of our underlying attitudes, beliefs and values as human beings: That our world economic situation is a fait accompli. If that's true, what does it say about us? Considering what we do in the name of wealth creation, how can we say we are civilised at all? But, there is a problem with saying 'money is the root of all evil'. For that saying to be true, money, and how we go about obtaining it, must attest to who and what we are and it is clear we are not all evil. Rather, the truth is that our darker primal human emotions are nourished and encouraged by what we see in our media and other sources of inspiration. Despite this observation, it remains true that the higher side of humanity is not interested in money, it's more intellectual. Our intellectual side seeks social connectedness and fulfilment. Money just happens to get in the way. Unfortunately, the two sides of us do battle every day and this is the source of conflict and social darkness in our world.

Fairness
The original intent of money was to create fairness in trade. However, the outcome has been something else.

The advent of currency has led to a global civilisation sorted, tiered and individually valued according to wealth. This has proved to be a dangerous war-torn strategy and our history of conflict over money speaks for itself.

Also, our global industrial economic system is now enormously specialised. I.e. we rely too heavily on greenhouse gas based energy, and problematically, our understanding of the past tells us that overly specialised species become extinct far more quickly than generalists. Moreover, what we have done is replace knowledge of how to live sustainably, which has intrinsic value, with a system of 'perceived' value, which allows little more than ivory tower building.

The outcome, of reducing the value of people to a notional number as we have done methodically and persistently by valuing wealth creation, has been conflict between individuals and populations who might otherwise be able to get along. How has this economic system been able to persist? It has because we brainwash each new generation to strive to sit atop the wealth pyramid by sending them to school where they learn the ways of the economic imperative.

It seems our modern day economic ideology is an ongoing expression of our distant history: a history in which competition and predation decided how we lived or died. In modern times, we compete for wealth with economic 'clubs' and financial 'spears' and see this as normal. It's not normal though, because the natural systems around us cannot and do not operate with any awareness of perceived value. I have to ask then, 'What is progressive about creating and exacerbating conflict by labelling people according to their affluence?' It may be the norm we are accustomed to, but it's not civilised or peaceful or likely to serve us well in the long term. In fact, if we consider the hardships people have and still suffer, we can say the so-called economic norm has never served us well.

It has been said that we work to reach a level of affluence we are happy with and stop there. But I don't think that's true either. Not really. Not if we're honest. If the opportunity arises, each of us is more likely to acquire more rather than stop accumulating or be happy with having less. More often, we are forced by circumstance to accept a level of wealth which is decided by the forces of competition and conflict.

Then at this point we can ask, 'does money create fairness in trade as per its original intent?' The observable evidence of social injustice and wealth inequity says the answer must be, 'No.' Further, it seems more accurate to say all we really have is an opportunity to compete within the wealth centralisation contest, and that fairness itself, is a myth.

Rat Race
Endlessly chasing more consigns us to living in an economic labyrinth. We might negotiate and escape the maze here and there, but we rarely do so in a way that leads to real freedom from the confines we are locked into once financial entanglement occurs. That is, once debt and expectations about affluence take hold. Can we actually leave these pursuits behind? Can we, in fact, would we even want to leave the economic rat

race? I suspect the answers to these questions depend on where we sit in the wealth pyramid and how much energy we have for the wealth contest.

Nevertheless, the means to escaping financial entanglement has to be a transformation of economic activity so that it works for us instead of endlessly powering the treadmill for the benefit of those sitting atop the pyramid. On this front, we could start by appreciating the massive amount of energy we put into acquiring wealth only to give it away again in the form of bills and payments. And if working and paying seems reasonable, if working to get wealthy still seems right and logical, be mindful that ultimately there is an ugly environmental end point to the economic treadmill. It will come when our resources give out. Not the ores and grains, but the biosphere we rely on for life itself.

On that front, attempting to raise the wealth level of an entire planet as we do now seems quite dysfunctional, illogical, unachievable and irresponsible, especially if we consider the environmental cost of delivering products and services to seven billion or more people. But hell, who cares about the environment, right? As long as we have money, all is good, yes? Well, no, because many of us are not happy, content, or satisfied with life. Work stress is prevalent in modern Western societies regardless of affluence. It does seem chasing wealth is not making us happier. Perhaps then we need to reconsider the set of values we live by.

Values

What we are doing to our natural world cannot be paid for with money. Once a species or habitat or resource is gone, that's it. Once an old growth forest is gone there's no bringing it back. At least not yet, but our science community is working on the genetic technology to overcome that problem.

Really? Seriously? I don't believe that strategy has a snow-ball's chance in Hell of working, partly because personal profiteering will get in the way. But moreover, one has to ask: 'How do we recreate the bewildering array of biodiversity found in a forest or an ocean?' In fact, the task is so difficult that we are planning to terra-form Mars because doing that seems more possible, manageable, and realistic than changing how our kind lives on Earth so as to save a simple grove of trees standing in the way of progress. That reality is astounding. It should be enough to scare us all into changing our ways. But it doesn't because we are too busy going to work each day. It seems money is more valued than the very biosphere we rely on for life itself.

On a different environmental note, there are seven hundred species of bacteria in our mouths and we understand less about them than flying to Mars or the Moon. That's astounding! Even so, we will profit financially by destroying bacteria with mouthwash, and, I suspect, right up to the day the last species dies out we will still have money. Right up to the last minute before we go to Mars because the earth is ruined, the last few people will be clutching a gold bar or dollar bill. They will be trying to find a way to smuggle a stash of cash aboard the spaceship even though the extra weight might cause a failed lift off. But hell, who cares, right? Who cares, as long as we are financially secure?

The really scary aspect of all of this is right under our noses. No, it's not the smell of mouthwash. It is that we accept the death of our planet is a part of profit making. Is this the hallmark of a civilised and modern people though? I can't convince myself it is.

Alarm

Our natural world is disappearing at an alarming rate, but we don't seem to care enough to stop the damage. Why is this so? I suspect it's simply because stopping would mean contemplating a reduced money flow. Looked at this way, it really does seem that misguided self-interest reigns in our world. And, the really staggering aspect is, we don't mind at all. We *say* we do, but we don't change *what* we do. In other words, in our modern economic religion a short-term money supply is more important than a supply of healthy natural resources. Bollocks! Money may be more valued by people, but to say money is more important is delusional.

Money is only possible if the environment remains enriched and healthy. Any thought to the contrary is a fantasy, but we don't see it that way because the damage happens too slowly to alarm us.

Perhaps the real source of our life stress arising from money worries is that we fear *being the poor* more than we fear how we will be affected when Mother Nature eventually has a breakdown caused by our recalcitrance. Let's face it; this is the fundamental basis of most economic rhetoric: be wealthy or be seen as losers so much so that, nowadays, almost exclusively, our self-image is based on our wealth. But, of course, money poverty is nothing compared to environmental poverty and it should be obvious the latter is a situation from which there is no fiscal recovery for our species.

Nevertheless, and without relenting, our daily economic activity goes on as if there were no danger. Our global actions suggest how to acquire our next investment property, car, toaster or mobile phone is more important than the environment we live in. Even so, these are only our monetary priorities and they ignore our biological needs. The bottom line is that, if we feel trapped by employment, debt, or financial entanglement generally, it's because we choose to participate in such a dangerous system. And, deep down, we know it's not sustainable but don't want to be alone in taking a stand. Of course, if we all think this way, there will be no stand.

Escape

To escape the money trap is simple enough. All one has to do is rethink one's expectations. It helps to get our ego under control as well and to make things easier, we might shift some of our thinking to the personal impact we are having on the planet.

These are the things this book is really about. It could bang on about environmental damage and statistics about seal pups and receding glaciers, however, that approach has been done to death and has not worked. I suspect what we really want to read is something allowing us to see through the illusions and distractions our ministers of economic dogma have preached for so many years.

It's interesting, isn't it? Ministers of the church and Ministers of Government. But those people are lightweights compared to the real culprits - Ministers of Corporations. And yet, even they are only guardians of the books of faith; of the documents of incorporation and the laws that protect them.

Corporations today are entities enabled by documents, laws and mission statements, not by people. That's because people die but corporations must live on, meaning people are just caretakers of the economic faith for a short time. In effect we have become the minions of the leviathans we originally created to serve us and raise our welfare. Sadly now our welfare comes second to that of the corporation.

Corporate entities pay tax and can be taken to court while

the people behind the corporations remain largely protected by the entity itself. Also interesting is that if kids speak of imaginary friends we take them to psychologists. Corporations are non-thinking, unemotional automatons that exist only on paper. They run our lives but they don't actually exist anywhere. Sure, we can see where they have been, but please tell me where to go to speak to a corporation. At best, we can try to approach its representatives. That is, we can speak to its minions who come and go while the brand logo and impact on humanity persists. Then, it appears that the rise of the machines depicted in the Terminator movies has nothing on corporations. Like the Terminator, we created them and unleashed them on our planet, and now corporations have taken over.

Corporations don't know we exist and that scares the heck out of me and no psychologist specialising in imaginary friends can help defend us from them.

Vision

The legal and mechanical means to disempower corporations and the stranglehold the economic paradigm has over us are presented in later chapters. For now the focus is on our motivation to go down that path. To start this process requires some introspection, some soul-searching, some honesty, maturity and vision. Bollocks! All it takes is to let go of wanting to be wealthier than the next person. This is the path to personal freedom that democracy promised, but failed to deliver. In other words, the notion that corporations deliver welfare and prosperity is the mantra of economic rationalists, and it's just bollocks! If what they deliver degrades our daily experience of life, degrades the environment and consigns us to a life of debt, how can that be considered an increase in welfare?

And, not so long ago, just a few hundred years back, churches were the corporate bodies of the day. They thought nothing of killing thousands during the Inquisitions and Holy Wars despite their mantra of peace and love. Will corporations go down that path if we stand against them? Hell, they already do! Corporations cause death and destruction all over our planet every day and we say nothing.

I have to say also, that I understand the pro side arguments. I see why it is believed corporations provide benefits. And, yes, I will concede corporations are people's playthings, meaning they can't really operate without human help. Nevertheless, I ask whether, on balance, we are happier and healthier today because of their presence in our lives. I don't accept they have raised our standard of living, not in a positive way. Social research agrees and casual observation of our world finds much darkness and risk as a result of corporate operations. Then, is it just possible we hide behind the brand labels and logos and the perceived benefits corporations are said to deliver and use them as justification for what is happening to our natural world? Do we smile and chortle at our purchases and pretentious outlook on life despite knowing what is really going on? Of course, that's obvious; it's exactly what we do.

This is what I object to. The hideous and uncivilised manipulation of an entire planetary population, and more so, that we sit idly by and allow it to happen because we have been brainwashed into thinking it's okay. It's okay for others to suffer and die to enable the ego and pride-driven prestige of a small minority. And, no it is not a defence to say, 'That's the way of nature'. Such excuses failed when we stopped throwing spears at each other.

In fact, the human attributes which have allowed us to accumulate and believe we have a right to lord over others, are the same attributes which allow us to know what we do through the corporations we participate in is not civilised, right, or likely to enhance our survival. Sucks doesn't it? As adults we are challenged by the very rules we scalded our kids for breaking: Meaning, we have to support the fallacy, the lie, that unbridled economic activity is inherently good, that infinite growth is possible or that there is no environmental reason to slow down.

Life must be about more than chasing affluence. It has to be because if there is nothing more than looking forward to the next income bracket we really are in for a world of hurt. If the futurists are correct and automation together with artificial intelligence relieve us of the need to work, what then? Will we be bored and will we have trouble finding meaning and purpose? We will unless we start the transformation of our values in the very near future. We will need to find a means to feel purposeful in something other than wealth creation because that way of life just won't be possible after capitalism ends.

Chapter Three

Released

Leaving a career and salary meant I could no longer walk into a bank and ask for a housing loan. Although it felt strange at the time, there was a pleasant upside. I could no longer chain myself to years of debt. That was satisfying because I was no longer helping to make the rich banks and corporations even wealthier. Of course, for this sin they cast me aside and thank God they did!

Being cast aside brought about the realisation that debt had caused my work stress in the first place. But debt is a part of life today right? We have no choice but to at least start our working life with some debt. I want to say bollocks again, but unfortunately, it's true, especially given that a simple credit card is a form of debt.

Also, we are all but forced to take on debt to buy a home or alternatively have wealthy parents. What other choice is there given rent is as expensive as purchasing, and what's more renting comes without the hope of a capital gain.

These days I better understand the dilemma faced by people who don't qualify for a loan. Their position often leads to a spiral of stress, unhappiness and in too many cases, violence or crime. So it seems now we are caught between a rock and a hard place. Both too much and too little money causes unhappiness, and yet the very purpose of economic activity is to raise the welfare of people. Here, I *can* say bollocks because none of this needs to take place, not if our societal values are truly civilised, not if social justice is the foundation of the economic imperative and not if our societies are truly democratic.

In fact, history tells us that we once built our own homes as a cooperative effort. We pitched in and created communities. A handful of wilderness people still do, but by and large our houses are built for us at great cost.

Nowadays, it is reasonable to say there are too many of us for those old cooperative ways to work: that we need systems to manage large numbers of people. Yes, that is exactly the point. There are too many of us on planet earth. However, who wants to talk about population control even though it's the painfully obvious solution staring us in the face. Furthermore, overpopulation is evidence for the argument that we humans are not as civilised or progressive as we like to think. That is, by allowing overpopulation to occur we are condoning massive inequity and huge levels of suffering as well as all the social problems that come with congested urban living.

Why don't we talk about population reduction? We don't because economic growth requires population growth. Wow, there it is: more people means more money and not even the threat of a catastrophic population crash due to resource stripping and biospheric degradation will shift economic thinking on the issue. No wonder there is fear in our world. Moreover, the anger and frustration caused when we become financially entangled in the economic paradigm - a system designed to create wage slaves through indebtedness - can be seen in a host of anti-social and self-destructive behaviours. Drug and alcohol abuse for instance.

Sadly, so-called capitalist 'democracies' foster anti-social behaviour by creating wealth inequity but provide no options or solutions to those who don't qualify for debt and so can't improve their lot.

The more I think about it, the less I'm convinced this arrangement makes any sense at all, other than to build wealth stockpiles for a very few people. These few people give us loans to make us feel better about ourselves. Wow, now that really is bollocks. The lenders don't give us loans and they have no interest in how we feel or what repercussions their loans create. Finance companies sell loans and the cost is enormous.

This is how the rich get richer: by controlling wealth and ensuring there are rules of admission into the wealth club. They use corporations to do their bidding and be the gatekeepers because, by hiding behind corporations, they are protected from personal liability and can avoid taxation. And, oh yes, the rules for entry into the wealth club change if the masses look like complying with them. To wit, we see the ongoing demise of the middle class with its occupants either falling into poverty or making it to the ultra-wealthy shelf.

To ensure the sifting of people continues, interest rates rise and fall but not in line with wages. This ensures some borrowers default on payments while others profit from that suffering. Is this coincidence? No. In fact, this is why there is a wealth divide: it's intentionally managed via the cost of finance.

What a revelation! The wealth system conspires to take from the poor and give to the rich. Robin Hood would roll over in his grave.

Moreover, it's not just the monetary shackle the lenders sell. They take away our personal freedoms because that's how they ensure their own. Be clear though, in our economic system doing this is perfectly legal, meaning there is no planned and organised conspiracy. Nevertheless, our freedoms are strangled by the economic imperative.

Our freedom, to expect an opportunity to have a home without massive debt, is gone. That's sad, it's engineered, it's uncivilised, but it's treated as normal, reasonable and just how things are. Our freedom to physically build a home for ourselves is gone too. That is, there are rules about how, where and when we can build: many rules telling us what to do. Wait on. We said earlier we humans don't like being told what to do. So what's going on here then? Are we seeing double standards on the part of the masses? It seems we don't mind being constrained by rules about finance and ownership, but baulk at any talk of environmental law that would actually and effectively slow economic activity.

It seems we are being somewhat selective about when and where we will refuse to be told what to do.

To make the economic maze even more difficult, the raft of rules and regulations designed to ensure we interact with corporations is all but endless. For instance, we are forced to connect to utilities and services, and, we are forced to abide by regulations in the form of by-laws, and, we pay crippling taxes which create questionable benefits to our existence. They put much money in the pockets of the wealthy though.

Mind you, perhaps we don't want to disconnect from the local water supply or other utilities. The point is though, that we have no choice and no freedom to do so. In many locations we must pay the connection fee even if we can't afford it, don't use it, or don't want it. But even this is not what freedom is really about.

Freedom
Slowly but surely the economic model has robbed us of our environmental freedom and our financial freedom as well as

the opportunity to be self-directed, self-providing or make lifestyle choices outside those convenient to the economic model. Even so, the illusion that Westerner's are free and that we live in a democracy is strong. We even speak of a free market economy, but that is just another way of saying the rich are licensed to get richer at the expense of the salaried or waged taxpayer.

The freedom narrative is delivered in our media every moment of every day, both subtly and overtly. However, the truth is that we can no longer be free of the economic paradigm itself and I believe this is what underpins the comments of discontent strewn in the conversations I listen to. As a good mate put it, *'The freedoms of the mega-wealthy minority (to design our social fabric to suit themselves) are only possible by diminishing the freedoms of the not-so-wealthy masses.'* The bottom line is, even though we say we don't like being told what to do, our economic system tells us what to do every moment of every day and our apathy on that front consigns us to being wage slaves.

To illustrate: This year, for the first time in the collection history of the Australian Census, a name and address was required on the form. Was there a choice not to comply? Sure, one could have refused and been slugged a fine of one thousand eight hundred dollars. This is our democracy and freedom of choice in action. I hear the word bollocks lurking again.

Changing that situation is what having freedom is really about, but it will come at a cost. We will have to bear the economic fallout if we, en masse, refuse to participate in the broad spectrum of economic structures. Rubbish and bollocks again. That thought is just part of the fear campaign used to keep us working. It is the language of the economic status quo: meaning fear of change is created where no fear should exist. Fear of change is reasonable until we accept that what we really fear is a loss of personal comfort should we attempt to change the system. This is why we see mass production of goods and services: because consuming makes us feel comfortable.

This is also the reason for the doctrine of affluence taught in schools; fostered in our media, and spruiked by our governments. With such pervasive access to our thoughts, it is relatively easy to control the mood of populations and avoid an uprising. All the economic imperative need do is offer messages (and the goods) of personal comfort and the masses will comply.

In financial terms, the effort involved in delivering these messages pays off because masses of low paid workers are required to prop up the system, and because with more comfort comes more population growth. However, the masses must endure a much higher tax rate than the wealthy and the corporations which double dip and prosper by paying less tax while tendering for infrastructure projects paid for with tax revenues.

Governments collect vast amounts of money and corporations lobby governments for public works projects to be created and then the same corporations tender because they are the only businesses big enough to take on the projects. Governments hand over our tax dollars to the corporations even though they are allegedly acting for the welfare of the people.

How is this fair? How is this a free choice, especially when one considers that most of the infrastructure is not needed, but we cannot choose not to have it. In fact, we largely believe it *is* necessary because from a young age we are surrounded by a social narrative designed to legitimise the economic cage we live in, making it appear to be the only viable choice.

Free Will

It's easy to get caught up in the day-to-day of our lives and believe what we do each day is vitally important. Even so, and accepting we have created a situation where we believe we need to earn in order to live; if the day-to-day we experience is less than pleasant; if work and the daily grind are not fun, why do we not put more effort into altering the system? This is where philosopher Sam Harris might be right when he says we don't have free will. Goslings don't have free will. They imprint on the mother goose and follow without question. In many ways we seem to be goslings. We replicate societal problems generation after generation and seem unable to change.

Perhaps comparing us to a goose is a bit insulting. Nevertheless, the analogy does seem to hold some truth in that we just keep on doing what we see others doing even though we believe we are acting individually and are free to choose.

For instance, would we build huge mansions if there was no one else doing so and no one to show-off to? I think not, meaning it appears that we are less able to choose what we do than we like to think.

Gods and Idols

One of our pet hates, taxation, could be far lower than it is if we chose to lower our expectations about our standard of living. Doing so would be indicative of having free will. But what about market forces you say? What about supply and demand? What about jobs, growth and the economy? How do we earn an income if we choose to re-engineer the economic system which is powered by taxation? Sure, I get it. We fear change so much that we prefer not to risk starting the change process. But I ask what of the Father, the Son and the Holy Ghost? Our economic words sound eerily similar to the religious trilogy. The economic paradigm, or at least the way we fear economic reprisal, is far too akin to religious faith and a fear of the almighty. I suspect all we have really done by having faith in the economy is replace worship in a church with worship in the marketplace. Both are predicated on fear. Fear is a primal emotion over which our intellect is allegedly emerging but our success in this is demonstrably questionable.

Our lives revolve too much around economic ideals (idols?) and financial institutions (churches?) and include an appropriate language of financial rhetoric, usually relating to a goal of independence and financial freedom (heaven?). We even have economic texts which speak in similar vagaries as religious books. For instance, we have idyllic supply and demand models and equilibrium theory which economists admit we can never see in the real world. More to the point, I have to ask where the independence and freedom we seek are to be found? In reality, our economic system offers one choice and that is to become heavily indebted (by mortgage payments or utility payments and more often both) to put a roof over our heads and then spend the rest of our lives as wage slaves to afford the interest payments and physical maintenance. And no, I have not ignored capital gains.

For now, it is sufficient to say, capital gains create an environmental loss. That's because capital gains are predicated on the flawed notion of infinite growth in a finite world being possible. If we included the environmental cost of creating capital gains, they would cease to be gains at all.

The brilliant deception employed by our economic gods has been to ensure we have just enough spare cash to afford the basic commitments for participation in our economies and communities, but not enough to escape financial entanglement. Workers believe the result of a lifetime of work will be an escape from the economic maze. This lesson we pass on to each next generation and they repeat the process as good goslings do until they too become jaded with the chase. It seems each generation fails to escape the process at all. Beyond this is the real bottom line, which is that our participation in this revolving door system is killing our planet. All the while, our way too high expectations are the very things keeping us from being happy or at least content environmentally, economically or personally. I ask, 'Who retires young, healthy, energetic and with the best years of their lives ahead of them?' A civilised society, a society founded on social justice and having left wealth accumulation as a measure of success behind, would be able to say, 'We all do, because we have evolved past the notion of retirement and the economic mechanisms associated with it.'

Instead, buying goods and services forces us to work and utilities are forced upon us at an enormous cost. Thus, we work ever harder to afford them. They get more expensive when corporations screw up, fail, or our markets have their all too regular collapses. And if nothing so dramatic happens, inflation ensures we pay more and more. Inflation though, is another nonsense of economic theory.

Why can't we price set? The only reason is that doing so would flatten the wealth hierarchy, and hell, we can't have that. We can't have wealth equality or social justice. Bollocks. Dismantling the wealth hierarchy is the only path to social justice, social equity and a sound self-judgment of civility.

Disconnect

Where is our freedom to disconnect from the wealth struggle and be self-sustaining? Where is our freedom to turn on the television and not be bombarded with advertising? Sure, we can turn the TV off, but don't step outside or read, well, anything, because propaganda telling us to spend is every-where. How, where and when did others earn this freedom to berate us with endless advertising campaigns, designed by psychologists, to manipulate and coerce us into spending? Actually, it's our apathy that empowers them.

Unless we demand change on this, or any other front for that matter, it won't happen. And, the propaganda is not just telling us to spend: it's designing our lives at every turn and level by appealing to our weaknesses. The very clever people who design advertising know exactly how to tweak our egos, our sense of self-esteem and our self-worth, not to mention our self-interest drive. We don't spend because we want to, we spend because someone else has told us to. Do we have free will? I don't think we can lay claim to that until we start redesigning our future rather than reacting to the herd momentum of our kind. To facilitate our claims to free will, we might consider reconnecting with the values that built fledgling communities long ago and leave behind the present ethos of profiting at the expense of others. If we were to reconnect with the real world and value it according to its importance to our survival, we would have the basis for a far more comfortable social fabric.

Inculcation

Real freedom, not the proxy used to spruik democracy, is taken away early in life when, so as to qualify for a loan in later years, one is exposed to educational dogma. *'Play-time is over. Work hard. Be an above-average student or your life is going to be difficult,'* children are told by people already in the system. This is the voice of inculcation. It comes from three sources. Firstly, parents who seem to want the next generation to do as they did in order to feel better about what they went through. Secondly, it comes from educators whose end game is to create a pool of workers for employers to choose from. Third, is the influence of the corporate sector on government education policies.

Education, or the process of breaking the curious and free spirit of children, sounds eerily similar to religious teachings in our history about following the path of God or Jesus or whatever deity happened to be popular at the time. Give your allegiance or suffer eternal poverty the ministers of religion and economics rant year after year. The parallels of today's economic teachings to yesteryear's religious dogma are astounding.

We don't hack the beating hearts from sacrificial virgins any more, but we do tear out our kids' individuality and childhood playfulness and replace them with a dull and uninspiring economic imperative.

Yes, I know, religion, superstition and spiritualism are pervasive in our world and have been for a long time. They are a part of the human psyche. In other words, we need something to believe in. That's my point: Why do we persist with problematic ways of finding something to believe in? There's no problem with faith, or belief, as long as it does not threaten our survival. Sadly though, in modern Western societies, faith in churches has largely been replaced by faith in governments as the organisers of society and these structures are threatening our future by failing to arrest out of control economic activity.

Some might argue that democracy and economic activity do in fact offer freedom and security and those same people might say also that we no longer fear men in robes in the way past generations feared the clergy. Bollocks! We fear what politicians will say and do every day. We fear what corporations will do, or magistrates for that matter when we cross the line of a financial law. And we fear not having the incomes we believe corporations provide, but only because we no longer know how to feed ourselves from the land. More than anything, we fear the economic God. On that front, governments and multinational corporations oppress people just as the churches did long ago, if not more so (and more efficiently). Conveniently, they do so in the name of 'economic prosperity' which we seem to find more palatable than considering the health of our planet.

Fear of the economy is used to organise us into believing in unaffordable and unreasonable expectations. The strategy has been to speak of freedom and liberation and rights but not deliver them any more than the churches did. Not really. The wealthy still lord it over the rest, perhaps more so now. The difference is that the masses are now given just enough wealth to keep them from moving against the ultra-wealthy, the new-age royalty and priests.

The problem though, is this: To keep so very many people financially happy means stripping our planet of resources and replacing our healthy biosphere with pollution and environmental death.

Changing Hats

The Father, Son and the Holy Ghost seem to have morphed into Jobs, Growth and the Economy. Why? We're told it's because without something to believe in - without goals - we suffer a debilitating lack of purpose. Therefore, the logic goes, we need financial goals because we have outgrown religious idealism. Bollocks! It's because we believe such rubbish that we're doomed to a life of working and a retirement of stress-induced ill health.

Then, after we pass, what's left of our estates when work-related illness kills us goes to our children, or back to the State.

I suggest we absolutely do not need financial goals to have a full and meaningful life. After all, purpose and goals are simply an expression of our sense of mortality. We are frail and fall by the wayside for a whole host of reasons and so we try to alleviate the fact we will die someday by over-achieving in order to leave a 'legacy'.

The reality is that stress-related illness (in all its variants) is likely to degrade our retirement years because of the pressure we put ourselves under. Our unrealistic expectations about the amount of wealth we must attain really are killing us. This is what consumerism critics call 'affluenza'. Watch for it, immunise yourself or it will kill you too, usually after years of suffering the symptoms. What lurks behind this affliction is deadlier than cancer.

How do we keep this system of accumulation running decade after decade? We exploit our children.

I will say it again, children are exposed to economic ideology (posing as education) from a very young age and we just can't wait to enrol them. They are infected with affluenza in the very first years of school (perhaps even earlier). Then they are thrust into the 'workforce' to create 'wealth for our retirement'. At school, kids discover there are things called 'must have' fashion items and this starts them on the path of consumerism. They compete for a place in their peer group hierarchy by using products as symbols of status. Their parents encourage this too, believing that 'social status' is a civilised goal. But some children end up at the bottom of the hierarchy no matter what parents do and that is particularly sad, especially when it leads to suicide.

We adults encourage them in their social ladder-climbing when we say things like, 'How did you go in your test today?' Those words confer a sense of relevance and importance on beating others and scoring high in the hierarchy climbing game. Is this the mark of a civilised society? No! Mum and dad will be happy though when a result is good. Higher is better, right? It's not, simply because it leads to a life of affluenza.

To begin addressing this problem, learning should be self-directed and children should choose their school subjects based on what appeals to them. I say, 'bugger the economic system and its manipulations that force kids to suffer years of agonising schooling that they despise because it lacks relevance to their life'.

Let's get back to children being children and let them do what they are good at. And we adults acknowledge and accept what they are capable of. That is, accept what children choose when they simply gravitate toward it. Encourage them to learn what they are naturally predisposed to be good at. Nothing more, nothing less.

To shape them in our image is to exploit their youthful vulnerability. Worse, to do so knowing the pitfalls verges on child abuse. Then perhaps it really is time for parents to take off their wise educator hats and return to being supportive and caring mums and dads. After all, that's all our kids expect from us. We betray them completely when we force them to listen to the words of inculcation that we were exposed to.

Rebels

At present, if children rebel against the school time they seem to hate, or heaven forbid if they refuse to take on the values taught at schools, they are less likely to earn enough money to pay out a home loan quickly. The primary reason for this is that lenders use employment status as a filter for finance applications. Of course, lenders are corporations whose only aim is to extract profits from our children. The predatory aspect to this is that they want us and our children to qualify for finance, but they don't want us to be able to repay the capital, just the interest. Our debt is their lifeblood. This is what Jesus referred to when he called the lenders in the temples 'parasites'.

The sad and unfortunate reality is that our education systems are designed to sort kids into various kinds of workers. However, real success at escaping this system is not profitable which is why education does not teach how to avoid debt. Why is this so? It's simple. Our economy (God?) needs to produce new generations of exploitable working-class people, on whose shoulders the wealth pyramid relies through the tax burden.

If nothing else, there should be a law against that! Seriously, the economic system does not care about who it rejects or accepts. Qualify or go without is the way of things, which sounds like extortion. School grades start the process of social tier-building and our adult employment status cements our social rank in later years. Affluence sorts the final grade, usually by placing a dollar value on our life's efforts at retirement age. We die with an 'estate' (hopefully) and mourners nod and say he or she was 'successful'. Or that she or he 'wasted their life' based on the value of the coffin the gathering cries over.

All of this process seems reasonable, until we find ourselves de-stressing on a beach, wondering how to tell the boss we've had enough, which hopefully happens long before the coffin becomes an issue.

What can we do? How do we combat the economic leviathan we've allowed to flourish and which now decides our value to society? I suggest it's remarkably simple: stop spending! Not on the essentials of life (food or water etc) but everything we don't need. Doing that simple thing would cut the head from the beast.

'Stop spending? That's easier said than done,' you say. Yes it is, but it's not impossible, not if we take pride in the knowledge we are saving the biosphere which keeps us alive, or that we are creating a viable future for our kids!

Chapter Four

The Time Before

Did we ever live without education and lenders working in unison to ensure debt driven wage slavery is considered normal, reasonable and right? We did, but not in times recent enough for most of us to remember. This is why an alternative understanding of history is so important. Sadly, the version of history we need to see in education, the history that might change today's circumstances, is suppressed in favour of pointless facts and figures about wars, personalities and so-called important events. Unfortunately, none of these banal facts and figures cause us to question the status quo of the economic paradigm, which is exactly the purpose of teaching it.

Also, looking at what *is* taught in schools, we could be forgiven for concluding that economic activity *has* improved the welfare of people over the centuries, and, economic rhetoric would have us believe the motivation was altruism. Yet the very existence of a wealth 'pyramid' makes that claim ridiculous given the wealth pyramid relies on a base of low paid tax payers. These people cannot be allowed to better their financial position for fear of destabilising 'the economy'.

Instead of crucifying the economic system for the inequity it causes, we incorrectly blame a lack of economic growth for

poverty and suffering. The reality is the system itself is fundamentally flawed because the very shape of a pyramid consigns
masses to endure low incomes.

Sure, the peasantry of yesteryear has been replaced by today's low and middle-class people who enjoy a higher standard
of living than ever before. However, the number of poverty
stricken people in the world is also greater now than at any
time in history, and, our societal problems are running riot at a
time when, if prosperity was delivering added welfare as
claimed, these social ills should be improving. These are the
threads of history we need to focus on.

And also, we need to acknowledge that as a result of relying
on capital growth to keep the middle classes happy, our entire
global economy is now dominated by the fear of running out of
new markets and/or resources to exploit. In fact, according to
Paul Mason, our current economic system is petering out.
Mason highlights five factors that are killing capitalism. One is
the previously mentioned onset of the information age in
which human labour becomes less and less necessary. Another
is the enormous cost of environmental repair, with the others
being the effects of an ageing population, looming planetary
energy depletion, and migration as millions relocate because of
rising sea water.

However, it is imperative that we go further and say that
economic growth is in itself a pseudonym for environmental
debt. To put that into context, as of 2013 the global environmental repair bill stood at US$70 trillion, while in the same year
global Gross Domestic Product or GDP was only slightly more
at US$76 trillion. If the pseudonym premise is accurate, and we
also accept that population growth is necessary for economic
growth, then simplifying the equation as a mathematician
would, we are left with one variable – population, meaning

there are too many of us on the planet! I.e. less people equates to less growth which in turn means less environmental debt.

Why and how has this happened? Why have we not managed our global population to be more survivable? I suggest the reason is that our daily thinking starts and ends in the economic paradigm and nothing is allowed to distract us – not even the lessons in our history or the threat of environmental calamity. There are a host of reasons as to why this scenario continues to play out. These reasons are biological and evolutionary, and are discussed in detail in later chapters. For now the focus is economic rhetoric within our daily social and business narrative and how such words are used to draw our attention away from sustainability.

For example, at a retirement investment seminar I asked the guest speaker (a renowned economist and investment broker) how the yearly profit figures he was spruiking accounted for the environmental costs not recorded in the balance sheets of the companies he recommended as investment vehicles. I added that if those costs were accounted for, none of the companies would show a profit. His answer not only avoided addressing the question, but he offered a completely tangential argument about investing in environmental clean up businesses.

A few minutes later during a break, I cornered the speaker in the foyer and asked again, this time being more specific about the environmental cost of production. His answer was again, 'We offer investments in companies whose business it is to clean up environmental waste.'

In essence, he was saying the economic approach to the problem is to accept environmental damage can't be avoided, and then to consume additional resources and create additional pollution via a cleanup process.

The level of denial of responsibility here is obvious. The speaker was so utterly entrenched in the economic paradigm that he could not (or more likely would not) bring himself to address the question directly. I am convinced he and others like him truly believe their laughable stories about sustainability – which in itself only speaks of cure rather than prevention. To live in that space, to gloss over what we know is happening to our world is to live in total denial of reality. And yet, when questioned about changing our economic system these same people will say, 'Get real, you have to live in the real world.'

The truth is it's them who don't live in the real world!

Sadly, many of us are guilty of accepting and participating in this flawed perspective on economic activity: a perspective that refuses to acknowledge responsibility for environmental impact. The real world is our biosphere, not our economic activity or our bank accounts or our possessions. The problem is that we have lived with the economic rhetoric of the growth model for so long that it has become part of our historical view of the world and that needs to change.

Coming back to the investment guru, he politely excused himself by saying he had more important things to do than talk about 'negative' ideas like the environmental costs of production, and walked away. This is the voice of economic rationalism - what can't be explained must be avoided and treated as nonsense or a waste of valuable income creation time.

Put in economic terms, the costs I refer to are labelled as 'negative externalities.' According to economic theory, pollution is a negative externality because while pollution can be assigned to specific business, and the pollution affects society as a whole, its cost is not recorded against that specific business. Instead, the costs are borne by consumers thus moving the burden from the corporation to the individual. This is another reason why life is so stressful with respect to making our cash stretch across all our financial responsibilities – mum and dad taxpayers are footing the bill for corporate irresponsibility. Ultimately, and more important than our hip pockets though, this practice means our economic activity is running up an enormous debt as if there were some giant environmental credit facility available to us.

Credit

Sadly, we have come to believe in a ridiculous twenty-first century notion the basis of which is that credit provides freedom. The truth is, credit is debt. All credit should be called what it is: an 'indebtedness contract'. One cannot avoid the fact, that the more we take on debt i.e. use credit facilities, the less freedom we have. The only real improvement between now and ancient times is that we can choose to default on our repayments without being physically whipped or slain! Even so, the consequences of credit default remain dire.

Perhaps more pertinent is that economic theory would have us believe debt is required for growth and expansion. Is it though? How can environmental debt be seen as growth or expansion in any form? How have we come to accept escalating global financial debt as being, in any way, progressive? And, more importantly and at the risk of being repetitive, all the Earth's resources are finite – there is no environmental credit card. Consuming the non-human world only brings us closer to a planet-wide resource end-point. Therefore, the dogma that touts endless economic growth as being sustainable is fundamentally flawed. It has been throughout the history of economic activity. The difference today, to times long past, is that our massive population has magnified the impact of resource depletion to dangerous levels.

The reason economic growth appears acceptable at first glance is simple enough. We look at our world from the perspective of our personal life-span. In other words, anything occurring outside our life expectancy, such as long term climate change, seems irrelevant.

But what about our kids and their future? What about the kids we say we love and want to protect and for whom we want to build security? What about our current circumstances for which we can only dubiously thank those who went before us? Thinking about these questions I ask, 'Do we exploit our kids by making them join us in the consumption of our planet?' Yes, of course we do: We are consuming their future and we are teaching them to believe it's good to do the same. Exploiting our kids in this way may not seem intentional, but it can't happen without, at best, deception and misdirection: At worst, what we do in the name of economic prosperity looks and sounds like child abuse, if not legally, then morally. I suggest on this front we need to seriously rethink our understanding of the past and apply history's lessons to the present.

No More Finance

It felt a little odd (after I resigned my sales job) to be 'unqualified' for finance. As a sales professional, the banks looked at my suit and tax returns, told me where to sign and a million dollars became available in a few days. A change of job meant I no longer presented as a risk-free investment and so the banks said, 'Don't bother to apply'. As mentioned earlier, that about-face had a silver lining because it delivered a sniff of freedom from financial entanglement.

Financial entanglement degraded my life from the age of about twenty-two when I took out a home loan. As the entanglement increased, I became angry and resentful at having to work only to pay out at least ninety-five percent of my income to one debt or another.

Being shackled to work was stressful regardless of the benefits of a salary. To offset those nasty feelings, year after year I spent what was left of my income after debt repayments on toys and activities for the singular purpose of venting work related stress. Of course, spending just meant it took even longer to repay the debt. Was I an obedient tax payer benefiting the economic system? Absolutely, because the system had a new wage slave chained to a place of work via debt.

I recall one of my bosses, from years ago, commenting on an employee who had just taken out a large loan to buy into the business. He said, 'Good! Now I have him chained to the desk.' Are we really emancipated as the slaves in our history books were? It's hard to say 'yes' if we define emancipation as freedom from the control of others. And no, it's not our choice to refuse debt - not any more. Not if we want to buy a home or a stake in a business.

Thankfully, today, the freedom I lost years ago has been somewhat regained, but not wholly because financial entanglement is everywhere these days. It is refreshing too, that the odd feeling of no longer qualifying for finance has been replaced with contentment.

Looking back, it is obvious now that the excessive products and services I purchased years ago did their job. That is, the tax office and my employers were very happy to have another contributor to the economy. Society was (presumably) pleased to receive a new set of shoulders to help share the cost of making others wealthy. But, from my perspective, society actually gained one more human-full of stress. It also seems obvious now, why there is road-rage and all the other forms of petty violence in our world, it's because our system of providing monetary wealth actually creates stressed and unhappy people. It creates discontent and encourages the use of debt in a vain effort to buy happiness.

Back in my petrol head days, I certainly added my share of (mild) road rage and participated in unsavoury antisocial behaviour before age mellowed my outlook. Why do we accept living with anger and frustration like this? It's because we exist in a 'winners' and 'losers' monetary system which cares nothing for the individual despite the altruistic flavour in words like *'economics operates to raise the welfare of people.'*

Thinking back, the motorcycles, hang-gliders and fast cars I purchased almost killed me, which is quite irrelevant other than to say that they certainly added to environmental degradation and kept me cashless, and so working. As is their design, the toys created financial profits so they must have been good, right? Because empowering the economic system is our purpose. No, that's just more bollocks. With hindsight, I now see that, ultimately, I worked to pay for the privilege of being stressed by debt. I added to and empowered the economic paradigm without realising I had been brain-washed into believing the 'stuff' of economic activity was worth chasing.

In reality, like most people I see rushing about buying stuff, the more I worked to pay for toys, the greater the stress load that I had to endure. Jesus H Christ, what a ridiculous situation. Actually, I think Jesus and I would agree here. He looked at the merchants and the money changers in the temples and chased them out. I want to do the same. That is, chase the money men out of the environment, the temple of our existence. I'm not religious though. I just happen to agree with Jesus on the issue of profiteering. It's parasitic, lacks a sense of the moral high ground and is uncivilised, unfriendly and leads to animosity.

That we don't see the current parallels to the past, the times of physical slavery, and do something about our economic slavery, is a mystery. For instance, long ago congregations gave to churches by way of the 'tithe' to keep the clergy operating. These 'taxes' were collected with a certain brutality. Fear of God was the excuse but it was really fear of a sword swung, not by the Creator, but by the employees of the wealthy and powerful. It seems not much has changed. Our communities today pay 'consumption' taxes (the 10% GST in Australia) and many other taxes to keep the government solvent. Prison awaits those who refuse to pay. Today, most of our taxes end up in the pockets of the wealthy corporations, not the clergy, but the result is the same.

Is collecting taxes a bad thing? Maybe it wouldn't be if the cash found its way back to the general population. But it doesn't. Mostly, it ends up in the hands of the 1 or 2% of people who hold 98% or more of the world's wealth. Nevertheless, we keep working and letting them take our wealth morsels.

Is this way of life really indicative of a society moving toward civility, equality and justice? Is it progress? I don't think so. And here's a kicker. We, and I mean you and I the voting public, allow it to happen when we could be the bringers of change. We empower the system when we vote for the status quo of Democrat or Republican, Liberal or Labor or whatever the major parties happen to be. We empower the wealthy elite by buying their unneeded, but desirable products and services. It seems religion and faith still prevail in our world: that we vote without challenging what it is we are condoning. 'God is good.' 'We must have a strong economy.' How is the latter different to any religious mantra? I suggest it's high time we voted for the environment, for civility via social justice, and showed we won't be deceived by economic hooks covered in sweet-tasting consumer goods designed to enslave our lives.

Petty Distractions

I find stress-relief from money and work worries in physical exercise. Some people drink to excess or party hard on the weekend. Others will try to hold it all in but end up on a leather couch talking to themselves for $150+ an hour. Whatever the choice, all of these activities are little more than distractions. They cannot resolve the cause of our stress.

Don't get me wrong, the toys and activities of our world are a lot of fun and therapists have their place also. But being stressed about money and thus consuming goods and services to release that stress only promotes and empowers more of the same. It's a circular process meaning spending cannot reduce debt. But we believe it will because economic rhetoric rationalises the earning and spending cycle. It is what we are taught by the social narrative also. For instance, we buy houses bigger and better than we could possibly need, then devote years to decorating or improving them. But I ask, 'Is it really *our* dream - to be indebted by housing loans?' Or is this simply something we absorb from our surroundings? The latter is more likely, but absorb is the wrong word to use. It is far too passive. Inculcation is a better adjective.

If the financial dream touted in modern Western society is not our individual dream, then whose dream is it? Is it the banks or the building industries dream that we happily accommodate, pardon the pun?

A handful of people are asking the question rather than simply accepting someone else's life plan. They are asking for change, but the majority are on-side with the economic paradigm, meaning it must be right, yes? That is to say, the majority can't be wrong – surely not. Likewise, a majority government has a mandate from the people to govern, right? Again, I say, bollocks.

The fact is our scientists have been telling us for years that our way of life is not sustainable. The majority, in this case, are clearly wrong and yet if I ask myself, 'Do I fear climate change as much as I fear being a low-income earner or not having a house that suits my ego?' the answer is, 'Well, um, ah, argh...' Dammit! There it is! Even I can't say 'yes'. This is the issue for us to consider, that affluence is so very attractive and that we promote it at every turn rather than prioritising the dangers it presents.

This happens so much so that it's at the forefront of every consideration, even the question of life itself, or in my case, writing a book about it. I guess that's why the rest of these pages are devoted to unpicking the aspects of our humanness responsible for making wealth so desirable. In short, our free will has been hijacked. Not by terrorists but by our human primal survival drive.

Where To From Here?

Change will only happen if we see the need and take action, and even then, it's going to be a slow process. That is because, as history tells us, our societies change gradually when there's no obvious pay off. This is so because we are genetically primed to seek out more. However, more nuts, berries and the occasional deer are a far cry from new phones, cars, pretentious houses and the like. This is the clever illusion perpetrated by our own evolution: by our need to attend to our self-interest. Our extraordinary minds have allowed us to be blind-sided about the point where having more becomes having too much! And, at the same time, to ignore the risks of excessive consumption.

Even the economists and leaders of our world, the people one might expect to understand how to shift to sustainability, seem unable, or unwilling, to do so.

Unwilling is probably the right word. They are unwilling because they fear losing their enormous salaries and positions of power. The very people able to enact rapid change fear voters will turn on them if they speak of reform. Why? Because that is exactly what we do. You and I, the voting public, are the problem and the solution. We are the rats trained to run around the maze without thinking, yes, of course we can climb over the wall and be out of this, dare I say it, rat race. But we don't. Instead, we run the maze every day thinking there must be more cheese, better cheese, grander cheese around the next bend: If we work just a little harder, a little smarter, and for longer.

Then one day, while sitting on a beach, we might ask, 'Why? Why are we still running after all these years? Was the cheese really worth all the energy we've expended?' The kids have left home, or at least we rarely see them anymore and working has lost its appeal. Even the toys our work buys are less satisfying. It's a problematic day because we want what money brings us but realise we don't really want to endure what earning it entails. Usually though, we are so financially entangled and so emotionally attached to our life's efforts by that time that we can't see how to pull back, and so, most of us find a way to rationalise the chase. We set goals and label our efforts with words like ambition, success, independence and financial security.

Who are we kidding though? Only ourselves.

Aha! This is interesting because human 'wanting' is reliant on expectations which means, if we could find a way to lower our expectations, there is an opportunity to bring fulfilment, meaning and purpose a little closer and maybe, just maybe, we can do that without massive economic and environmental debt. The first big 'aha' then (well, it was for me), is to avoid allowing others to set our goals for us. Advertisers and marketers (the merchants), educators and corporate management (the economic priests) tell us what our goals should be in all manner of overt advertising and subtle imagery and language. And we don't question that such thoughts are not our own, in fact, we take on the language of the economic imperative very readily.

The content of that language has become our complex multi-layered social fabric which values social status and perceived importance over substance. A less thought of, and perhaps not so obvious instance of this, is personal grooming. Not personal hygiene, rather the image we try to emulate when we look at successful people and copy how they present themselves. For an important meeting, our hair has to be just right to meet the expectations of the boardroom or interview etc. But does it really matter? To what extent should we judge a haircut? Is a person able to make sound decisions with bad hair? Of course they are, just look at Sir Richard Branson. More important than thinking about the socially acceptable hairdo though, is our lack of consideration of the vast array of industry and production required to supply hair products. This goes unquestioned. It's quite pathetic that we consider neat hair so relevant to our lives that we will produce toxic chemicals and consume vast amounts of resources just to conform to social or business expectations.

The first step to real freedom then, is taking back the power to say 'no'. To say, 'No, I don't need to conform to the profit motive masquerading as fashion or corporate culture or a host of other unsustainable motivations.' I say, let there be long, unkempt (but clean) hair.

Saying No

I'm passionate about life, happiness, people, community and sharing even though the words here may sound critical, cynical, dark and self-serving. However, being negative and derogatory toward degrading our planet is not cynical or dark at all. Rather it is pragmatic. Accordingly, the story here is really about life and health. The truth is, our new-age economic priests are the true dark deceivers because they deliver nothing but degradation of our life giving resources.

These issues, I mean saving our planet, protecting ourselves from rampant consumerism, avoiding being wage slaves and so on, are probably too big and too well-entrenched in our humanness to expect significant change soon enough to save our kind, but try we must. Ouch, that really is sounding bleak. Still, we have to ask, 'Is the criticism warranted? Is it valid? What are the risks?' That's good business sense, right? I mean we should identify risks to our survival and weaknesses in our social fabric and move to mitigate them. In fact, I suspect, our capacity to deal with this line of thought may well determine the survival or not of our kind.

Next Gen

I tell my son (and anyone else who will listen) how to avoid losing happiness to financial and environmental indebtedness. He looks at me while dragging his attention away from a computer game and says, 'Sure dad, whatever.' To be fair, he listens but is drawn back to his games. He's not alone. We workers do the same. In fact, most people I speak to accept there are many social and economic issues to deal with but feel compelled to work for a living even though they can't justify the disconnect between the environmental damage and the economic benefit of what we do. Nevertheless, the power we need to disconnect from mundane, repetitive, body and soul destroying work is close at hand. It resides in our vote. Voting for change takes a few minutes every few years. It's not a great impost on our time. Having voted for real change, we can sit back and watch our elected leaders put initiatives into place knowing we won't turn on them at the next election.

Yeah sure and pigs can fly! At the first hint of an economic impost to our daily lives, we turn on politicians and oust them.

One day my son, and hopefully his generation, will realise just how much our present mode of economic activity actually costs. Not money. The cost is habitat, resources and personal freedom which translate to an enormous financial, social and life energy burden. I tell him of the dangers, but I don't think he will fully realise until he's paying the bills himself. By then it will be too late for him and others like him to avoid financial entanglement or, tragically, to save our natural world. But one must remain chipper, positive and energised, right? Why? Because we humans are not drawn to pessimism or criticism. If that's really the case, if we really can't suck it up and make the changes needed to protect the future, I say, 'Bottoms up! Cheers. Chin, chin have another beer and forget about the world.' Seriously folks, being an environmentally responsible person entails very little effort. And what's more, it certainly means gaining more than we've been led to believe we would lose.

Creepers

Money-stress (because beer gets more expensive every day?) creeps up on us throughout our lives and the infiltration starts at a very young age. For example, who would question drinking alcohol? My cousins started at age nine. Their parents laughed. I guess that's the point, who questions these things? Who campaigns for change to the point of sacrificing income opportunity in order to speak out and create a different social narrative to laughing at drunken kids? I suggest we need to question far, far more, and on many fronts. We might question why we work so hard but don't get ahead? And even if we do get ahead financially, where the heck are we going? Bigger house? Better car? To which I say, 'Ho hum.' Honestly, 'Ho frick'in hum.' So your car is faster than mine? Wow. Guys, is your penis bigger too? I'm not sure what women compare, maybe boobs? Regardless, should a life be measured in horse-power, a better lounge, or a designer hat? Is this the pinnacle of human evolution? I hope not.

These trivial values (sneakers, designer clothes, etc) are imprinted on our kids at an age long before their minds are able to see the trap set for them by consumerism. This is why I speak so much about education from here on. Accordingly, and to reiterate an earlier point, education is a training camp for consumerism and we eagerly enrol our kids. Yes, sure, we teach kids a great deal of seemingly important stuff, but not how to say 'no' to consumerism. In fact, we drum that out of them as soon as we can. Odd isn't it? We teach little Johnny to say, 'Yes mum, no mum,' and then wonder why he ends up locked into a dead-end job doing as the boss tells him. Why don't we teach him to question? The answer is because Johnny has to consume or he won't enjoy economic growth. Wait, no, we tell him to consume so others can enjoy the growth he creates and so they can have more.

Yes that's more accurate.

Wait on, this sounds like another load of bollocks creeping in, and it is. The entire economic growth argument seriously lacks maturity or wisdom. I want more, more, more, is so childish.

I would like my son to have a choice: A choice about the addiction to money and consuming he is confronted by. Unfortunately, how our world operates at present makes it difficult to get a word in on the subject. Especially when, to argue the case risks sounding like a grumpy old guy, or perhaps a soap box preacher on a street corner who is eventually arrested for disturbing the peace. I ask 'What peace?' If I am to be arrested for disturbing the peace, it's only fair there be some peace to disturb.

Preaching

If the metaphoric guy on the soapbox defies the economic paradigm, the legal system works to soothe the disgruntled economic deity by making the guy disappear. For instance, recently a Lord Mayor in Australia asked the public not to give money to street beggars because the money they gave enabled the beggars to stay on the streets. Is it not quite bizarre that the Mayor could not conceive of the reasons why the beggars are on the streets in the first place, or how to help them? None of which was mentioned in the report. This is the not so subtle language of the economic system. It is the message saying, 'We don't want to see, or hear, about the processes designed to shift wealth from where it is needed most, and into the pockets of the wealthy where it is needed least.

The eviction of the beggar happens because they prick our conscience and, for that, the preacher, the beggar and the homeless person must be silenced or shunted out of view. Jesus was. JFK was when he threatened to end the very profitable cold war. Mandela spent thirty years in prison. People who don't conform to the economic norm are quickly ostracised and swept under the carpet. Some resist and some die in the process.

At the individual level, just look at the poverty stricken people we ignore every day, preferring to work to feather our own nests with opulence than lend a hand in the street.

We participate in this ostracism even when we simply over-look the poor instead of giving them some of our excess wealth. We are complicit when we fall back on rationalisations such as, 'They need to work harder,' or this, 'I have worked hard for what I have, why should I give?' These are the thought processes of the economic paradigm, not evolved and civilised humans. And, don't ever think our laws are about anything other than ownership protection.

Owning is power. Owning is wealth. Owning is self-image. Owning is demonstrating one's superiority over others. It need not be, but we find it hard to resist the feelings of pride, ego and empowerment that have always been associated with advertising our wealth. Nevertheless, this practice is abhorrent if you consider the suffering caused and ignored. And, sadly, owning is not possible without conflict and violence.

Ownership laws are violent because, for one person to be protected by ownership laws, another has to be excluded by en-force-ment. Any force is by definition violence albeit it is often non-physical.

If a person suffers hardship because they don't have enough; because a law enforces the fact one person has more right to resources than another, how is that not violence? Don't confuse legality with civility either.

Legally owning is an expression of our primal and animalistic heritage where we jousted physically for food, territory and a mate. Lower animals own by force, but we are more evolved, right? No, that's just more bollocks. Our history is filled with violent conflict over ownership.

Honestly folks, if we are to self-assess our societies as civilised, we need to rethink the notion of ownership and all the negativity that spew's forth from it. Let's face it, when we die we can't take anything with us, so can we really 'own' anything? The better thought is that we are temporary custodians (of resources) meaning we could develop a custodianship morality and a raft of resource-ethics text books to replace ownership laws. Sadly though, and due to our inculcation into the economic paradigm, owning the stuff of economic activity has been made more attractive than discussing why or how to avoid consuming it, or for that matter how to deal with the real costs, or even admitting there's a problem.

This is the social dilemma of our era. It's not drugs, crime or human trafficking and so on. These are just symptoms. And these symptoms are really illusions and distractions - they are ways to make money and to justify ownership and laws. Social reform rhetoric loves these distractions because they are nebulous, endless, and consume the attention of the masses. For instance, how long has the war on drugs been running? 'Hell, let's not target the real cause,' we say, 'there's no money in that.' Instead, let's distract the population from thinking about the underlying reasons for the problems of our era by targeting the symptom and even then not addressing them in a meaningful way.

The more I think about these issues, the more I ask, 'What the heck is life all about?' Surely it was never meant to be about pollution, degradation, money, stress, financial goals, market crashes or global warming and competing for bragging rights. But my God, look at our world! Where can one go and what can one do without at least some money or seeing the impact it is having? Somebody owns every thing and every place, on

Earth. What if someone comes to own the rights to the air we breathe. What then?

The Core

One might say, 'Everything we experience today is geared around encouraging us to spend and thus grow The Economy.'

Stop! Hold the bus. Wait a minute.

This is the core issue in my view: That our thinking is money-oriented in the first instance. Nevertheless, I hear a voice in my head saying, *'Get real, money is everything.'* The voice screams at me, *'Money this, the cost of that, etc etc.'* *'If I just had more money.'* Can you hear it? That's the voice of our economic paradigm, the voice of social conditioning, the voice of economic rationalism. It's the voice of the econo-God that has been melded into the very core of our experience of life. So much so, that we take it for granted. Money is good; money is important, wealth, affluence etc, etc. The mantra is so familiar. God is good. Praise be to God. Forgive me father for I have sinned.

The religious words are different but the underlying intent is not.

Money is the new-era tool used to control people through faith and belief in its innate 'goodness'.

I recall a preacher, a real one, not an economic robe-wearer, telling me that to invite God into my heart and then reject him, was to live in Hell on Earth. His message was a guilt trip and it worked particularly well at the time. I was young then and I felt guilty for years.

It was not until I realised God had never left me that I healed. Again, no, I am not religious, but I accept God is that part of us which yearns to be friendly, considerate, social, amiable, tolerant, compassionate, inclusive, forgiving, fair-minded and so on. These qualities are in all of us, but money, in all its manifestations, suppresses the best in us and brings out the worst. And no, I am not going to say money is the Devil's work.

But I will say again, money and wealth are expressions of our primal emotional evolution. Economic activity is an expression of that part of us which seeks out the food, water and shelter we need to stay alive and is willing to fight for it, but goes too far. That's why we can still find Hell on Earth: Because we foster and nourish our primal emotional drives rather than putting them aside at every opportunity.

Should we all become logical unemotional 'Vulcan's' like Mr Spock from Star Trek? Of course not! However, we believe, wholeheartedly, that our species is making progress towards being civilised, even though there is so much evidence to the contrary. I think Spock would say, 'That's most illogical, Jim.'

Social Progress

Unfortunately, human social progress is at present an illusion. We are certainly more technologically capable, but that capability has not reduced human suffering. More people live in poverty today than at any time in history. Also, the idea that we are happier, more tolerant and compassionate, forgiving or content really does not stack up against the evidence.

Moreover, what we teach our kids to do to others in the name of economic competitiveness is abhorrent. To ensure they carry out our will, we put them through years of educational torment and justify doing so for money and wealth reasons, not love. We wrap our insistence up in what we convince ourselves are defensible intentions saying, 'Education is for the good of the child.' We tell them, 'You must be competitive,' even though we know competition is a path to stress and violence, and that, by definition, it can't be anything else. We blindly insist they learn the ways of our new-found faith. It's no wonder so many kids don't like school. It's no wonder they act out. They can see our hypocrisy. They just don't have the skills to put what they see into words that will move us.

And, what's more, we make it clear we don't want to hear if they do. Perhaps we should listen more? In fact, how to avoid the manipulation of our emotions by our economic system is something our schools should teach, but don't. That's because we can't have kids smart enough to avoid becoming the next generation of consumers. Can we? The better question is, 'Can we afford not to teach them?' That's the question of survival I want to see debated at elections, in the streets on soapboxes, and in universities.

Bad Weather

It's been a clever snow job, the manipulation of our desires in the name of improved living standards. However, I don't think it's perpetrated by anyone in particular. Rather, evolution has brought us to a point where we are vulnerable to our own innovations and curiosity. Because our survival instincts tell us comfort is good, we have never stopped seeking it in greater and greater amounts. But I think most of us know the storm clouds are forming. At the same time, the reality we don't want to accept is that we just don't need what we have now. And, of course, yes you guessed it our planet can't support everyone having such a high standard of living.

And so I ask this, 'Is life about choosing between chocolate and vegetables?' The healthy choice is obvious, but chocolates sure taste good! Is life just about growing up, leaving school, getting a job, buying a car, getting married, buying a house, having children, experiencing a mid-life crisis, retiring, complaining about the younger generation and the cost of living, aches and pains, politics and dealing with the kids issues, then fearing and denying death? Or, is life about creating happiness, smiling and enjoyment (but only after working), worrying about money, planning for the future and avoiding tax and traffic fines? Do you see the dilemma? Happiness is trying to break through but we hold it back using financial restraints. The most effective restraint is where we fall into the trap of admiring and trying to be one of the people wily enough to exploit others. We fear our kids not being educated enough to deal with such people, but the education strategy has not worked - ever.

Then, perhaps, we need a new strategy, one which will avoid the approaching mega-typhoon of environmental feedback that the economic imperative is creating.

Is it possible to reduce our worry, stress and the years spent paying back borrowed capital? I believe it is. But that would mean rethinking our ideas about where we find contentment and intrinsic value in our lives. The real world, the world of fresh water, snowfields, forests and habitat is vanishing before our eyes. And, with it, what we need for our biological survival is disappearing: This being the very source of our economic wealth also.

Sadly, we have fallen in love with the perceived value of financial wealth and discarded the intrinsic value of the biophysical world other than to convert it into perceived value.

Today, we prefer to look at the biophysical world on a Smartphone than actually go there. No, perhaps not 'prefer'. Perhaps it is better to say we can't afford to go there because we have to work... to pay for the Smartphone, to tell us about the illusion of going there. And, after struggling with that dilemma for a while, we borrow the money and go whether we can afford it or not. Then we regret the debt as we sit at our workplaces reflecting on the images on our phones.

Of course, the environmental cost of our travel is not even a consideration, but it is the more dangerous issue we face going forward.

Caring

I suspect very few of us have an 'I don't care' attitude about the natural world and the welfare of each other. It's just that there are more pressing and more enjoyable issues to deal with from day to day than hugging a tree. Or are there? Ah yes, here it is again, the language of the economic status quo. 'It's just that there are more pressing issues...' A comment like that legitimises economic activity. The better thought is to say that, 'We are distracted by seemingly important issues.' The difference is a recognition of a more survivable set of priorities. Destroying our environment cannot be thought of as normal, not if we want to survive.

Unfortunately, we all fall into using the language of the economic status quo too easily, which is not surprising given how often it is used and the volume of education designed to ensure we learn the mantra. The choice is between chocolate or broccoli though and it seems based on the state of our world chocolate is destined to cause a heart attack.

Then what to do? How to make change palatable seems to be the burning question. Actually, it's probably not a question at all for most of us. Life is just too darned comfortable to bother with such dreary issues. And, of course, there's no money in them! Right?

Chapter Five

Where Are We Now?

Unlike any prior time in history, humanity is at a technological cross road. Futurist writers tell us that in the coming few decades human genetic engineering will extend our life spans beyond one hundred and fifty years. We will be immune to most diseases and will be smarter and have more acute senses, not to mention dermal machine integration which will see smart phone functionality implanted under our skin. Living longer might sound wonderful until we stop to consider our global population would double or quadruple in the very short term. There will also be social issues to deal with such as potentially working in the same occupation for more than one hundred years or having our kids live at home for fifty plus years.

More importantly, if such a dramatic population increase eventuates we will very quickly create fish bowl earth, meaning we will risk a massive population boom then crash due to a lack of capacity to feed fifteen or twenty billion people.

Rather than starting a debate about natural attrition or birth control to manage our already too large global population, we manipulate our environment to feed more and more people. To support even our existing population, we have deployed highly mechanised agriculture which relies on chemicals to make crops grow in depleted soil. However, these chemicals destroy waterways and kill aquatic creatures. We have built fleets of enormous trawlers to scour the oceans to find the last of each food-fish species we send to extinction. We drill many kilometres into the Earth's crust to extract fossil fuels locked away by nature to protect us from the carbon they store. And yet with all these attempts to raise the welfare of people, millions are starving and living in abject poverty.

In very recent times, we have turned to genetically modified (GM) crops and livestock without understanding the long term impacts. The perfectly logical extension then, as predicted by futurists, is GM people.

GM Wars

Given our predilection for racism, war and conquest, will there be conflict between GM's and 'normals'? Of course there will! However, the 'clone wars' will be different because GM people won't occupy a nearby nation or land that normals can invade. They will be amongst us and will, over time, outnumber, outthink and outcompete Homo Sapiens. According to Noel Yuval Harari, at that time Homo Deus will replace Homo Sapiens and this new species of super humans will take over planet earth.

During the transition we will fall into conflict. It's inevitable. It's how we humans deal with people we see as different to us. We kill them because we fear they will kill us, or we simply want their territory or the resources those territories offer. It's an inarguable historical fact. That said, and as tempting as it is to persist with the genetically modified human thought trail, and because this is not a sci-fi novel, we must return to what is real in the here and now.

The technologies we already have today serve one ultimate

purpose and that is to demonstrate our superiority over the rest of nature. This is the statement of intent to be found behind genetic modification. It is an extension of the 'sanctity of human life' belief which itself stems from Christianity and other religions.

It is this line of thought which will see human clones at first grown for spare parts (assuming fish-pond Earth allows us to live until the technology is ready). We will clone ourselves because trying to cheat death is a part of our species' ego complex.

In other words, we have claimed a greater right to life than other creatures, and, how we operate at present says we don't want to play by nature's rules. We prefer to lord it over the natural world and assume we can bend it to our will. Then it's not a great leap to suggest we think we are as smart as God. I don't know if God exists or if he or she created the Earth, but it seems obvious that there's a design for our planet's operation which we don't fully understand and that tampering with it is dangerous. Where did that design come from and how does it work? Until we know that, adopting a precautionary approach is probably the best option. We might sit back and say, 'Until we have resolved the uncertainty around what we are doing, we had best stop doing it.' Sadly, that looks unlikely to happen.

The difficulty with our air of superiority is this: If we accept that we are reliant on our environment, we then have to accept we can't afford to abuse it. If we admit to being on equal terms with and thus reliant on our biosphere, we must protect the breathable air, fresh water and arable land needed to stay alive. And that means we can't afford to financially profit from it as we do at present. We would have to care for our pond. Hmm, I think I see pigs flying over the horizon, but sarcasm is not acceptable is it? It's not acceptable in this instance for the same reasons that a bad hairdo is not acceptable in the boardroom. In other words, it speaks of a truth we don't want to acknowledge. In fact, our world is replete with truisms that upon closer examination flounder and fail.

For instance, my son came home from a university class and announced this little gem, 'The business of business is business.' I suppose it's true, but the comment is so ambiguous I'm not really sure of the point his lecturer was trying to make. I would have thought the business of business is to make a profit. That is, profit at any cost, even the cost of the business itself when negative environmental externalities ruin the balance sheet and make the business non-viable: and life in general non-viable too, but we can't say that, or we risk being seen with a bad hairdo, right?

Instead, we turn a blind eye to incomplete accounting because doing that prevents the balance sheet reading so badly. At least that will be the case until the accountant's incomes succumb to environmental pressures, but I suspect even then they won't admit they've screwed up, not even when the numbers tell us we are playing with forces beyond our control. Not supernatural forces, rather we are messing with nature's life giving system of cycles by not accounting for the impact we are having on them.

Each technological band-aid we adopt on the survival front causes a new wound. Like the rat in the maze we run in circles licking those injuries. No, not licking any more, now we pour on broad spectrum disinfectant without considering our reliance on the microorganisms we massacre. Too often, if not always, overlooking our dependence on the relationships between us and the bacteria, the amoeba, the snail, the sparrow, the dolphin, the chimpanzee, the wetlands, rivers, snowfields, forests and permafrosts, and that all of nature is required for the Earth's system of life to operate in the long term. If we kill the bacteria, we ruin the inter-connected system. Nevertheless, if it suits our short-term financial aims, we will displace or eradicate creatures and habitat to access resources we see as vital to the economies which pay for our technologies. What we have done on this front is self-destructive, but we turn a blind eye because a strong economy is allegedly more important. Is it? Really? Absolutely not. How can it be when economies rely on environmental health?

The Colour of Elections

I stood at a polling booth recently, wearing a green T-Shirt, handing out how to vote cards. It was quite amusing to walk up to the area where the party faithful assembled all dressed in different colour T-shirts. Red was for Labor and as I recall the Christian Democrats were in yellow. The scene reminded me of my early school years when different factions were herded onto the sports oval for a day of competition. Red, green, yellow or blue, we all battled for supremacy. We were good little maze running rats... ah, I mean, obedient kids. Hmm, yes, 'rats' is probably more appropriate.

Perhaps those school days are why we are still running around the economic maze wearing the logo and colours of corporate support. No not 'perhaps', definitely, it's a learned behaviour. It has to be. I can't accept we are born that way.

At the polling booth (the kids now adults), most nearing retirement, found ourselves wearing the colours of competition learned at school. That's a pity because it says we have not broken away from our childhood conditioning on the sports field (an overarching ethos of competition). I walked up between two different coloured shirts and after a few awkward moments started talking about the school sports carnival. Soon we all laughed about the silliness of not wanting (at first) to talk to each other because of our differing political allegiances, which leads me to the woman in the blue T-shirt. Blue is the Liberal Party colour by the way. She was interesting.

A successful business woman, highly-educated and sharp of mind, she suggested the pro-environment Greens should align with the pro-business Liberal Party because sustainable business innovation was the way forward. What a lovely piece of rationalisation that was. 'For goodness sake,' I thought, 'it's the mind-set of business growth and profit that has led us into our environmental and stress-filled life circumstances.'

More of the same is not the answer. And adding 'sustainable' somewhere in the argument does not legitimise business-for-profit at the cost of our environment. Why? Because business is not sustainable unless we remove the idea of growth and even then we are already over taxing our natural resources meaning contraction is needed to reach anything like sustainability.

As an aside, I talked to her about how we rate the importance of others on a diminishing scale in order to justify what we do to strangers. That is, our regard for others falls away as their social connectedness to us diminishes. I asked, 'Why would I care about John Fitzpatrick (or any person I have no connection to) in Ireland compared to a co-worker or a family member? I know I should care for John, but do I really? What is John in Ireland to me? If I was given the power to determine if John lives or dies, what would I decide? I think most people would say he has the right to be alive, and who are we to judge, but we might put a caveat on that decision based on what John has done. Is he a serial killer? What if his continued life means someone closer to us must suffer or perhaps die at his hands? What would our decision be then? The point is, we weigh up decisions in light of the significance of others and the situations we encounter them in. With that process in mind it's hardly surprising we don't give much thought to worms, gnats or scorpions or people of other nations whose resources we exploit in order to make business profits.

The unfortunate part of this scenario should be obvious. Worms, gnats and scorpions are just as important, if not more so, than John or I because insects represent a larger part of the biosphere. But, and here's an inconvenient kicker, these small critters contribute in a positive way while the vast majority of people don't. It's a tough question to consider perhaps, but I ask, 'What do we humans contribute to the biosphere in a positive way?' If we take into account our pollution and all the other negative impacts we impose on the natural world, what do we do to enhance the biosphere? We could do so much, but consciously choose not to.

Do we turn the soil as ants and worms do? Do we constitute a food source for other creatures as herbivores do? Hearing this, the lady in the blue T-Shirt decided I was a bit loony and so she laughed and changed the subject. That's educated Liberal thinking in action. Thinking that she could not see a profit in the words so she dismissed them out of hand. And her reaction is typical of the response I hear from most people. Interestingly, that response comes from our socialisation, which says humans are special and stand alone at the pinnacle of evolution: that we have supreme rights over the non-human environment. Apart from our self-estimation though, nature does not rate us differently to any other species.

And that thought brings me to a recent TV show explaining why a pod of whales beached themselves in the Bahamas. A researcher happened to be on a beach when several whales swam ashore.

With some help, he pushed one whale back into the water, but it turned around and beached again, then died. He decided to take some heads of dead whales and scan them to find a cause for the suicidal behaviour.

He found bleeding in the whales' inner ears and the only explanation he could come up with was the onset of a sudden and enormous, sound/pressure wave. His conclusion was that a human activity created a sound so loud it ruptured the whale's auditory systems. The source was probably military sonar.

It was suggested the whales were in so much pain they were trying to get out of the water. We can't prove that last point, but it makes sense given the whales sought the land as a refuge. In fact, a search revealed there were no more whales in the nearby ocean, meaning their suicide was not the result of disorientation amongst a few individuals. All the whales in the area located a beach to swim onto rather than go around the islands. That certainly sounds like a desperate en masse attempt to get out of the water.

Later in the program, the researcher described how whales are a critical link in the ocean fish-food chains. Without them, we lose an entire food chain that we rely on to feed millions but, of course, we also know sonar is a product of economic activity and a means of providing national security.

Allegedly, we need the military to defend us from other humans who want to take from us, meaning sonar is important to our welfare. Sorry, but this is just more bollocks. It is the language of the economic status quo again. It is more rationalisation and legitimising of the economic dogma of ownership laws which define how we live. This is something we need to move beyond as a global community; that is, assuming we want to claim civility, progress, wisdom, or maturity as a people.

It is likely we think in terms of conflict and competition first, because for millions of years we've modelled ourselves on animals we see taking from one another and jousting over mates and territory.

This is the dilemma of being human. On the one hand, we consider ourselves superior to other creatures, while on the other hand, we imitate them in so many ways as to make our distinctiveness hard to see. How's that for a question of survival? That is, how to reconcile our predilection for thinking we are superior, while we behave more like the animals we seek to be distinct from, than enlightened beings. My goodness being human is complicated.

The dollar cost of new technologies such as sonar, needed to drive our economies is high, which is why we have encouraged our population to grow. A large population spreads the financial burden (and gives us a supply of people to send to war). At the same time, a large population also means greater pressure to compete for living space and resources. As a result, much conflict darkens our world. Still, provided we are one of the lucky ones living in middle-class suburbia, life seems pretty good. It's not perfect. It's stressful, expensive and congested but we don't go hungry or cold and so we are not likely to complain enough to bring about change.

This is the insidious aspect of economic activity. It offers just enough to keep us believing we can be happier if we work a bit harder and for a little longer, but delivers so little of intrinsic value. This sounds like a story about a donkey and a dangling carrot; or maybe a rat and some cheese in a maze. And to make sure our goals are never completely met, economic activity creates an endless list of 'wants' by putting ever more appealing products in front of us. Admittedly they are difficult to resist. Nevertheless, they remain wants, not needs.

Wants are hard to resist until we take stock of the real cost. Yeah, you're right if you say, 'Even then they are still attractive.'

Demand

Economic theory would have us believe that consumers 'create' demand for products through purchases and that production is a response to demand. However, it seems obvious that we cannot purchase something we do not know about.

Hence, our media is constantly filled with advertising designed to tweak our curiosity by putting new products under our noses regardless of the intrinsic value (or harmfulness) of those products. Thus, it is better to say demand is driven by persistent and highly targeted media content created by advertisers who are keenly aware of how to ensure the viewing public confuses needs and wants.

Perhaps we should make a law against advertising unnecessary products in ways that lack moral fibre. That is, ways designed to mislead and deceive – especially children. Just stating 'buyer beware' should be no defence or acceptable rationale for manipulative sales techniques. In the absence of controls, regulations, or a code of ethics, advertising and marketing is free to employ every psychological trick in the book: the aim is to shape societal values and attitudes toward products and services. This applies particularly to children who are targeted long before they are old enough to defend themselves. Parents allow this to happen and so we are as culpable as the advertising agencies. Is this the mark of a civilised people? I think not!

What's more, it's painfully obvious this 'created' and 'manipulated' product demand is slowly killing our planet and therefore us. Knowing this should have already brought about changes to how we assess the value of products and services, but doing that would be sacrilege against the econo-god. All hail the econo-god!

'Wait,' you say. 'Life is good, why would I want to change the vast array of products and services that I enjoy? I have many modern conveniences and comforts. Why would I threaten my opportunity to have these things?' Ah yes, this is the well-sold illusion. That we can have all the feel-good stuff of this world and not pay the piper.

To ensure we participate without question, we are educated from a young age about how to be proud of our achievements, but not how to evaluate what we do from a sustainable perspective, the moral high ground, or an environmentally friendly position. This is the purpose of education: to ensure we are inculcated into a social ethos of effectively being proud of ruining our planet.

Pride

What has pride got to do with demand theory? Well, in my experience, making a comment about the environment or more so the need to reduce our consumption of resources will dull the mood of just about any group of people. It's a real conversation killer at a party or celebration and that is a shame. I believe this is so because comments about conservation fly in the face of the economic imperative. That is, such comments fly in the face of just about every economic activity our communities take pride in participating in.

Perhaps then, rather than speaking of the problems we are causing, the better topic might be: 'What the heck are we going to do without becoming sad, depressed, angry, defensive, or much worse, dismissive?'

At this point we need to come back to the woman in the blue T-Shirt because the conversation with her provides a perfect example of the wall of resistance our human pride puts up.

We talked about climate change and she agreed it is a problem and that we should be doing more to avert it. Then I said, 'according to research I've read the next ice age will start by 2050.'

The Liberal lady was instantly dismissive saying, '2050? No way!'

This reaction is typical when we talk about environmental consequences happening in our own lifetime. That's because we want to hear that climate change 'doom and gloom' is a long way off. This is our very human ego defence mechanism attempting to protect our pride. Accordingly, she insisted the environmental downside of our economic activity would come around 2100 or later, meaning her generation would not be directly affected, although she did at least accept it was coming.

Then, here we have an educated Liberal person, who understands climate change science, but who, at the same time, would not entertain the idea she would have to make any changes. I asked why she thought the onset of an ice age was further away than 2050.

She replied, 'Because ice ages take many years to onset and we should be seeing changes by now if it was going to happen.'

The reality is that researchers observing receding glaciers are finding flowering plants, frozen while they were in bloom long ago, emerging from under the ice as it melts. This tells us the last ice age onset started in one season. That is, during one season it was summer or spring and then the flower was snow bound for the next ten thousand years or so. Will it happen so fast again? I don't know, but hell, I don't want to be responsible for accelerating the process!

The last time an ice age started there was a tipping point. As far as we know the cause was fresh water suddenly released from the North American Great Lakes region. The water flowed into the North Atlantic where it stopped the great ocean current. The current is the heater for the northern hemisphere. Warm tropical water flows north from the equator and surrounds Britain preventing severe cold.

Will the current stop again? It hiccupped in the 1990's due to the polar ice caps melting faster than usual, so it is clearly possible. As well, we know the arctic polar ice cap is still melting and that's a lot of fresh water flowing into the North Atlantic so it would seem such an event will happen at some point. But the blue T-shirt was having none of this argument. It was just too inconvenient to her business model and of course it meant her life time would be affected. We agreed to disagree and changed the subject. I suspect she remains in ego defence mode to this day.

More important than talking about what might happen though, is action to mitigate climate change. How do we put some runs on the board with respect to protecting what's left of our environment? The short answer is we can place our individual support behind Green politics. However, I have to admit, as I re-read this paragraph several months after writing it, I was taken aback by the sudden reference to 'Green politics.' So perhaps it needs some explanation.

In my view, Green politics is not about *who* we vote for or what party we support. It's about *what* we vote for. In other words, policies are more important than parties or popularity. It's about demanding a sustainable future from politicians whatever colour T-shirt they adopt, and, the same from businesses. This being the case we might consider voting for policies that protect our long term future rather than our short-term hip pocket nerve.

Neither is Green 'thinking' about chaining oneself to a bulldozer; rather, it's about personal freedom and intrinsic sustainability. And, I accept, we typically don't change our political affiliation easily. We need to be convinced over time. In fact, we need a good reason to change our minds on any view we have held for a long time because our ego will try to defend our position as was the case for the lady in the blue T-shirt.

Usually, and sadly, those reasons boil down to monetary considerations because we want to know that changing what we are doing won't cost us financially. Also, talking about politics is touchy in itself. And, as already discussed, telling people how to vote, or anything else for that matter, is problematic because we don't like being told what to do. And yet, I hear so many complaints about life, work, and/or the daily grind. So many are asking the question, 'What the heck is life all about?' It's only logical that if the question is being asked, an answer might be expected even if it is political. However, I think what people are really saying is this: 'How the heck can I have my cake and eat it too?' The simple answer is, we can't.

Goslings and Climate Change

Are we head-in-the-sand ostriches and imprinted goslings, or sentient beings? It's hard to tell sometimes. I know I started out in life a Liberal gosling: I simply followed my father's vote. It took fifteen years to break that imprinted-goose-like behaviour.

Being a gosling is not uncommon though. We often vote as our family or significant acquaintances vote. Yes, I accept that's a gross generalisation, but I think there's some truth in it because the two major parties in most countries revolve in and out of office over and over: usually without achieving anything substantially different to each other. This situation is evidence that the majority must be voting for them, despite these major partys' inability to deliver significant improvements to life. To defend that situation we say, 'What choice do we have? We say, 'The minor parties can't form government' or offer up some other equally flawed rationalisation. Are these ego defences based in fact? No they are not, but pride will get in the way of admitting to the need for change.

Considering this, it's not surprising that the political majors are look-alikes, because, apart from the party name, the ethos they operate from is identical. That is, they all fall back on the perceived importance of growth, jobs and the economy because this is what the voting public seems to be influenced by. I think, on this matter, we need to transition from goslings and ostriches to future-oriented thinkers.

Shoot to Kill

Some all-but-extinct North American Indian tribes, who were killed off in the name of progress, were future thinkers.

Those tribes considered the impact of any change to their society and if in their view it would not create a problem for the coming seven generations, they went with it. Otherwise things stayed as they were. That outlook was clearly sustainable, at least until they met Europeans. Their outlook was far more sustainable than the philosophy of the missionaries who came and tried to convert the Indians into Christians. When that approach failed, the military followed the priests killing many thousands in the name of the militaries' religion, namely, the economic model of the civilised world. Ouch, has anything really changed since then? We are still displacing people from their land in the name of profits. For instance, North American farmers' lands are being ruined by fracking, effectively forcing them to walk away from their livelihood. Some residents in California have no running water forcing them to truck in water or walk away from their properties. Their drinking water has been diverted to orange orchards. Armed US troops practice crowd control manoeuvres on home soil in preparation for civil unrest over wealth inequity. All of these situations occur in the name of greater profits.

More, bigger, better, faster. These words are designed to appeal to our ego and pride. These words are protected by laws and vigorously enforced by litigation and violence. This is the ethos of progress, growth, jobs and the economy and such concepts form the gospel of the new corporate gods who instruct the ministers of government on how to ensure the masses bow before them. Surely, we can see the problem with such an arrangement and move to better it. If the socially acceptable and predominant mantra seen in our media was less, restraint, contentment and community, would we not gravitate to that as well? The point is our ego wants to run with the crowd, meaning we need a new direction and new mantra for the crowd. Without that we have little to look forward to with respect to social reform.

How can we make better use of our ego and pride? How can we experience the appeal of a more cooperative social fabric? Actually, it's easier than one might suspect.

Try this at home. Have your family or some friends come together and make a rule to apply to conversations for an agreed timeframe – say, two weeks. The rule is this: No comment in a conversation can start with the word "but". No one is to start a reply with 'No, you're wrong..." or any other contradiction. For two weeks use some of these instead: 'I understand, and yet...'; 'Yes, I see your point, however..."; Agreed...so what you are saying is...'; 'Okay, so what you are saying is...'; 'I hear you, however, what do you think of...'

It's a pretty simple change to make. The idea is to validate the other person's perspective and not attempt to bring them down as a first response. Each person should still have their own opinion, but find a way to be constructive and explore ideas, not respond by burying each other's point of view. By engaging the other persons point, we reduce the risk of conflict.

This experiment worked wonders for a group of friends I talk to three times a week. Our conversations went from each person waiting to contradict the other, to an exploration of ideas and it was brilliant where we ended up sometimes.

Saying, 'Yes, but...' is our ego trying to be superior and assert our will, usually for no better reason than that's what we've learned to do. So much more is possible if we listen and reflect instead of stomping on the opinions of others.

Ego is not something we can eradicate, but we can turn it to our advantage rather than let it destroy conversations. There's nothing worse, in my view, than a social conversation where each person is simply waiting to have their say and no one really listens to, or reflects on, what is said. Then here is a way to change our world. We can educate our kids about how we speak to each other so that we nip anger in the bud, rather than teaching competition and conflict as the economic imperative would have us continue to do.

Sleeping Better

At present, rather than engaging our minds in discussions designed to find solutions to a host of problematic aspects of our lifestyles, evidently we prefer to switch off and accept our financially entangled circumstances. This happens because education does not teach us how to introspect in a way that would bring change to our daily routines. In fact, education teaches us there is no need to mount a challenge to the economic status quo. This happens when education suppresses our capacity for critical questioning which might embarrass the establishment, and it also suppresses our uniquely human desire to be more than worker drones in the economic factory of industrialised life. This suppression is achieved via a constant and ideological mantra which is entirely focussed on success, achievement and status when all the while our pursuit of these goals, which require us to strip resources and create pollution, is ruining our planet.

So all I can do is ask, 'Why is it so?' and ask you to ask yourself the same thing and talk about it with others. Why do we work until we retire, die a few years later, and leave what we've accumulated to our children? It feels right to do it. I'm doing it also, but question why. Am I simply copying others? Yes that is probably true because a better and more believable reason remains elusive. Or, is what we do because of something beyond pride and beyond the superficial economic motivations that presently drive our daily lives. For instance, are we genetically designed to be as we are? An answer to this question might help a lot of people sleep better.

Sand Castles

Why do we humans so often want more than we have or need? Why do we innovate and change everything around us regardless of whether a thing needs to be changed? Is it simply because the world is there to be changed? Perhaps it is. For instance, watch children on a beach building a sand castle. They will spend enormous amounts of energy digging and piling, then lose interest and walk away, or on a whim destroy what they have built.

Children are not alone in this pursuit. Adults often do much the same. For instance, many of us spend a lifetime building a career, then walk away from it and die. What's the point? Other than money I mean? We might say ambition, purpose, meaning or sense of achievement are the reasons, but I suggest these reasons are learned rather than being genetic. If that is so, we have the opportunity to unlearn these unfortunate habits.

In fact, I suspect we've become the dominant creature on our planet because of the traits we see in an innocent child's play. We have become dominant because we understand how to build the metaphoric sand castle. That is, we can envisage what the end result will be before we start.

Yet, perhaps we have moved past the point of being clever to a place where our cleverness is now going to be our undoing. We do seem to be building problems with no solutions. Perhaps the way to stop is to train our kids to consider the impact their sand castle efforts will have on their lives, before they build them.

Are there alternatives? Can some of us realistically expect to go off on a tangent and create a lifestyle different to the rest of society? This is the question behind thinking about sand castles. 'Is there a realistic option, an option to create a different society, one we can all enjoy in the knowledge it is beneficial to nature and so ourselves?' One with less stress and less focus on financial entanglement. Can we build a society that has no natural resource endpoint. Change is certainly possible and our climate scientists are telling us such changes are urgently needed, but we too often ignore scientists because, even if we factor in the downside of our hectic lives, the lure of having greater affluence remains too powerful. It seems thoughts of a significant change to our way of life are quashed by an ever-present array of economic distractions and social illusions which foster and nourish our egos, our ambitions and our curiosity. What is the result of this endless charge? Our sand castles are no longer sustainable because we have never been satisfied with them and keep reinventing such structures with ever more negative consequences.

I think this has happened because, regardless of the cost or threats or risks we know about, our humanness is only concerned with the here and now, with feeling good in the moment and with how big our sand castle is or how it compares to everyone else's efforts.

We are not well equipped by evolution to consider the long-term, even if ignoring the long-term means putting our future at risk. That's curious in itself.

History tells us all previous empires have disappeared for much the same reasons as we face today. And yet, the situation today is different to the past because of its scale and impact. What we are doing threatens the very viability of our planet to support life itself.

Derek Jensen (1999) points out in End Game: The Problem with Civilisation, that the carrying capacity of our planet is about one-fourth of what is required to support our current population at North American middle class standards. Still, knowing this, or any other environmental statistics for that matter, does not inspire us to change our ways. We have not yet been able to take our attention away from the comfort and convenience that economic activity tempts us with. Much has been written about this problem. As much, has been ignored.

Why? Well, that's the real question. If we can find that answer, perhaps there is an opportunity to prevent our kind joining the list of extinct species in Earth's future history.

Chapter Six

History: An Unorthodox Perspective

The important messages in our history, the messages telling us what not to replicate, are largely overlooked. Those messages are replaced in education, our media, and our days of remembrance, with versions of events that appeal to our ego and rouse our pride. This focus is needed to legitimise conflict and competition that costs millions of lives and destroys or degrades great swathes of environment.

Knowing the dates of wars and conquests or who came to power when, is of no value unless we understand whether or not we are repeating history, and then make changes to prevent a repeat of tragic events. The more useful aspect of our history is to realise, for instance, that no past empire (no matter how many soldiers sadly and tragically died to defend it) has survived. Why then do we persist with repeating the process of empire building without ensuring each new empire will serve us better than the last? That is to say, 'Why would we expect today's empires to be any more likely to survive the test of time given their foundations are no different to the past? And, in particular, I have to question why soldiers agree to die to protect empires. Why don't we send the warmongering power brokers into battle instead of sending members of the public?

The answer is that we allow our patriotic fervour to rule

over our better judgement by erroneously accepting we are proudly defending our nation. Now that really is bollocks, because in most cases wars can be avoided by addressing the social and political causes long before they fester to the point of open conflict.

The fact is, soldiers do not defend a way of life, rather the 'will' of the wealthy is defended, and the soldier's real function is to ensure the economic imperative is allowed to go unchallenged. Protecting the average person's way of life is nothing more than a plausible cover story. Did war protect the lives of the French, Polish, British or German civilians during World War II or any other war for that matter? Of course not, but such is the primary rhetoric of the war mongers.

It seems we prey on the testosterone charged egos of young men, who know nothing of history other than lies about patriotism and heroism, to give them the courage needed to face enemy machine guns.

They die and that's tragic and sorrowful, but more tragic is that we don't send the real culprits to do battle or, better still, let's head off wars before they start. Let's indict those who sit behind a wall of wealth and dictate that cash-strapped young people should die on their behalf. They get away with this at present because the average person in the street swallows the story that wars lead to greater economic wealth.

Then, once a year we hold a solemn service to remember the glorious death of our fellow humans, rather than avoid the complete waste that war is, or prosecute and persecute those who sent them to die. Ah yes, it's true, we hang or shoot a few dictators who we conveniently blame for starting wars, but never convict the real culprits: the manipulators and connivers who orchestrate the dance of war.

The bottom line is this. If we delve into why wars start, the reasons rarely (if ever) have anything to do with the welfare of the masses and everything to do with ensuring the wealth and power pyramids needed to support economic activity are maintained.

For instance, history tells us the Roman Empire fell partly because the Roman people (meaning the soldiers and their families assigned to border outposts) lost faith in an administration that was demonstrably more interested in their own personal pleasures than in running the country. Another cause was the sheer cost of Rome's armed forces. Maintaining a military umbrella (as the Romans did and as the USA has done since World War II) is unbelievably expensive. The cost eventually crippled Rome.

US government debt has reached staggering levels, largely because of its military expenditure. Will the US population lose faith in their leadership? I suggest, based on media reports, that large numbers of Americans already have, but don't know how to challenge the establishment. As a safeguard against the common person having an effective say, the US voting system is entirely geared to protect against any legal reprisal by commoners. To wit, we can ask, 'When was the last time a candidate stood without millions in campaign funds behind them?' And today, US armed forces stand ready to quell any broad-based citizens' physical protest.

Patriotism, nationalism, parochialism and economic ideology are the tools used to exploit the emotions of taxpayers and keep commoners loyal to the economic paradigm. Sooner or later though, the burden will become too great for the US (and other countries) to bear. Then another superpower will crumble just as the Soviet empire failed when the social and economic impost of its military grew too large for its people.

One only has to look more closely at the cost of the US military to understand the extent of the problem. According to Derek Jensen (1999), during the first Iraq War alone, US bombing cost the American taxpayer $1 billion per day. Also, fifty percent of all the fossil fuels used in the United States are used to mobilise the armed forces from day to day. The taxpayer funds this expense and their tax dollars become profits for the arms dealers and oil companies.

To placate taxpayers, economic rhetoric tells us this process creates 'economic growth' and 'national security'. If so, one has to wonder why as reported by Hope Yen in 2013, '...*eighty percent of (American) adults struggle with joblessness, near-poverty or reliance on welfare for at least parts of their lives, (which is) a sign of deteriorating economic security and the elusive American dream'.* Evidently, the wealth of war is not reaching those who need it. It is the wealthy arms dealers and their subsidiaries who scoop up the dollars, and, parochial patriotism operates to ensure there is little objection to this process.

Uncertainty

One result of economic conflict and physical war which are now capable of affecting our entire planet is 'economic uncertainty.' This benign label is misleading though. Economic uncertainty is actually a deep seated and highly consequential fear of economic loss. This fear drives volatility in financial markets and volatility is required to create profits from those markets. Without volatility cycles there are no winners and losers and economic markets effectively cease to function as a wealth centralisation vehicle. Sadly, swinging volatility is a mechanism which facilitates the legal acquisition of what little money mum and dad wage earners have squirreled away in financial market investments and superannuation. Also tragic, are the losses working class people endure when so-called expert investment houses take a hit.

Volatility is and must be created; meaning market cycles and crashes are an integral component of the wealth centralisation process. It may be too much of a leap to suggest market crashes are engineered; however, any market trader worth his or her weight in salt knows how to take advantage and eagerly awaits the opportunity to profit from others misfortune when markets swing.

The pertinent problem is that financial markets are 'winners and losers' systems founded on financial conflict. We sanitise this conflict by labelling it 'healthy competition', 'market forces' or 'financial cycles.' However, in any pyramidal competition there can only be a few winners and a large number of losers, meaning a few ultra-wealthy people end up controlling the vast majority of wealth. The rest are truly losers, or rather, as we are labelled to avoid the stigma of being called losers, workers and tax payers. In fact, the reality is that we are wage slaves: people whose time is effectively owned and directed by those people we work for.

Yes, I hear you say, 'some make it to the big time'. A few more are comfortable and others are 'okay with their level of wealth' so where is the problem? The issue is that none of us are really winning if we consider the unacknowledged environmental cost, the personal stress, or the impact on family life that economic market activity imposes.

Despite this situation, if we have even a modest level of affluence, and even if we know having our unequal share requires us to live with uncertainty, affluence remains a powerful motivator. Why? Because economic rhetoric convinces us that gaining ever higher affluence is the central purpose of life no matter the cost, no matter the risk. That is, for too many people success is embedded and enmeshed completely, entirely and only in the economic paradigm.

But I ask, 'If we sit in traffic snarls breathing polluted air, deal with our daily frustrations, put up with economic and environmental worries and uncertainty, and work long hours away from our loved ones, how are we winners?' The situation is not black and white though. Nothing we humans participate in is as rigidly defined as yes or no, right or wrong. Except to say that, if we continue to destroy our planet as we pursue more of everything our economies offer, ultimately we all lose. That much *is* a certainty.

How do we explain this situation? I believe it is an issue of our minds structure. It is how evolution built us. We are genetically programmed toward satisfying our now wildly out of control self-interest drive rather than pulling back and showing restraint. In other words, our search for nuts and berries that once kept us alive, has taken us to the point where we are no longer satisfied with picking the crop. Now we want the whole tree and the other guy's tree as well. Bugger that, we want the entire population of trees, worldwide. Corner the market and clean up is the economic modus operandi.

If it feels good do it, has been our way but it's gone wild. This is history's first lesson: that we can't keep 'doing it' just because 'it feels good.' We need to look at history not to find new ways to turn a profit, rather to see how to avoid the dangers of our self-interest drive. Of course, challenging three million years of evolution won't be easy.

Hunter Gatherers

The drive to hunt and gather has been with us for a long time and has its origins in our distant ancestry, a time when our survival hinged on being successful in the wild. At that time, we had little choice other than to keep busy and seek new sources of food, water, shelter, and find a mate – this by definition is our self-interest drive. Today, as has been the situation throughout history, without it we would perish.

Despite being forced to survive in the real sense of the word, our ancestors had choices; they had real freedom to do as they pleased; to provide for themselves, and the very real opportunity to experience the direct rewards on offer for fitting in with nature. And clearly, given their small number, they were unable to degrade the biosphere more than it could recover: meaning their way of life was truly sustainable.

Our nomadic and tribal survivalist days are behind us but our urge to be purposeful remains. However, today that urge is regularly misinterpreted as ambition, and, modern human ambition is far too focussed on the economic imperative. Ambition can be of benefit, but only when it increases our chances of a healthy and happy life. The problem with ambition is that it can be blind and so too often results in negative consequences. Understandably, we can only see this if our frame of reference is set to value biological health rather than financial wealth. Chasing financial wealth is a distraction from happiness and contentment, and, finding rationalisations for maintaining the economic status quo can't resolve our biological needs. Equally, economic ambition, competition and conflict cannot satisfy our human need to have purpose and meaning. A new plan really is necessary.

To satiate our remnant genetic ambitions (collecting food, water and shelter) we have changed our focus from using clubs or spears and finding shelter as we negotiate the landscape, to obtaining cash and qualifying for credit (becoming indebted) as we try to survive in today's economic jungle.

To create perceived wealth, we build towns and cities which take from the land and return little, if anything, to the environment. There's no circle of life in cities, just consumption and waste output. You might say cities are a one-way street. Boom, boom! To build them, we use energy to transform Earth into metal and glass, trees to toilet paper, habitat to concrete and bitumen, forests to suburbs, and free people to wage slaves.

To prop up the survival of cities we educate (enslave?) our children to ensure they participate in city life as we've done. Why? Because we find comfort in ensuring we are all in the same boat, even if the boat is sinking. We enslave our kids so they can compete and so they won't be enslaved by others with more education...wait on, it seems, either way, they are slaves. If that's so, what to do? Well, for one thing, let's not raise our children in our own image. Instead, let us make sure they have a very different outlook on life and what the heck it's all about.

At present life is about rushing and doing in order to separate ourselves from nature, rather than being satisfied and co-existing. We do this because a close connection with nature reminds us of our mortality. Denial of our mortality is popular but it is irrational because we are inseparable from nature. No matter how much economic propaganda states we can use our technology to give us an edge over nature, we can't escape our reliance on everything non-human. But we work harder and harder as if we *can* be separate. As a result, living has become habitual instead of fulfilling and meaningful.

Quietness Hurts

Nowadays, if we make a conscious effort to be quiet for a few minutes the experience can be somewhat disturbing, especially if a looming deadline is on our mind. We feel compelled to get busy. The reason? Others want to profit from our labour and us from theirs, so we all try to outdo each other. The idea that we cannot afford to stop without the risk of falling behind and being labelled a loser is frightful and highly motivating, but it is a competition where no one wins. Strange though it may sound, I like fitting the description of a loser; it's a peaceful place to be. There's no rushing about; no stress filled days; no need to compete or be envious. Try it, you might like it. It might feel good.

Instead, for most of us, if we take the opportunity to be quiet for a moment our minds wander to what we will do next and almost unconsciously we find ourselves doing something, anything, rather than remaining still and quiet. Whether it is making a cup of tea or coffee, thinking about the future or fidgeting with a leaf, a pen, or some other nearby object, we find a way to occupy our minds.

This is the legacy of our evolution. We see it in children building sand castles on the beach. Then years later, we see them building skyscrapers and dams and wonder what drives them to do it. The answer is us - parents. We taught them to be like us. Again I say, teach kids to be different, to have more sustainable, relaxed and enjoyable values.

Too much of our daily media content is about economic competition, one-ups-man-ship and, sadly, the violence which arises between people and nations when they compete. I'm convinced this is because our drive to ensure we have sufficient daily food and shelter etc has evolved into a stressful and damaging global competition to have more than we need. Economic activity, the label we have given to our financial battle with each other, creates monetary profits but comes at an enormous cost. The tragedy is that our drive for comfort and convenience is now threatening our very survival and we seem unable to pull back or change direction. Were the environmental impact to show its hand more quickly, as quickly as new digital devices come into our lives, we might react differently.

Considering this, I think there is merit in asking if there's a better way forward. I have to believe there is and a framework for that path is set out in part three of this book. However, in order to appreciate such change we need to better understand our past, ourselves and why we have become so busy. That understanding might just enable us to achieve the survival goals we set millions of years ago when our earliest ancestors first picked up a hand tool to make life easier and more survivable. However, at that time convenience and comfort were not the motivators of what our ancestors did. Such motivations obviously came much later.

Small Beginnings

Our present way of life evolved from meagre beginnings, a time when our ancestors decided to give up their nomadic life and settle into villages. That move went well at first because those early communities had to cooperate to succeed.

Up until the time when populations reached around one hundred and fifty, everyone in a community was able to know and work with everyone else. The opportunity to take unfair advantage of someone was low. As populations grew (past 150 or so) it became impossible to know everyone.

Breaking the personal and close connection with people in this way made it possible to do wrong to others without remorse or concern. In other words, anonymity arose. Since that time, crimes-against-neighbours have escalated dramatically, social connectedness within communities has declined, and we have created laws in an attempt to control inappropriate behaviour. Coincidentally, to create fair trade between people who had no personal connection with each other, currencies and markets developed.

Today, we see the end result of those early years, and in many respects, our societies have regressed since then. We care less about others than ever before as is evidenced by profiteering which has become the acceptable means of taking advantage of others. Profiteering is by definition, a deliberate action to take from others in an unfair but legal way. It usually occurs in transactions between people who don't care about each other. Would we take an inappropriate profit from our mothers, fathers, sons or daughters? Would we knowingly and intentionally charge our family or friends more for an item than it's worth, just to make a profit? I suppose some might, but I have to believe most would be fair-minded. Regardless, the point to be made is that profiteering is a fundamental tenant of an uncaring and cold economic system, and is the antithesis of mature, evolved and civilised societies.

Profiteering is deemed normal simply by its predominance in our world, but it's predatory, it's uncivilised, and it's immoral. The outcome of this strategy is distrust, dislike, fear, uncertainty and all too often, conflict.

The social contradiction of profiteering is all around us but is rarely if ever challenged and more often these days is over looked because it's become 'normal'. Then the issue to consider is our frame of reference. Today it's askew, awry, and problematic because it flies in the face of the values we teach our children and aspire to as caring communities. This suggests we may have found the source of the wealth divide. That is, in order to maximise profit, we need to be personally disconnected from others.

Also, to avoid retaliation from those we profit from, to maintain a high standard of living, and to make businesses profitable, we need to be shielded by finance transaction laws. However, and this is the kernel of our social ills, such a comment is deeply entrenched in economic thinking. That is to say, our standard of living today is only high in monetary terms. On every other front, we are worse off. We endure more stress, more risks, more troubling decisions, long working hours, a dying environment, disconnected families, worry about the future and dissatisfaction with work, the list goes on and on. Certainly, our concerns are no longer centred on, for example, being in a coal mine at nine years of age, but are we truly better off?

Much of our work is mundane, repetitive and uninspiring. It is also as dangerous as a coal mine if we accept the negative impact on the world that comes with economic activity per se. To think otherwise is to be an ostrich. I suggest also, that relying on contract law is not the way to build cooperative, tolerant and inclusive communities.

That is not to say we don't need laws. We do. People need boundaries. However, our laws are designed primarily to define ownership and accumulate wealth rather than creating equity or protecting resources and building connected communities. Laws attempt to be black and white. Yours, mine, don't cross the line is the ethos when a grey solution, let's share, is the better option. Sharing sounds soft and lame doesn't it? That's because we are no longer accustomed to hearing such words. An anecdote is useful here.

Recently, I built a new boundary fence next to my home. While the old fence was down I talked and chatted with my neighbour. Since it went back up, we have not spoken a word. That's because the fence represents a legal transaction and a social boundary. Laws (such as property laws) absolve us of responsibility for the impact we have on others and the responsibility to communicate with them: well that's the illusion at least. The reality is laws are a massive problem we can't address unless we recognise profiteering, made possible by ownership laws, is the fundamental problem in our social fabric. History tells us this is so and yet we persist with such a damaging system.

Today, owning and defending ownership feels right because such words and habits are the language of economics that we have heard from birth. Not because ownership contracts are the best way to arrange our communities but rather because being insular, separate and independent have become the norm.

The lessons about laws in our history, are perverted such that they seem to justify having more laws rather than fewer. The truth is, we don't really enjoy being insular and isolated even though that is what laws attempt to achieve. Sadly, laws are accepted because we have taken on the prevailing economic ideology which convinces us aspiring to be independently wealthy within our communities and social circles are our purpose in life: laws give a false sense of independence.

Strange isn't it: that, as we become wealthier, our social circles change to omit those who don't keep up with our status, while observable evidence all around us says we are incredibly social and emotional beings. We need, in fact we thrive on, being validated and having our ego stroked by others and yet we live within an economic culture of separateness. This culture places a dollar value on human and all other life and non-living resources. We have become a culture of wall builders. So much so, sharing has become an antiquated if not forgotten word in our business dealings and lives generally.

Even so, living with our natural world is a give-and-take relationship and we might be well advised to consider that nature knows nothing of money and ownership or emotions or contract law for that matter. In fact, I would say, the survival of nature now relies on our kindness and willingness to share, which perhaps explains why the natural world is suffering. We've stopped caring and hardened our hearts and that situation is fostered and reflected by how we conduct and encourage financial transactions.

Laws have come to replace trust between people as well as compassion and tolerance for that matter. Laws, particularly finance laws, which include taxation law and property owner-ship laws are the new swords-of-kings wielded to shift wealth from the poor to the wealthy. On that front, little has changed since the dark ages in that the poor still pay more tax than the wealthy. What is the result of this social regression?

The idealism contained in our constitutions and welfare policies aimed at creating wealth equality and social equity are failing as is evidenced by the growing chasm between the rich and the rest.

Interestingly, if all the wealth of our economic world were placed into a single bucket and evenly distributed only 2% of our population would be less wealthy. However, like the lotto dream we prefer to compete in a race we are unlikely to win (to be in the 2%) than we are to share and be content. It does seem we are as motivated by the chase today as we were when we used clubs and spears. Our loin cloths cost a lot more now though.

Then it is evident, the switch up to financial tools is merely a veneer of technological change rather than social progress.

In many respects, the outward display of our civility has been eroded in real terms. That is, we now have the means to assist the less fortunate, but choose not to. As stated earlier, the clever and I would say the insidious nature of our modern economics, is its ability to offer just enough wealth to the masses to prevent a serious challenge to the system from being mounted. And at the same time, economic ideology convinces us that destroying our environment to enable the economic paradigm to continue is a reasonable trade-off.

Outspoken Critics

More and more we are hearing prominent people speak of the need to address climate change. US President Obama, Sir David Attenborough, Dr Bob Ballard, celebrities such as Harrison Ford and many others talk about the problems we face. However, it is the voting public who hold the key to our future, not familiar identities. At the end of the day, public opinion drives political decision-making, meaning without our public support politicians cannot hope to overcome corporate influences. This is not to suggest corporations are evil conspirators, but, it does say businesses have just one goal, economic survival at any cost. We know our greater concern is environmental survival, but the industry funded sceptics have turned us away from such thinking.

I believe we can have a healthy environment and financial security at the same time, provided our businesses are focused on repairing the damage we have done as well as respecting our biological reliance on nature. At present, the vast majority do not.

Our vote, or our political allegiance, is our most effective and efficient means to put a solution in place. But as stated already, garnering a green vote will mean accepting change and change is difficult for we humans simply because we don't like being told what to do. Maybe my writing lecturer was correct after all when he said, 'don't try to deliver a message, your audience will hate you for it.' I can only hope he was wrong.

Either way, it seems we really are creatures of ego and personal pride and it is unreasonable to expect us to up and change at the drop of a hat. At the same time, the environment is more important than our individual pride.

In other words, we simply cannot afford to consider ourselves separate from nature. We know we are different to other creatures and we seem intent on displaying that difference. Still, if we are endangering ourselves along the way, it's a bit hard to say we are 'progressing'.

To keep us focused on the oil-based economy and all its trappings, the climate change 'sceptics' have leveraged our fear of economic loss. The result is that simply discussing environmental issues feels like criticism of who we are. And so now we are caught between a rock and a hard place. We don't like being criticised. We don't like being told what to do. But we also know what we are doing is, well, wrong. We scald our children and make them admit to their mistakes so perhaps it is time to practice what we preach. Does that sound like criticism? It probably does.

The question is: 'Can we take the criticism on the chin and use it to energise a positive outcome? Or simply close this book and walk away?' I would like to say it's a choice like chocolate vs broccoli, but bear in mind nature has no interest in such human concepts as choice or like and dislike.

Chapter Seven

Don't Criticise

Pleased to see the first edition of this book in print, I was somewhat deflated by my wife's darkening expression as she read the words I had so carefully constructed. In her estimation the story was saddening, the tone was angry and she felt the finger of criticism being pointed at her. I suspect her sentiment arose partly because the words challenged the fundamentals of the accounting profession she chose years ago, and partly because she wanted to be entertained by a fun-to-read book.

The first edition was just too critical and did not provide the escapism she sought after a day at work. This is interesting in itself because her need to escape is indicative of not being happy, not being content or satisfied with one's daily routine. The temptation to argue that point with her was strong and I have to admit we had a few words.

Ultimately, she was right of course. Even so, her reaction was typical of many when challenged by a call for environmental protection in our lives, or any serious look at how we conduct our day to day economic activity for that matter.

Similarly, when I look around the world and see the economic and social problems we have created, I am saddened: My mood darkens because I see people struggling and suffering when things could be so much better.

Happy vs Content

Is it realistic to want to be happy all the time? Or put more accurately, can we be as happy as the advertising on television works hard to convince us is possible. The answer is an unsurprising no, and that's because happiness is momentary. Still, the expectation of endless smiles as seen in product advertising is created nonetheless. The better understanding is to realise any state of mind can only be experienced by contrasting it to another. Happiness is only possible if we experience unhappiness and so on.

This is why products are designed to fail. They fail in order to keep us running the emotional roller coaster of highs and lows as we spend and re-spend on products in order to get our next spending high. It should be obvious then, producers can't afford for us to be happy with their products because happy, content people consume less. Hence we see much planned obsolescence.

Considering this situation we might say that being content is more sustainable. That's because while contentment is not happiness, it is more enduring, and it keeps unhappiness at bay. Even better, contentment is not something we can buy. It comes from our mind-set, our attitudes, values and beliefs. And, that's not to say we should give up on being happy, but perhaps finding the middle ground will be easier especially since it does not involve spending and consuming. In other words, seek contentment rather than buying into the myth that we can be happy all the time simply by spending on the stuff of economic activity.

That's brilliant. We've found a way to free ourselves from the consumer trap. We just have to be content with what we have. The bonus being there will be more cash in our pockets.

Of course, under our present economic system contentment is actively discouraged at every turn. It has to be or our system of making profits will fail. In fact, we are taught from a young age that to be content is really a lack of competitiveness and ambition.

Obviously, we need to eat and clothe ourselves meaning some spending is unavoidable. However, there is a great deal of spending on unnecessary products and services which serve a singular purpose and that is to ensure we keep chasing more cash to feed our consumer addiction. In turn, our spending feeds the tax system.

Prestige

Our self-concept, self-worth and social status are all too often linked to ownership of prestigious items and an outward display of our consumption of less significant items - driven by fashions and fads - when the better means to achieving self-worth is a content state of mind. Who and what we are is not determined by the size of our bank account, the size of our house, or the products we purchase, but our economic system ultimately relies on us thinking that it is.

This is the basis of the consumer trap set to ensnare our humanness and it has been very successful. It has captured our happiness and contentment and sold it back to us, but at the cost of our future. We might even say capitalism sells us unhappiness. At least that would be the case if we had a conscience about the state of our environment.

To reiterate, the advertisers and marketers have convinced us their products will deliver, but obviously, they do not. If they did, we would need but one or perhaps two or three products and these would make us eternally happy. Instead, fashions change, meaning the new toy purchased today is obsolete tomorrow and must be upgraded and so we work ever harder to earn more cash only to give it back to the corporations when we purchase more stuff. Seriously, what is wrong with last year's products? If we stayed with last years, we might not need to ask, 'What the heck is life all about?'

Research

Published and peer-reviewed social research supports the notion that wealth, products and possessions do not bring happiness.

Stutz & Mintzer (2006) found happiness with life fell away as personal wealth increased beyond meeting basic needs. It seems a low figure, but according to the 2006 study, reported well-being did not rise as incomes increased beyond a base level of just US$22,000 per annum. The reason? Material affluence does not meet all our human needs such as being socially connected or having freedom and being understood.

As put by the researchers, '...*people assume acquiring a higher level of affluence will bring more and longer lasting happiness than it actually does*' (Stutz & Mintzer, 2006).

It is apparent that we work hard to gain economic security from higher incomes, but and herein lays the source of our unhappiness, at no time do we feel completely financially secure. As well, all the while there is the nagging thought that we are a part of the problem we see in our environmental, social and economic circumstances.

Nevertheless, we fear economic loss more than environmental loss because the effects are perceived to be more immediate. Equally, we do little to challenge the reasons for our fear of financial hardship preferring to participate in the daily competition for more wealth.

This is the conundrum of our times and I hear it expressed in the by now familiar question, 'What the heck is life all about?'

How we make progress toward being content with less over the coming years has become our new age environmental question of survival.

Chapter Eight

Uncomfortable Bedfellows

What drives our inner happiness? Psychology tells us our minds are a complex mix of emotions and intellect, and while our intellect works hard to make sense of how we feel from day to day, sometimes it succeeds, other times it doesn't. The end result is that we live in a social and economic minefield of emotionally charged opinions and points of view which often clash. They clash because we like to have our opinions validated, and also, we easily fall into defending our point of view especially if we have a lot of time and effort invested in arriving at that perspective. Where has this left us?

If our allegiance to our opinion is strong, ideological if you like, trouble is likely to follow a challenge to our position. Two key questions arise out of this circumstance, namely: 'What are we doing to improve this situation?' which is a question aimed at social policy and the content of education, and, 'How can we maintain an opinion without falling into conflict over our individual beliefs?' The latter is particularly important because getting emotional or angry prevents clear thinking. Moreover, having a strong and ideological conviction about any issue is a path to violence, because being ideological closes off our acceptance of alternatives, solutions and options which would otherwise be considered.

Being ideological especially closes our minds to concepts like compassion and tolerance which are the best tools we have to avoid social problems like bullying, road rage, terrorism and even a simple argument.

Tolerance and compassion have become far too aligned with losing and so they are undervalued in today's world. They are certainly seen as soft words and as such lacking a sense of superiority. And yet, compassion and tolerance are in every way superior to entering into conflict. Clearly, it takes far more courage to go against the popular rhetoric of our peers and against our primal emotions, than to acquiesce. Especially if taking a passive stance involves being perceived as soft and gooey: if that happens, our ego will scream at us to find a socially validated position.

Shifting Ideologies

The key to dealing with a strong attachment to beliefs is to know we are free to shift and change our life ideology whenever needed. There is absolutely no shame in changing our position on a topic, despite the counter-intuitive feeling which may accompany doing so.

This is a form of wisdom our education systems do not teach. Instead, education encourages a rigid, usually economic ideology based on competitiveness, the importance of money, the pursuit of prestige, as well as, feeling superior. This is why our world is darkened by conflict, stress and worry. Our incredible human persistence has been, and continues to be, captivated by economic distractions and the high which comes with competing, rather than being content with less.

Ultimately, stress and worry arrive in our lives when we see our striving for success is not panning out as we expected -

when we are not validated for our efforts.

Our emotions and intellect really are strange bedfellows. We often know the appropriate thought, behaviour, or better reaction to a circumstance, but feel compelled to go in the socially expected direction or wherever our emotions drive us at the time. Should we, will we, do we, choose broccoli or chocolate is the question? At the end of the day, it seems we acquiesce to a learned and concocted ideology of success and consumption, even if it means creating resentment in others, stress in our lives, or degradation of the world around us. It's time to deploy our capacity for humaneness and consider the merits of choosing broccoli more than we do at present.

Togetherness or Independence

I wonder if John Fitzpatrick in Ireland would consider himself a friend were we to meet and have a conversation. Would we offer each other a greeting based on mutual trust or be guarded and standoffish?

The point is we understand and accept our efforts to create and maintain friendships are unlikely to succeed if our strategy in conversation is to tell others what to do, what to think, or why they must accept our views. Then, this would not be a way to endear ourselves to John (assuming he is a real person).

Likewise, the words in this book so far are not particularly complimentary to our species and likely are perceived as quite directive, cynical, dark and negative. It may seem the theme so far has been one of condemnation of humanity. But that is just more bollocks. Every word is intended as an encouragement to move toward a happier and more content life. Every word is a path to a vibrant, healthy and self-sustaining way of life. To hear the words so far as dark and depressing is to be firmly held in the grip of economic ideology and its dark and destructive end game. To embrace economic ideology, is to be as spellbound by mysticism as the people of the dark ages were when they feared the clergy, God or the Devil - and as well - before that when paganism's raft of gods directed human social consciousness.

In what realm of consciousness is it possible that speaking of protecting our natural world in order to keep us healthy and alive is dark and depressing? What realm indeed? I suggest it is only possible if we really are ideological and parochial economic rationalists. This is the persona that should be offensive to John in Ireland, and indeed to all of us.

A Stranger Arrives

If we are ideological and parochial economic rationalists, then it follows that if one day someone comes along who has opposing view to our own; a view which is contrary to the fundamental beliefs that have been instilled by a childhood exposed to economic propaganda; and to whom we are perhaps only vaguely connected, we might struggle to accept or adopt that view. No, not struggle, our immediate gut reaction will be to dismiss the view out of hand.

Regardless, the person's view may contain something useful and worth considering, suggesting it is important to keep an open mind. And of course, the different view this stranger has will arouse an emotional response, usually fear, resentment or anger. That's because the view challenges the legitimacy of our ideology and may even challenge our concept of who we are.

Despite this, it still remains possible the other person's view has merit. We don't have to like the perspective or agree with it, but it usually pays to listen to alternatives, and depending on the setting, social rules may dictate that we listen or be seen as rude, or worse, arrogant. I suggest it would be an unfortunate missed opportunity if we dismissed the views of others and perhaps missed friendship opportunities or information that may be of great importance simply because the opinion of the new acquaintance does not immediately validate our thoughts and activities, or stroke our egos. This is the mark of our era. The mark of economic rationalism: The notion that thoughts about profits are able to decide the formation or not of friendships.

Too often, social groups with differing outlooks on life enter into conflict to resolve differences because of parochial ideology. Here again, we see a social contradiction. That is, we see people forming cooperative groups which become identifiably different to other nearby groups, and subsequently, these groups fall into conflict. This is a worrying reality. That we are willing to close our minds to alternative world views in order to maintain *our* world view. In this, I speak mainly of racism and bigotry which arises from parochial patriotism and nationalism. Argh, that's a mouthful. Put simply, far too much conflict arises due to perceived difference where none actually exists. Accent, skin colour, spiritual or cultural beliefs, even environmentalism hardly constitutes a defensible reason for any form of conflict or bigotry.

Still, nation building and defence of borders (defence of egos?) is rampant in our world today and has been for many thousands of years. What chance then, does the stranger who comes into our midst bearing a message such as environmental protection have of being heard and appreciated? This person may look like us, sound like us, even be a long-term member of our community but still be ignored. Then perhaps something other than physical differences or different languages or cultural beliefs is operating to create the ideologies we see between individuals and groups.

The real cause is this. Our quest to build safe communities has been perverted by profiteering. The result being, we have created perceived differences between the peoples of our planet that are convenient to profit making but not to peace and community bonding. We have created ownership laws which only make sense if we expect to profit. The problem is we have become subservient to too many laws, especially corporate law.

Corporations own just about everything of monetary value and are protected by laws which ultimately empower these non-human entities. My god, what have we done? I think we have lost the capacity, will and/or gumption to challenge the system. We have lost it through exposing each generation to propaganda and social conditioning (posing as media and education). Even more so, we simply find the comforts offered by the affluence our inequitable laws makes possible, too attractive.

Under this arrangement we have come to expect others who sound or look different are to be shunned, even ostracised or as is common now, physically excised. Why has this happened? It's so that we can exploit them with a clear conscience. For instance, consider the poverty experienced by the children of the low-paid workers, who live in squalor, to make cheap sports shoes available. The crazed insanity of this industry is the enormous price consumers are willing to pay for a shoe that the manufacturer paid a few cents for. Even the death of children forced to drink water contaminated by sports shoe factories does not break through the conditioning imposed by economic rationalism.

Corporatisation and nationalisation of our society are only possible where we accept the notion that one group deserves, or has the right to be more affluent than another. That right is supported by you and I, the consumers and voters of our world. We enable corporations with every purchase and every conservative vote.

A sense of right-to-access (to other nation's resources) and a feeling of superiority are the underlying reasons for border disputes and nationalistic parochialism. Establishing right from wrong and being able to meter out sanctions is the basis of ownership law which powerful nations impose on others. And these laws are only possible if we empower them by participating in the consumer trap. We teach it in schools and we are inculcated by our media services. In light of this, again I ask, 'What chance does the stranger, who comes into our midst bearing a message such as environmental protection, have of being heard and appreciated?' How do we break through a lifetime of social conditioning which most people don't give consideration to from day to day? I think the answer is we must appeal to human self-interest. We must appeal in the same way consumerism does. We have to ask, what would make us feel good and thus serve our self-interest and make life better at the same time?

Radically reducing our spending and so ridding ourselves of financial entanglement feels good on many fronts. It seems so simple, to say *spend less*, when breaking our affluence addiction will be anything but easy. Perhaps a deeper understanding of 'self-interest' will help.

Self-Interest

According to research published by Griskevicius et al, 2012, in the Journal of Public Policy and Marketing, we are genetically wired with a predisposition to ensure our individual survival by exploiting resources. This is our self-interest drive operating to ensure we eat, drink, and find shelter and a mate. No surprise there. In fact, it seems blatantly obvious that we have no choice other than to consume resources if we are to stay alive. But today, our in-built drive to 'gather for the winter' is preyed upon by manipulative advertising and marketing and is in overdrive. Our ego gets involved too. It wants us to feel good about what we do regardless of the dangers of over consumption. This is a conundrum because inevitably over consumption leads to financial entanglement, stress, worry and a reduced life experience.

Then, if there is a suggestion that we should show some restraint, our ego immediately sees that as a criticism; it makes us feel bad. When we feel bad our ability to use sound judgement diminishes. If simply feeling bad becomes anxiety and then turns to anger, all bets are off. We become emotionally charged and unlikely to think clearly at all. Still, we are usually more rational than emotional aren't we? Bollocks! We are emotionally charged 24/7! It's just that we sometimes 'lose the plot' and really 'go off' and these extremes are seen in road rage and so on. The rest of the time, the average days, our intellect struggles to stay on top of our emotions.

Every waking moment, our internal judgement engine, our ego, is working its magic to influence our decisions and opinions on all issues we consider, and usually without our conscious awareness. Combine this with the human urge toward self-interest and self-preservation, which is now very much enticed by consumer goods, and we have a mighty challenge ahead if we are to pull back our overuse of Earth's resources. It is doable though. It has to be if we are to survive as a species, and fortunately we have powerful allies – others who think as we do.

Causes

We are a species largely motivated by trends and common

causes, meaning we can rely on each other for motivation when we get together to support a cause. Perhaps then, all we need is the human herd heading in the right direction. No, not the right direction, it's better to say, the safe direction. That is, the direction of life which means caring for the real world as opposed to the consumption and pollution of it.

If our social group embraces a cause, we are likely to join in and all over the world a growing number of average people are shouting the demand for change. Conversely, and at the same time, the rest of the global 'crowd' is consuming ever more goods and services. The latter is a bit mindless though, isn't it? As a reason to be alive I mean? How can we say we are individuals with an identity and free will, or that we are independent, if all we do is consume because others are doing so.

Sadly the dangers of overconsumption have been watered down by a small group of self serving profiteers who undermine public opinion about climate science. Despite a 97% consensus between climate change researchers found in a landmark study by Cook et, al. (2013), telling us that climate change is caused by our consumption, we are distracted by the remaining 3% (the industry funded sceptics) who lie to us. Why is this so? It's because our media corporations give 97% of their attention to the 3%! And of course, the sceptic's words encourage our consumption while the 97% appear to be telling us what to do.

If a call to support the climate cause is considered indelicate, how *do* we approach discussions about protecting our environment in a calm and effective manner? How can we raise the issue and discuss it without treading on individual sensibilities or creating anxiety?

The aforementioned social research by Griskevicius, which

looks at our reactions to research data, suggests we need to tread softly and encourage rather than direct. Even so, perhaps we cannot afford to overly soften our approach about climate change just to feel good. Perhaps we need to take the criticism on the chin and ignore the remnants of our primal minds - our self-interest drive - if for no other reason than the immense importance of environmental protection to our future survival.

How we deal with individual sensibilities is a conundrum which has plagued the economy versus the environment debate for many years, but perhaps a common goal of wanting to stay alive will change things. I believe a desire to stay alive is behind the massive mum and dad support for environmental protection that has grown in recent times. You won't hear about it in commercial media though. The owners of our media have no interest in raising such awareness because ultimately it threatens their income stream. Consequently, to be aware of this movement requires us to search the internet and see the ground swell of support for green initiatives for ourselves.

Albert Einstein understood the conundrum we face when he said: 'You cannot solve a problem with more of the thinking that created the problem.' In other words, technological Band-Aids are not the answer to climate change. It is you and I the average consumer who need to sit back and ask, 'What the heck is life all about?' and consider what our lifestyles are doing to the present and the future.

Perhaps the *meaning of life* is about shortening the journey from youthfulness to the wisdom of hindsight without becoming fearful of economic loss, without becoming cynical, sad, or dismissive of environmental protection initiatives. I expect this is only possible if we are surrounded by like-minded people who have left behind the affluence race, preferring instead the contentment which comes from cooperating at having enough rather than having more, more, more. Wow, that's a big ask, right?

It is, but nevertheless, and no matter how daunting the task seems, asking what the heck life is all about is the exciting starting point of an amazing journey from the land of parochial economic ideology to appreciating and nourishing the real world - the non-human natural world. This is a pursuit rewarded with life instead of planned obsolescence, with less stress rather than more financial entanglement.

So, we might ask; 'Where do we start on this mammoth task?' I suggest education is one place. Not just education of kids, but adults too because we don't have the luxury of enough time to wait for generational change. Our planet needs all of us now! I've already talked about the power of our vote in creating change. Add to this a public call for a new curriculum in education, with a central focus on sustainability, and we will have addressed two enormous components of the much needed drivers of change. 'But,' I hear you say, 'we have to work to earn a living...there is so much to do from day to day...life is good why change anything?' The peer reviewed scientific reply is simple enough, 'Everything we value at present is at extreme risk if we don't change.'

Chocolate or Broccoli?

'We work because that's what we do.' 'Life's like that.' 'You get that.' 'Such is life.' 'It's just how it is.' It's probably fair to say we have a common sense understanding of these sayings, and others like 'I hate school/work, why do I have to go?'

I suspect most of us have heard grumbles like those above more than once, but I have to wonder just how much thought has been given to exploring why kids and adults alike are saying these things.

Fortunately, it does not take much scratching below the surface to realise grumbling about school is children's way of saying school is not relevant to their lives. Of course, adults grumble about work for similar reasons. Nevertheless, both activities carry on regardless.

The crazy thing is that economic activity was designed to serve us, not us serve it, but the evidence is that we are now very much bonded servants i.e. wage slaves. How else can we obtain the money needed to buy necessities? The answer is to shift our values, attitudes and beliefs about how to provide the basic necessities for life and move to make them free. The impetus for this shift comes from asking just three simple but critical questions:

1. Who stands to benefit from the way our world operates now?

2. What is the motivation for what they do?
   and

3. What is their reaction to anyone who opposes them?

These three questions will usually uncover the reasons behind any activity whether it is education, the production of chocolates, building and using missiles and bullets, even invading countries, or simply going to work each day to pay for broccoli. If the answers point to a handful of people benefiting while the majority are exploited; a handful of people making laws that benefit the few, and the use of force to keep the rest in line, then perhaps we have the basis for expecting and seeking change.

Socrates wanted to answer the three questions above. He encouraged the youth of the day to question the establishment and saw the profiteers in the markets as parasites on society (as Jesus did). This suggests our history books really do hold some clues, such as providing evidence of how we repeat the problems of yesteryear time and again.

Today, we can look back on the times of Socrates, note the array of gods in the belief systems of his time, and perhaps discount his words on the basis that we no longer worship gods and idols. We see his time as archaic and irrelevant and our own as modern and important. And yet, today we revere a powerful array of economic structures, jobs, growth and profit margins to name a few.

If these economic structures govern how our lives operate and we fear and revere them and show unerring faith in their relevance to our lives, have they not achieved the status of a god? Do we not in fact worship them? We certainly fund the leaders and minions of economic ideology from our meagre wages, which means in truth we are still making offerings to the gods or paying a tithe.

In fact, it may well be true to say all we consider about the human condition today has been discussed in the past. All we need to do is inquire into our history to understand how to deal with who we are and why we have arrived where we are. It seems clear that history is a powerhouse waiting to be tapped.

Instead, our schools focus on economics, accounting, science, English and math as it applies to generating wealth, with no regard for sustainability, personal growth, or moving away from the systems history tells us are problematic. Then, when our economic systems crash or stagger we say, 'Wow what happened?' Usually, our next move is to point an accusing finger at our governments regarding their management, but we don't look at the real cause of the volatility: which is that economic growth assumes infinite resources can be taken from a finite world, that infinite population growth is possible and that new markets will always be available. This has proved to be flawed thinking particularly since the Global Financial Crisis (GFC). But we still have faith. I want to say bollocks again, but won't. Oh hell, yes I will, the economic paradigm is a load of old cobblers. It's bollocks. In all honesty, I think we know it is, but the lure of chocolate over the health of broccoli sees us willing to sacrifice our future to have the candy-like technologies on offer.

Ultimately though, if we fail to learn from the past and so reinvent the wheel over and over, then history has been wasted, as has our education in general.

Moving Ahead

Rhetoric in our media says as a global society we are advancing our moral compass, but are we really? For instance, a recent television news report presented three stories in the following order. A cold snap is chilling the south-east. A man was killed on the freeway. Beer prices are higher in this state than anywhere else in the country.

Apart from the obvious juxtaposition of a life lost amongst petty reports about prices and temperatures, the report said nothing of the causes of the extreme weather or the man's death. It mentioned nothing about the cost of freeways that are dangerous to drive on; it mentioned nothing of work deadlines or economic pressures etc even though they are the cause of such deaths when people rush to meet such deadlines. It mentioned nothing about infrastructure serving to provide profiteering opportunities for wealthy businesses using tax dollars. Also, climate change, the reason for extreme weather, was not commented on at all. That's the same climate change caused by traffic emissions on freeways.

What purpose does the news report serve if nothing changes because the report lacks reference to the causes of the problems? If people keep dying on roads and the weather keeps getting more extreme, but we don't acknowledge the cause, what's the point of reporting such events? The news becomes nothing but a trivial distraction.

Working on It

I oppose suggestions we are working on the problems we face, or that we simply need more time to resolve horrible social and environmental issues. If that were true we should be able to see measurable progress, but our natural world remains in a state of decline and our societies remain riddled with problems.

Interestingly, if we need a law to enable a new tax, it is created in record time. But, if we are looking at an environmental law, it takes years for nothing to happen. There is around ten thousand years of history to review, dissect and consider. Nevertheless, the symptoms of a troubled system are still with us. I ask then, 'Where is the progress?' It should be visible all around us. Instead, we are surrounded by conflict over resources and other social ills.

I believe there is always an alternative solution to conflict and the suffering it causes provided our expectations, values, attitudes and beliefs are in order. That is to say, were we not to value material wealth over the health and welfare and often the very lives of others, conflict in all its forms would struggle to find a foothold. This is where we can choose to surround ourselves with a new social narrative. We have the opportunity to fill our media with messages of cooperation, consideration for others and restraint on technological change. Combine this with modified laws dealing with ownership (the fuel of profiteering) and the change to a less competitive world would follow.

Also, we might ask why some outspoken critics of the establishment are treated so harshly? Jesus had words of wisdom and challenged the establishment and, like Socrates, he was put to death. More recently, some say US President Kennedy was assassinated because he was about to end the Cold War with Russia. Martin Luther King comes to mind, as does the gaoling of Nelson Mandela. But one does not have to be a well-known identity to fall victim to character or physical assassination.

Our military forces kill tens of thousands of civilians in the name of democracy and freedom every year. The question is, 'Whose freedom are we protecting?' I suggest it's the freedom of the wealthy to take from whoever they choose. If that's true, we have not progressed at all from the days of lords and knights wielding swords. The only change is how the power mongers go about taking what they want, meaning they truly have evolved their modus operandi. That is, they give a little more to the masses to keep us placated, and no longer have to pay knights with swords to collect the tithe. Today, we pay enormously inequitable taxes all but voluntarily despite having political systems through which we have the right to protest and create change.

The process of normalising our complacency relies on us being distracted by daily life, and daily life is truly very distracting. The big distractions such as nationalism and patriotism, for instance, are not questioned mainly because we have swallowed the story that we are supporting the delivery of democracy and justice. Whether what we deliver is wanted by the incumbents of the land where democracy is imposed is of no importance, which in turn creates the need for armed forces. It creates conflict while simple day to day responsibilities see us totally absorbed in often inane tasks, meaning we accept the conflict as part of the system.

Nowadays also, when there is a serious challenge to the imposed hierarchy of power and control, verbal and physical violence inevitably erupts. This is often labelled as terrorism. The terrorism label is used as an excuse for invasion, or war and killing, or suppressing of those whom we too easily call radicals. No doubt some deserve the title, but I suggest if we look at the interference by superpowers in the affairs of smaller nations, we will too often find an understandable reason for so-called terrorism. Such was the failed search for weapons of mass destruction in Iraq. On the home front, strikes and protests over wages go largely ignored, and, as for protests about the unhappiness generated by our economic systems, there are no protests.

However, marketers and advertisers, sales professionals and producers all rely on recent history to tell them how to extract wealth from our pockets. They can do this without direct violence or reprisal because of apathy on the part of the average person with respect to instigating change.

There is an abhorrent misuse of knowledge by marketers and advertisers but most of us take that process for granted only because we accept the practices of our economic system rather than questioning them. This exploitation of our knowledge of the past and of our humanness is especially heinous when the techniques target our children. Advertising of dangerous products is immoral and uncivilised and when that advertising is aimed at children, it is child abuse.

Is marketing to children considered radical? No, but it absolutely is. Even so, we are numbed to it and so don't question. I suggest understanding more of our history might just bring about change on this front and so histories' importance is discouraged by those who set the curriculum for education.

A Little History

What can history teach us? According to historian NS Gill (2012) the Roman Empire fell due to factors including the effect of Christianity, social decadence, lead pollution of the water supply, economic pressure and military conflict. These reasons are ominously similar to the issues our modern world faces.

In Roman times, many thousands of soldiers and civilians died in battle when nomadic groups invaded Roman territories. Today thousands die to defend democracy.

The Roman Emperors sacrificed legions to defend their borders and their economic power base. The cost of maintaining the military umbrella was enormous and eventually crippling. Today, superpowers face the same problem. The USSR was unable to afford its military spending and collapsed. The United States spends billions on its military might, while millions of its citizens live in poverty caused by their tax burden and a lack of funds to provide assistance. It seems the US has not learned from history or even recent events.

However, more relevant than economic collapse itself, is the myth suggesting economic pressure is responsible for the death of people. We need to be mindful that economics can bring about the disappearance of an administration but it cannot take a life. Empires may disappear by title, but the people of the empire rarely do. Everyday people certainly suffer as the process plays out though while the wealthy corporations remain largely protected. The point is that when empires fall people die while others live through very difficult times, but economics does not kill or create that suffering. The better proposition is that the attitudes and actions of people determine who lives and who dies when a lack of money stands between people and the food, water and shelter they need. And today, more than ever before, corporate structures need our attention because in many respects they are the empires of our era.

Where civilisations have physically disappeared, for example, the Maya or Aztec, the American Indians, or Australian Aboriginals, it was the thinking-of-people not economic activity per se which decimated once large populations. The quest for gold, gems, territory and resources are the economic reasons we cite for these events, but beneath the surface is a disregard for life itself.

Those who suffer or die are victims of how we humans see little value in the lives of people who are, typically, from across a border. (Hello John Fitzpatrick, can you hear me?) This is another painful lesson from history which we prefer not to discuss, ostensibly because it questions our civility and also because it questions our economic priorities and dents our pride. It questions our nationalism and our patriotism also.

The sad fact is that these social structures are illusions and distractions and they have been employed by parochial economic rationalists to make killing and polluting seem reasonable. It is worth saying again: if we choose not to render aid, people die not because of their economic circumstances but because of our attitude toward helping them in their time of need.

Our history clearly shows our attitude toward money has been more important than our desire to protect life in any form.

Be mindful though, none of this is a victimisation of the individual or people in general. It is an indictment aimed at our global economic ideology. An ideology which surrounds us with a daily narrative reinforcing the idea we must profit or see ourselves in a negative light. Winners are grinners, is the colloquialism.

This is a most dangerous aspect of our humanness. It is the

result of our survivalist heritage left over from when we sought to meet our needs in the wild. This is now manifesting in the economic imperative as we try to satisfy our infinite wants, but I do not believe it is a decision individuals make consciously. Rather, the anonymity associated with living in a large population allows us to rationalise that someone else is responsible. That we are not required to have compassion for those we put at a disadvantage.

We believe an aid agency or government body will pick up the slack where poverty exists. At the end of the day, we make a chocolate or broccoli choice. It is a decision preferring comfort and convenience over personal restraint or sharing with others, and yet we call ourselves civilised.

It is choosing power and control before cooperation and caring. It is opting for personal wealth building over equality or social justice. These are the symptoms of civilisations in the late stages of development. As Gill pointed out, Rome fell for many reasons, amongst which were; military conflict, the effects of the economic imperative, and decadence. All of which are rife in our modern civilisation. I will say it again, citing economic reasons as viable justification for a human life sacrificed or the metaphoric tree removed defies everything being civilised entails. It is possibly true then, economic activity really is a reflection of our values, attitudes, and beliefs.

Our economic theory makes this point by definition when it says: economics is a reflection of the behaviour of humans going about their daily routines, and economics is the study of how to satisfy our unlimited wants with limited natural resources.

The futility of the latter part of this definition is self-evident and may well see us added to the list of past civilisations in our history books. I ask though, 'Who will write the history book after the global environmental calamity takes its toll?'

To ensure a more palatable outcome, there is an urgent need to re-prioritise our current hierarchy of important issues and place parochial economic ideology low on the list. To do this, we need only use some hindsight, and there is an abundance of it waiting in our history vaults. Progressive use of that knowledge would allow us to turn the tables and have economic activity serve us as it should.

Ambition

Although it has already been discussed, ambition requires further clarification because ambition drives technology, and it underpins the economic imperative to race ahead.

The Australian Aboriginals, the American Indians, and other indigenous peoples who we see as primitive, but who were highly sustainable, perhaps did not suffer from ambitious personalities. Or alternatively, they may have mastered the art of contentment in order to coexist with nature. Either way, it seems they were happy with their social structure because those structures did not change for thousands of years. Rather than learn from them, we have destroyed their cultures and inserted our own onto the landscape. Who are we? We are the economically ambitious people responsible for destroying the planet. Again I say, 'Many indigenous cultures remained sustainable and technologically similar for thousands of years, suggesting they saw little reason to change anything about their way of life from year to year.'

Perhaps they did not have ambition or possibly they saw the danger it posed and avoided it. We will never know for sure because they are gone. It is sobering to think of the knowledge we have lost because we slaughtered these people to financially profit from their lands.

Yes, I accept we probably don't want to live in the manner the indigenous tribes we killed did. Surely though, there is a happy medium. A point of enough comfort, but not so much that we wreak havoc on our planet.

I wonder, if by some miracle we could travel back in time, if we would kill off those peoples again given the hindsight we now have?

Hindsight

A review of the literature surrounding what has now become known as the Climategate scandal of 2009 reveals the impact vested interests have had in perpetuating denial of human caused climate change (Sceptical Science, 2012). In short, Climategate is about the efforts of hackers who accessed climate scientists email accounts and published out of context comments suggesting there was division in scientific opinion about human involvement in climate change. The intent was to discredit climate science. Sadly, the lies shifted public opinion and regressed environmental protection by at least thirty years.

The profit motive, has not too surprisingly, emerged as the ultimate motivation behind this dangerous tactic, and also not surprising, we find the climate change sceptics are very often funded by the fossil fuel industry. The myopic, self-centred and exploitative activities of these relative few people in our recent history have lured the rest of humanity down a dangerous path, not only toward self-destruction at the hands of environmental impact, but they have also ensured a life of servitude to the economic machine.

Affluence is certainly a powerful lure, but even the devout economist cannot rationally exclude the effects of environmental degradation from a discussion of the benefits or otherwise of economic activity. And yet this does not prevent economic rationalists insisting on doing so. It seems, from an economic standpoint, that there is no reason to protect our environment. Profits must come first.

And don't be fooled by the distraction of 'job creation'. That phrase is simply a proxy/excuse for profiteering. This is the essence of the argument throughout this book: That, despite all the rhetoric to the contrary, our economic activity itself is not reasonable or rational. How can it be if it places us all in danger?

The chasm between what we do and what we need to do to live sustainably remains enormous despite our modern and digitally enhanced hindsight, knowledge and intelligence.

At the same time, taking a 'green' stance does not require a return to life in caves and igloos. That would be irrational and it's unnecessary. But it does entail finding new ways to maintain our existence. It involves a new social narrative. A narrative put into action rather than it residing in well meaning policy riddled with loop holes to allow business as usual.

At any given moment there are mounds of legislation and policy documents all filled with good intent. However, very little of that intent leads to reformed law or is converted to action on the ground. This is the strategy of the economic machine at present. It is a strategy of much lip service but little commitment to real change, and we the voting public are falling for the well sold story that it will all be okay. However, already climate change is affecting our lives albeit in subtle ways for the moment.

Chapter Nine

The Seeds of Conflict

From time to time dictatorial and malicious national leaders or violent groups trouble the world. Dealing with these people is often seen as justification for sanctions, forceful intervention or outright military invasion. Admittedly, there are times when conflict seems unavoidable. And yet, if we turn to history and scratch below the surface of the cited reasons for these people becoming problematic, often the popular and apparent arguments fall into disrepute.

For example, according to the Global Policy Forum, Saddam Hussein was on the Central Intelligence Agency payroll from 1959 and was supported by Britain and the US in the 1980's. The stated reasons for supporting Hussein's rise to power involved Iraq being seen as a key buffer region between East and West during the Cold War. It is on the public record that years later, many lives were sacrificed in the process of removing Hussein from office. This action had an enormous environmental cost given the oil fires which burned during the wars and the enormous carbon footprint of military mobilisation. The financial cost caused by the consumption of war materials was massive.

In another instance, and according to the CATO Institute in a 2002 report, the United States financially supported the

Taliban during 2001/2002 by way of a US$43mil grant in recognition of an anti-drug program. However, drug production in Afghanistan actually increased in the same year. It became apparent the Taliban used the supposed crackdown on drugs to force up the price and then pocketed the US$43mil as well. That's easy money!

One has to question the logic and motives of superpowers when they install and later evict leaders in this manner. Media stories have indeed questioned, and have exposed some inconvenient truths such as the weapons of mass destruction (WMD's) fiasco. Sadly though, meaningful public condemnation of those responsible remains all but non-existent, evidencing the effective use of parochial patriotism and nationalism to ensure the puppeteers are not reigned in.

Evidently the reasons for war, sanctions, and other interventions are rarely as simple as two opposing armies meeting on the battlefield and are always paid for by the voting public. This cost, I suggest, should incite active public outrage from taxpayers. However, it seems we are too distracted by our personal economic pursuits to raise our voices in protest at the hikes in taxation needed to fund wars and ill-conceived meddling in the affairs of other nations. Did the US invade Afghanistan to stop the drug flow? No, but it did invade Iraq to manipulate the flow/price of oil in the region, and ousting Hussein - the guy they installed – using WMD's as an excuse, was a sham.

Looking further back, the people of Germany supported Adolf Hitler before the Second World War. They did so mainly because he offered to alleviate the enormously harsh economic environment in the country. Those conditions arose due to the cost of reparations imposed by the Allies after World War I. Perhaps, an enlightened and peace loving group of nations (the

Allies), that is, nations enjoying economic wealth, could have stepped in and relieved the economic pressure burdening the German people. This perhaps would have averted their affection for Adolf Hitler. The cost of such an economic relief effort would surely have far under weighed the cost of the subsequent war which engulfed the entire world.

In fact, financial aid *was* given to Germany after the Second World War. Rather than again imposing reparation payments, the Allied powers rebuilt Germany's infrastructure, thus removing the threat of yet another charismatic leader bringing the nation to war again. It seemed the lesson had been learned, but alas, there have been many wars since. However, these subsequent wars represent a new breed of imperialism not seen prior.

Post WWII, many nations have been invaded under the auspices of removing an unwanted regime. In the process, and I would say quite intentionally, the nation's infrastructure is crippled thus forcing the unfortunate country to accept economic aid offered by the invaders.

It is difficult to reconcile the level of self-interest needed to send soldiers to war over blatant grabs for territory. Narcissism is the pathology, but it is disguised as democratic and patriotic intent, which I suggest, makes it all the more abhorrent.

Today, those with vested interests in how our nations are run are as active if not more so, than at any time in human history. Despots and dictators are difficult to separate from post-World War imperialists in terms of their intent to gain power and control.

Ultra-wealthy and powerful individuals quietly but persistently work to ensure our social fabric remains to their financial benefit, their vested interests, and soldiers must die to defend that circumstance.

According to economist Thorstein Veblen, 'vested interests' perpetuate an individual's belief in their superiority, using economic activity as a means to display that superiority (Veblen, 2005). The result is those with vested interests occupy the top of the pyramid of personal and financial power. In the lower echelons of the power hierarchy, the levels where the rest of us squabble over the financial scraps, there exists a process of inflating and deflating expectations about success. Should the upper echelons be threatened by newcomers, the goal posts are moved or changed. Moving the goal posts in this manner is a significant source of frustration and anger in our world.

The conflict this causes can be seen in politics, finance, sport, the workplace, and even personal relationships where people compete endlessly. While there is an innate and perfectly reasonable human tendency to protect or enhance one's own position – ostensibly to satisfy our self-interest about food, water and shelter - the lengths we go to in the process is typically magnified by how much wealth is involved.

Take away money, which was invented to create fair trade by the way, and our self-interest would refocus on our survival needs. In other words, we would have to rely on each other again instead of head butting. Now there's a novel idea.

Instead, today we see millions of workers whose aspirations for success are high, being forced to compete. In other words, competition within and between businesses is often little more than a palatable proxy for physical conflict. Using pen and paper rather than a wooden club is accepted as progress and the mark of a civilised society. Bollocks. It's not progress at all. Those in positions of power, the leaders of our nations and financial systems, demonstrate a quickness to use economic manipulation to their advantage and will resort to military aggression as required to achieve their aims. This hardly represents a species keen to be peaceful and cooperative.

It is also important to appreciate that conflict is inherent in legal contracts, selling, and business negotiations. That is, we need to be careful not to perpetuate conflict by creating complex legal systems which serve little purpose other than to provide a platform for profiteering. To this end, laws are generally designed to protect the interests of one party over another and that ultimately means protecting ownership. High wealth allows access to the premium legal representation required to consistently win legal battles and so our laws serve the purpose of ensuring the rich preside over the poor. Whether we use a club, a spear, or pen and paper, the intent and result is the same.

Were we to place less importance on ownership, and in particular the ownership of items designed to portray superiority, the fundamental reasons for protecting ownership would evaporate. It does seem quite illogical that we expend so much energy fighting legal matters over ownership in one form or another. If there were no wealth and power hierarchies; if we all shared resources and ensured the betterment of others before ourselves; if we at least moved toward this goal we would have less need for laws and jails except perhaps as a means to control those who find it impossible to control themselves.

At present, prisons are predominantly filled with the socially and economically disadvantaged people who commit crimes because of unbearable economic stress imposed by vested interests. These people are not the disturbed psychopaths for whom jails were designed.

It is puzzling to look back into history and wonder why we have not made it our imperative to minimise competition at all levels of human interaction. It is particularly difficult if one has empathy regarding the pain and suffering which arises from conflict. This is overwhelmingly puzzling if we consider the basic aim of religion has been the fellowship of humankind! Nevertheless, we have tossed out religious rule in our world in favour of governments and the economic imperative but the outcome has not been for the better. The same social issues still riddle our social fabric.

It is unreasonable to suggest or expect there has to be a better social structure than the conflict inherent in free market capitalism. After all, there is nothing free about that system, other than an expectation that one can exploit. It just makes sense, is pragmatic, and is logical to want to remove exploitation from our humanness, but that means we have to overcome our evolutionary self-interest drive which has become a troublesome superiority complex. However, this is not a conundrum of evolution as much as it is a matter of establishing a new set of values, attitudes and beliefs about our purpose on planet Earth. To this end we can consider the following:

Firstly, and surely, our purpose is not to go to war.

Secondly, and surely again, our purpose is not to destroy our planet.

And third, our purpose cannot be to have our lives guided by something as empty and cold as a financial system.

The reason these problems exist is that early humans copied and modelled themselves on the animals they observed around them. Competition and jousting for supremacy were everywhere in the animal kingdom. However, the animal kingdom has (arguably) only one self-aware, sentient, intellectual creature – us. Surely we are capable of seeing the difference between humans and the rest of the animal kingdom and earnestly work toward letting go of our animalistic urges. A useful place to start on this journey is to have a voice opposing all forms of exploitation. That voice will be heard at the polling booth, via social media and in face to face conversations. There really is nothing difficult about the task of speaking out against exploitation of others and our resources.

Perhaps a short review of conflict in our world will provide some incentive to speak up in favour of meaningful progress toward a truly civilised global village.

The Cost of Wealth and Power

Not too long ago in South America, it was deemed perfectly normal to cut the beating hearts from citizens as a tribute to the war gods of the day. The Mayans and Aztecs were convinced sacrificing the life of an individual would bestow prosperity upon those who still had their hearts. We understand now that this practice maintained the authority of the chieftains and shamans through instilling fear and superstition. Equally though, in modern Western societies we fear our chieftains and what they will do, meaning little has changed other than the blatancy of the physical act.

In one four-day festival, the Aztecs allegedly sacrificed eighty thousand lives to appease their God (New World Encyclopaedia, no date). While scholars debate the exact number and some claim it was as low as three thousand, even three thousand people sacrificed to appease a god is abhorrent by today's standards.

And yet, during World War I the first documented British infantry charge against well-entrenched machine gun positions occurred. The charge cost the lives of sixty thousand troops before lunch that day. From this, the British commanders learned little more than to alter tactics from the full frontal charge, to trench warfare. Social progress indeed!

Throughout the ages, we have sacrificed lives to defend one

belief or another, usually to maintain power, prestige, wealth and control. Witches were burned at the stake because they represented a challenge to the power structure of their day. Also, there have been holy wars and inquisitions resulting in massive suffering as Christians and the Catholic Church respectively ensured their power base was not threatened.

However, these unimaginable events pale into insignificance compared to the number of lives sacrificed in the First World War alone. Numbers vary depending on the source, with some putting that number at more than sixteen million. Since the lessons of the First World War, also known as the first modern war and the war to end all wars, the Second World War cost the lives of over seventy-two million.

Can we compare the Aztec and World War sacrifices? I suggest we can. The Aztecs lives were shaped by their belief in gods. By comparison, today we have left the pagan practices of South American ancients far behind and replaced them with a rigid and well defended belief about the value of the economy. Is this not our modern god? It certainly appears we revere the economy, fear the economy and worship the trinkets it offers and make offerings to its markets. Were the World Wars fought over a god, or rather a set of political and economic ideals so entrenched in our belief system that they now receive our reverence? Economics certainly appears to be the faith of our times.

There is a new war on Earth today though, and it threatens to be far more deadly than any prior conflict. It is the war between pollution and the environment and left unchecked it will kill billions.

The World Health Organisation, 2014, tells us casualties in this war so far are calculated at seven million deaths due to atmospheric pollution in 2012 alone, with the annual rate before 2012 being two point one million. It seems the battle is already being lost.

Today, we consider the Aztec and Mayan sacrifices were barbaric behaviour, and obviously, today humanity has progressed from the time of the South American pagan tribes because we no longer condone blood sacrifice in our modern society. Bollocks.

The truth is we no longer perform ritual sacrifices at the stone altar, but we remain prepared to allow millions to die. Since the end of WWII, over 230 million people have died in wars (Leitenberg, 2006.)

It seems we are still prepared to accept the pain and suffering of entire populations in the name of prosperity and accept death and destruction in the name of wealth creation. Then we can say very little has changed since the time of the Mayans.

Also, it's fortunate the starving and poverty stricken peoples of the world don't have mobile phones or we might be hearing from them, and as well, the civilians in Iraq during the US bombing raids probably had a reason to complain. And even when war is not being raged, approximately nine hundred and twenty-five million people in our world go hungry every day (United Nations Food and Agriculture Organisation, 2010) all because we won't give up a little of our prosperity to feed them.

Allegedly, we have advanced past thinking god-worship outweighs the need to spare individuals from pain, hardship or death in the name of power, ownership, religion or control.

To that idea I say Bollocks again. If that were true, the 9/11 attacks in the US and the two subsequent invasions of Iraq must have been peaceful protests. The search for WMD's in Iraq, which preyed on the fears of a nation for its justification, must have been an aberration. To date, there is no agreement on the cause of 9/11 (Rockmore, 2011) and no weapons of mass destruction were found.

Thank goodness we humans have advanced past those primitive times when we bled innocent young bodies to satiate our fears.

World War I, World War II, the Korean War, the Vietnam War, two Gulf Wars, the IRA conflict, the Somalia conflict, the Afghanistan Wars, the Syrian conflict and atrocities in Rwanda, Uganda and Libya and suicide bombings, are just a few of our recent peaceful confrontations where peace loving humans have progressed beyond the need for bloodshed in order to maintain prosperity for some while others languish.

None of these conflicts could have been fought over power, wealth, resources or religion, could they? If they had been that would mean we could not claim to having progressed since the days the Mayans held a knife aloft and plunged it into an innocent chest. Is this social progress? I think not. The litany of tragedy goes on and on. In fact, there has not been a year in the last fifteen hundred years when war was not being waged somewhere on our planet (Kennedy, 1987). And yet still, we claim we are making progress. For a full account of our peace loving history see The Rise and Fall of the Great Powers by Paul Kennedy because I have barely scratched the surface here.

The following event from World War I borders on the bizarre. However, it serves to ask the question: who starts wars and why do soldiers participate?

The Christmas Truce of 1914

'The initial force behind the Christmas Truce came from the Germans. In most cases, this began with the singing of carols and the appearance of Christmas trees along the trenches. Curious, Allied troops, who had been inundated with propaganda depicting the

Germans as barbarians, began to join in the singing which led to both sides reaching out to communicate. From these first hesitant contacts, informal ceasefires were arranged between units.

For the most part, both sides returned to their trenches later on Christmas Eve. The following morning, Christmas was celebrated in full, with men visiting across the lines and gifts of food and tobacco being exchanged. In several places, games of soccer were organized though these tended to be mass 'kick abouts' rather than formal matches.

Private Ernie Williams of the 6th Cheshires reported, 'I should think there were about a couple of hundred taking part...There was no sort of ill-will between us (Weintraub, 81).' Amid the music and sports, both sides frequently joined together for large Christmas dinners.

While the lower ranks were celebrating in the trenches, the high commands were both livid and concerned.

General Sir John French, commanding the BEF, issued stern orders against fraternizing with the enemy. For the Germans, whose army possessed a long history of intense discipline, the outbreak of popular will among their soldiery was cause for worry and most stories of the truce were suppressed back in Germany.' (Hickman, 2014).

Stories of this nature may be few in our history, but I have to believe the soldier's sentiment is innately human and demonstrates our deep-seated preference for peace and goodwill.

Then the question becomes, 'From where or from whom does the cause of war arise?' It certainly seems war is orchestrated within the high ranks of our leadership and the need for it is not necessarily shared by commoners – those who die for the cause. It is highly likely, given the choice, the armies of Germany and England in the trenches would have packed up and gone home once they realised the horror not included in the recruiting rhetoric. But, they faced a firing squad if they refused to be shot by the enemy.

Is this democratic choice operating? Absolutely.

One might conclude the men and women who signed up in 1914 were not aware of the reality of war because they did not have access to electronic media at the time. However, today, the real face of war is displayed in our homes as it happens. And yet, only a few years ago American families were shocked by the death of their sons in Iraq, suggesting having access to such information is not sufficient to raise awareness of the realities of war. During that war also, the Iraqi soldiers in many cases abandoned their positions and ran. This was reminiscent of the World War I Christmas day story and suggests the fighting soldier really is less interested in war than those who give the orders.

Ultimately, I believe the reasons we are looking for to explain war are related to a blending of nationalism and patriotism. The blend is actively encouraged by parochialism to ensure a plentiful supply of armed personnel; ignorant and misguided armed personnel; ignorant because our education systems have failed them by not teaching how to avoid war.

There have been 120 wars every 50 years in our more recent history (Jeanes, 1996). Since 3600BC, more than 14,500 major wars have killed close to four billion people or two-thirds of the current world population (The Peace Pledge Union, 2014).

That's two wars every year for five and a half thousand years. Incredible! Yet still, we lay claim to being peace loving civilised humans. The claim is just more bollocks.

Each century in our history the technology used in and the scope of our wars increases and so the consequences escalate. We created the atomic bomb to end a war and deter further wars. Now we live in the shadow of nuclear threats, but conventional wars persist. The threat is not so much from bombs but from nuclear power generation facility disasters and radioactive waste management. Ah yes, we humans and our sense of connectedness, our stated love for our children and our families, our neighbours, and our sense of community. Lowbrow sarcasm aside, I believe, despite all the evidence to the contrary, there is an innate goodness within humans. Of this, we can be sure because without an inherent goodness families could not operate to propagate the species. However, it takes very little threat to our economic way of life to turn us on each other.

The challenge then is to reject the flawed arguments of the established and accepted patriotic, nationalistic and pro-competition rhetoric. We need a better system than warring over economic goals. War, in this context, includes the board-room, the local business, the workplace, and the classroom where we do battle with each other every day.

Such rejection of conflict can only arise if each and every individual sees the treachery of our social order and speaks out on the subject. Of course, the real war to eradicate is that which is waged against our environment. The reasons to reject this war are immensely more pressing than any previous human-on-human conflict because what we do to the environment cannot be healed by tears at memorial services.

So far though, achievement on this front has been hampered by a socialisation process which places the pursuit of financial reward above the value of human life itself. And while many of us accept and believe our daily lives do not involve the sacrifice of human life, there is a reality that begs to differ.

Another choice we make every day is our support of global warming: The two main sources of greenhouse gases being the great herds of beef cattle which emit methane, and the use of fossil fuels which emit CO_2. Unfortunately, our ongoing support of these industries is closing the door on our future as rising global temperatures threaten all life on our planet.

The global average temperature is around .8 degrees centigrade higher since we started producing carbon dioxide in large quantities a few hundred years ago. According to www.climatecentral.org the rate of increase is accelerating, with new average high temperatures records being set year on year. July 2016 was the hottest (global average) on record since 1880.

Four degrees hotter is the maximum upper limit where we can possibly survive. Six degrees ends all life on Earth. Four to six degrees is the forecast temperature rise before the end of this century, meaning young children today may well not die of old age. It is a sobering statistic and it is one we are ignoring.

Chapter Ten

Ego and History

What the heck is ego all about? And what does it have to do with our history, environmental protection or our economic systems?

Well firstly, the word 'ego' is often used in a derogatory sense when we accuse a person of being egotistical which is where the negative connotation associated with the word ego arises. In everyday use, we judge people as egotistical if they persistently display an attitude of superiority. However, that use sells our ego short. Our ego's real purpose is to make us feel good or bad about our decisions. It is a judgement engine which allows us to improve over time by seeing our past thoughts and actions as superior or inferior, meaning we are less likely to repeat the inferior.

However, as is the case with all aspects of being human there is more to our ego than a short definition can explain. We need to put the ego into context of our daily lives.

To this end and at the risk of generalising, it is probably fair to say that individuality is important to most people. That is, we like to be our own person and see ourselves as somewhat unique. Another generalisation might be that we desperately want to belong to, and be accepted by our close social groups. What is possibly not so well known is that maintaining this balancing act between individuality and group acceptance is largely down to the judgements our ego makes about our social interactions. As put so nicely by Srini (2010), our ego operates to create a sense of separateness for our personal identity to exist within. Or in other words, we work at being unique individuals but do so within the socially acceptable behaviour defined by our social circles.

Yet another generalisation is that we like to have our ego stroked by praise or compliments. Here's a kicker though. Our ego is not interested in our thoughts in the present moment. It is only concerned with looking at the past to help us plan our future actions. If we think about past decisions and see them as mistakes, our self-esteem is usually dented. If this happens repeatedly we form a negative feeling about whom and what we are. This is our ego in action. It will assess comments from others and decide if the comment is praise or criticism. A negative assessment will cause anxiety.

Freud argued anxiety is generated by our ego. Stephen El-liot author, inventor and life scientist, writing on Coher-ence.com, 2008, suggested the opposite is true: that our ego response is determined by our level of anxiety.

Whichever is the case, and as inconvenient as it may be, we cannot change what we have done in the past, meaning to be truly free of a negative self-judgement by our ego we need to be able to look back and find little to be critical about.

However, with respect to the state of our global environ-ment we are all contributors to the problems we face, meaning there is implicit criticism in any information about climate change and environmental degradation. Hence, the bad feeling our ego generates will drive us to deny responsibility, rational-ise our individual culpability or in some other way defend our position. Regardless of the strategy used, this is likely the source of depressed moods when the environment is discussed. Our ego is telling us we need a better track record.

To achieve the required positive shift, we can fill our media with messages designed to direct our energy away from overconsumption and toward a more relaxed lifestyle which values the preservation of all life more than a fist full of dollars.

A simple way for the individual to start this process is to reduce our personal spending by setting our expectations lower: Doing this, will slow economic activity and our pace of life, both of which will lead to more contentment and better health. The question that remains is, 'How do we get started?' Fortunately, the answer is not difficult, expensive or overly time consuming.

Tools for Change

The anti Vietnam War lobbyists changed the course of history in the 1970's. That movement grew from a handful of concerned students to an enormous global voice in a very short time, meaning we can create change much more easily than one might think. By adding our voice to present day environmental movements our ego can arrive at a positive assessment because joining them *is* what the masses are doing. In other words if the majority are involved we are more likely to consider our participation as the right thing to do. This strategy fits with our inherently human need to have our ego stroked and our deep seated desire to be socially accepted.

What else can we do? What concrete action can each of us undertake on a regular basis without putting a huge impost on our time?

We can vote, divest, join, click and speak up.

Firstly, our **vote** sends a powerful message. Then we might vote for green-minded politicians and policies regardless of the colour of the T-shirt standing behind such policies.

Second, **divestment** is a growing worldwide movement backed by an increasing number of retail banks, superannuation funds and financial institutions, as well as, the International Monetary Fund and The World Bank. The www.350.org website provides all the necessary detail to participate in divestment. Put simply, it involves instructing our superannuation providers not to invest our funds in fossil fuels. It involves changing our bank account to a fossil fuel investment free bank and not buying shares in high carbon companies.

Joining green organisations raises their profile and influence.

Clicktivism is a relatively new phenomenon made possible by the Internet. There are many organisations and movements now seeking little more than the couple of mouse clicks needed to sign on-line petitions. Joining these movements offers an opportunity to contribute between elections. For example see www.gofossilfree.org, or, www.350.org. There are many more.

Speak to others and spread the word about voting, and about spending less. This will disempower the corporations' capacity to pollute and exploit.

Speak up in support of environmental protection and be as unrelenting as the pro-economic rhetoric we hear from day to day. Instead, base conversations on the values which have kept us alive for millions of years and reject economic dogma suggesting affluence is more important than habitat and the life it gives.

Such words will build a movement aimed at a new set of values for our society. And let me be clear, this is not a call to completely walk away from economic security. However, it is a call to develop vastly different types of finances - systems which would create many jobs in activities designed to rectify

the damage done so far. The bottom line is we can all participate by simply realigning our values.

What do we Value at Present?

Gold, currency, ownership, power, control, comfort and
convenience are some of the labels we use to describe the ideals
of our economic paradigm. We might add shopping, holidays,
sport, television, hobbies, financial achievement, etc, etc. All of
these things have been the central focus of economic activity for
as long as money has existed and yet all of these things have
only perceived value.

Gold for instance, is used in electronics and so it has a particular utility, but the vast bulk of gold on this planet is kept in
vaults by the superpowers and banks where it sits doing
nothing useful for our survival. Currency too, is stockpiled by
the ultra-wealthy. Neither has any life-giving capacity, i.e. they
have no intrinsic worth with respect to nourishing us. Given
gold is no longer the basis for US currency (Bordo, 1981) one
has to wonder why it is so coveted.

The explanation is that our fondness for precious metals
and gems evidences an underlying distrust of notional bank
accounts, fragile economies and volatile financial markets. In
fact, rather than trust these mechanisms we are forced to tread
nervously around them like we might the school-yard bully.
Not wanting to upset the bully, we pretend to like them
because it seems impossible to avoid them, but all the while it
is our participation that empowers the economic blaggards.

No other creature on our planet seeks out gold or currency.
Put side by side with a food source, a bar of gold or any other
precious commodity would not be disturbed by anything other
than humans. And yet, put beside a seedling, gold diggers will
trample over the seedling to take gold, even though the

seedling is a life-giving fruit tree. The reason for our attraction to precious metals is simple enough. They have perceived value.

Jungles, permafrost, rain forests, the ocean floor, none of these intrinsically invaluable environs are safe from the mindless excavator operated by people who think nothing of destroying the very ecosystems which give us life, in order to find commodities which cannot. That being the case we have the opportunity to shift our values and see the benefits of creating wealth based on intrinsic worth.

To that end, recently a judge in Britain ruled against a coal mining company seeking to open a new mine. The judge ruled the company had not taken into consideration the global warming caused by burning coal. A similar ruling in Colorado, USA, suggested there is some non-financial value being placed on our environment (Berwyn, 2014). However, in many other cases, high court appeals have overturned the rights of state governments in favour of miners. Similarly, laws established to allow fracking below farmland and residential areas have created massive pollution issues. The laws remain in place despite the horrendous environmental damage they allow. Vast areas of prime farmland have been destroyed or made unin-habitable by methane gas percolating up from the fracked Earth below. These situations reflect the manner in which the economic paradigm values doing anything but ensuring the natural world stays as nature intended.

Can we Take Back Control of our Lives?

The challenge for each of us then is to wrest back control of our future which has been hijacked by the lure of our perceived needs.

The truly satisfying and sustainable pursuit in life is to encourage rather than destroy the systems which have allowed us to evolve from furry mammals into sentient creatures. This is a far cry from the baubles economic activity offers us. And, while we keep attempting to go our separate ways, despite our connectedness to each other and the world around us, it's hard to envisage our kind surviving much longer.

Certainly, we have the potential and the skills to take back control of our destiny. Although, I suspect many will say we are already in control and that our growing civilisation proves the point. But I keep coming back to our quality of life. Is the down side of the economic imperative really a worthwhile trade for what we have to give up? Wars, conflict, aggression, money worries and so on are all around us at a time when we are told things have never been better.

Who or What is to Blame?

Should we look at our historians, our past and present leaders, and/or the financial world for a cause for our circumstances and blame them? No, because, without a doubt it is far more productive to understand what we can do going forward than to undertake an inquisition or seek a scapegoat. In keeping with that thought astrophysicist Neil De Grasse Tyson points out a clear and present danger when people in positions of power and influence are also climate science deniers. Tyson also suggests politicians are duly elected, meaning it is the voting public who empower politicians. Hence if there is any blame to be laid, it must fall at the feet of the voting public, but we must also ask, 'Are voters informed enough to see the folly in their decisions at the polling booth?'

This is why Tyson, as he stated on national television, has a personal mission to connect people and science because he believes many are interested but have not been exposed to science in a way that makes the impact of science on our lives obvious and relevant from day to day.

Also not relevant in our day to day thinking are the activities of climate change sceptics and the misinformation they propagate in a way that makes it seem like peer reviewed research.

For instance, since the aforementioned Climategate (Sceptical Science, 2012) controversy of 2009 engineered widespread denial of human involvement in climate change, particularly within the North American population, social progress towards sustainable economic activity has regressed.

Also, knowing sea levels are forecast to rise by a predicted seventy-five meters as the polar ice caps melt (CGER, 1996) is too easily cast-off by comments such as, 'I won't be around when it happens.' Yet today, the ocean is steadily rising at the shoreline of low-lying Pacific Islands and at Miami Florida, meaning it is rising worldwide, but unless we are personally affected (and even then) it is unlikely we will see our complicity. It's far easier to think we will simply move to higher ground! Of course that ignores the massive loss of arable coastal land that will occur. That cost will be massive and in all likelihood will cause widespread food shortages.

Also, standing in the way of more affirmative action, is the oft used excuse that keeping the family fed and the bills paid takes priority over focusing on our natural world. Time constraints also remove our personal opportunity for quiet reflection on such issues, or for that matter campaigning for change. I suggest the more pressing questions are, 'Can we really afford not to take an interest in our environmental welfare,' and, 'Can we afford not to utilise our unique human capacities to avoid the consequences of climate change?'

Part Two

Evolutionary Heritage

Chapter Eleven

Human Superiority

According to Stephen C Rockefeller: *'Humanity may destroy the possibilities for life on earth unless the freedom and power that we have acquired are channelled in new creative directions by a spiritual awareness and moral commitment that transcend nationalism, racism, sexism, religious sectarianism, anthropocentrism, and the dualism between human culture and nature. This is the great issue for the 1990s and the twenty-first century.'*

We humans consider ourselves qualitatively different to other species, or perhaps it's better to say, we *simply know* we are 'superior' because we are more intelligent. This claim, to greater intelligence, is supported by references to human culture and technological achievements which are supposedly the mark of a civilised people. As suggested by Stephen Rockefeller in the above quote, it is arguable that *the only* difference between humans and the rest of the animal world *is* culture itself. I have to ask though, 'Is it true?' Are we really the superior species or is it possible that despite all the hallmarks of our civilisation, we act more like the animals around us than sentient beings? There are obvious references to be made here. For instance, our violent past and for that matter our violent present, are indicative of animalistic urges rather than civilised behaviour. Add to this a culture built on valuing people according to their wealth, or the value of the resources under their feet, and our claims to civility rapidly diminish: particularly given the lengths we will go to in order to take those resources. Despite these obvious problems though, we humans remain convinced of our superiority. However, the ability to outthink another species in order to destroy it, displace it or ruin its habitat is patently problematic if we consider the declining state of our biosphere. This suggests there must be a better way to qualify how we humans are different to the non-human natural world.

To explore the *human difference*, this chapter looks at several popular measures of humanness that are often taken for granted but don't necessarily stand up to scrutiny, before settling on a new frame of reference.

Firstly, at the biological level, we are not all that special. We don't run fast. We don't have big claws or teeth and we can't climb or burrow as specialised animals do. And, as is the case for all creatures on Earth we rely on a particular set of circumstances to make life possible. That is, all life including human life requires an energy source (the Sun) and an environment to exist within. All life requires time to adapt to environmental changes and requires the opportunity to reproduce, to eat, drink and sleep in one way or another. In these respects, all Earth's creatures are in the same boat, or more importantly, the same biosphere. None of this is about culture though, meaning we have to ask what is it about humans that enables us to have 'culture'.

Perhaps the more relevant human difference is that we are

the only species able to contemplate such concepts and yet ignore the dangers which accompany our capacity for such thoughts.

This suggests that, on the one hand our humanness has given us an enormous advantage, but on the other we have disconnected our daily experience of life from appreciating or very often even consciously experiencing the natural processes which keep us alive. By and large we have done this through the use of technology.

Our freedom to choose this path, that is, to be self-directed rather than respond to instinct is called free will. Not too surprisingly though, philosophers have debated for years whether free will actually exists. From a religious perspective, Christians suggest God gave us free will and we chose to ignore his advice and that decision explains much of the hardship our kind has endured.

On the contrary, philosopher Sam Harris suggests we have no free will at all - we simply respond to stimuli albeit our responses are complex and intricate thus giving the appearance of self-awareness and intelligence.

Whatever the explanation for human behaviour, we cannot escape our reliance on the natural world if we want to stay alive, which again raises the question, how are we, or indeed are we at all different from the non-human world? We certainly *appear* to be more evolved and intelligent than other creatures. And yet, if we have greater intelligence one has to ask, 'Why are we facing persistent and ugly social, economic and environmental problems?' Is it not reasonable to say our intellect, the hallmark of human distinctiveness, should have already overcome the need to compete with each other; destroy the resources we rely on; or fall into conflict year after year?

At the same time, a balanced review has to accept that our

history is not all negative and bleak and that we have made some progress. However, despite our advances with respect to being civilised, the most recent 1,500 years of human history are replete with war, preparation for war, empire building and subsequent failure of those empires with all the associated trickle down effects, and importantly, blind eyes turned to the suffering that ensues.

In other words, if our hallmark intelligence is not able to overcome social ugliness issues, then perhaps we are not so different to other creatures we see jousting for supremacy amongst their kind. Perhaps instinct is directing us more than we like to admit, meaning our difference to other creatures really is an illusion. The mere fact that we kill each other so readily is quite animalistic and yet other mammals fight and compete, but rarely kill each other and certainly not by the millions, nor over wealth and power issues.

Why is this fact important? Well for one thing, if we can understand the reasons behind our warlike behaviour, we may find a way to become more content, less fearful, less stressed, and so lead more fulfilled lives with less conflict. That outcome would seem worth the effort involved in understanding our humanness a little better.

To that end, we might consider that the human mind is able to deal with abstract concepts such as seeing ourselves in the third person. Also, we can plan for the future whilst knowing of the past, and yet we seem unable to use our knowledge of history, or our understanding of our psychology, to avoid repeating the darker parts of our history. Hence, we see the persistence of social issues such as crime and violence, or even a simple inability to get along with others. We also see racism, bigotry and the simple fear of people who are different, causing social problems.

Most higher-order animals live in social groups with status hierarchies based on age, gender and experience. We humans differ in that we use money and the perceived status it creates to determine our position in society. In this process, how efficiently and successfully we accumulate wealth is largely determined by our individual ability to manipulate information to our advantage. This is one way we are quite different from other creatures. That is, to the extent of our capacity to store, recall and manipulate information from day to day. In fact, this is why our history is so vital to our future. There is no point in having highly developed storage and recall abilities if we don't use them to improve our survivability.

Moreover, our misuse of our memories explains how we are able to expand the frontiers of technological innovation, create wondrous music, art, and thought, and in the same lifetime kill each other by the millions and not feel motivated enough to campaign against such atrocities. That is, our manipulation of facts about the past means we can rationalise what we do very easily and allocate validations, for instance blaming dictators for terrorism, without accepting any responsibility for enabling the perpetrators to come to power.

So, while we have a great deal of information and intellect, it is apparent we lack a social fabric or a social narrative conducive to using it wisely. In fact, I suggest, we have a basic operating system or code which reads, *if it feels good, do it*. This is not a conscious thought, but rather an underlying autonomic tendency which is at best moderated by intellect.

This idea is in keeping with Freud's theories. He suggested that children seek instant gratification, but as we mature we learn to delay rewards provided the deferral seems worthwhile. However, if Freud was correct, we have to ask what influence in our lives could override our intellect telling us to provide a safe environment (biosphere) for our children. What is it that allows us to expose ourselves and our children to the ever rising risks of overconsumption and overpopulation or for that matter, to allow school yard bullies, corrupt public officials or malevolent national leaders to exist?

The answer to this question is the ongoing manipulation of facts, or in other words our history, by people only interested in profiteering. In support of this idea Richard Dawkins (in The Selfish Gene, 1976), suggests the Darwinian process of natural selection now favours the survival of money oriented people in a world where money and finances largely determine our quality of life. Hence, by natural selection, we are breeding more and more money oriented people. Of course, and despite evolution, for this to be the case, people have to make con-scious decisions about how to use wealth. That is, we will apply our superior human intellect. Sadly though, this applica-tion typically sees us 'wanting it all' and 'wanting it now', and we will go to great lengths to have what we want. In other words, we really are operating by the idiom, if it feels good do it. It seems our supreme intellect has not prevailed over our primal and animalistic urges.

Then perhaps Freud was wrong about our capacity to delay gratification. However, I suggest what we have really done is not covered in Freud's work. What we have deferred is our individual responsibility to the future and our responsibilities as custodians of planet Earth in the here and now.

To facilitate and nourish human wanting, there has been a clever misdirection over the last forty years or so which says we can leave out the environmental cost of business and not fall victim to a global environmental margin call someday.

Thus, it appears from simple observation of our world, that our endless drive to reproduce and provide a secure place for our young has overstepped the sustainability mark and is coming back to haunt us. Ironically, the information we have used to keep us not just alive, but living in outlandish luxury and thus see ourselves as superior to the rest of nature, has become deadly. This trait *is* uniquely human.

As stated earlier, the pleasure principle says if it feels good do it. And yet that principle fails if we ask, 'Does going to work every day feel good?' We might also ask, 'What feels good about *any* of the financially entangled activities in our lives?' Debt certainly does not feel good. Being forced to work to repay debt does not feel good either. It appears, that we really do undertake a huge array of unpleasant tasks in the crazy mixed up belief they will result in pleasure. Then the question becomes, 'How do we account for these crazy decisions?'

There are two possibilities. The first is that our information processing, or in other words our decision making is awry. The second is that the information we are receiving has been manipulated or is not in our best interest. However, the latter can only be problematic if the former is true. That's because our human intelligence is completely capable of dealing with information but our primal desires will torpedo our decision making if that information looks like it will bring us pleasure despite any dangers inherent in that information.

To resolve this dilemma we need to unravel how the various aspects of our uniquely human intelligence can best be deployed in order to see through any questionable information we might come across: Doing this will highlight how we humans think differently compared to non-humans.

Intelligence

Inuit Indians living in the polar ice world that is their native land would likely struggle to survive in a tropical jungle without time to adapt. Likewise, city folk might struggle with being thrust into a wilderness of any type. However, neither of these situations reflects intelligence (IQ). This is because the above scenarios, or for that matter the question and answer tests used by psychologists to measure intelligence, typically measure a person's volume of culturally specific knowledge rather than intelligence itself.

For example, one might ask who wrote Faust? This question is part of an intelligence test aimed at middle-class Westerner folk. The answer is Goethe. But does knowing this answer measure intelligence? Does it make us more likely to survive? I think not. It is more likely a simple measure of literary knowledge.

Further, intelligence tests do not ask city folk to identify the hundreds of different types of snow Eskimos have to understand in order to survive, or for that matter, how to live in a rain forest with no outside help. Accordingly, if we want to accept intelligence is at all useful in making humans unique, we might ask, how long can one live with a plastic bag tied over one's head? This is a simple abstract concept only humans can comprehend, but the important point is we all understand it equally. Of course, the typical response to this question might be to laugh it off and say something to the effect of 'don't be ridiculous.' And yet, our planet has a thin veil of atmosphere wrapped around it and everything we do in our daily lives has an impact on the quality of the air we breathe within that thin veil, meaning the plastic bag analogy is quite valid, albeit somewhat crass at first glance. In fact, the analogy demonstrates a key human intellectual capacity which separates us from non-humans; it is the ability to discern.

Hence, we have found the first identifiably and uniquely human difference to other life on our planet:

1. The ability to **discern**: the ability to 'recognise' or 'find' meaning when presented with information that is difficult and complex or where meaning is obscured. This is an intellectual process where evolution is seeing our intellect slowly take over from our primal urges.

Problem Solving

Does our ability to problem-solve uniquely separate us from non-humans? At first glance that may seem to be the case. However chimps, crows, dolphins and octopuses to name a few are quite capable of solving problems, albeit not at the level humans are capable of.

Crows, for example, have been seen dropping nuts onto traffic light controlled intersections. Cars break the shells and the crows wait for a red light to retrieve their meal. Octopuses can open screw top jars to retrieve a meal and rats can negotiate complex mazes with complete memory retention of a maze after a single attempt.

Nevertheless, it is obvious that humans solve much more complex problems than other creatures. The truth is though, most of the problems we struggle with are created by us in the first place. That is, crows don't need to solve the problem of atomic warfare, and chimps don't need to wrangle with answers to nuclear waste disposal problems. Complex problem solving, where the problem is self-inflicted, is the only uniquely human aspect of this skill, but it is difficult to see this as a positive attribute. In fact, our problem solving makes us unique in that we create problems we can't solve.

Abstract Thought

According to Dr. Mark Ylvisaker (2006), philosopher, lecturer and speech pathologist, another generally accepted defining human ability is our capacity to understand abstract concepts such as freedom or justice.

However, and quite inconveniently, dogs, some great apes, chimps, bears and even pigeons are capable of abstract thinking tasks. As an article titled Many Animals Can Think Abstractly by Andrea Anderson in the Scientific American (2014) points out, while different species use different strategies to undertake abstract tasks such as matching pairs of photographs; they are nevertheless, able to pair them correctly. Even so, the task of matching pairs of photographs is a far cry from understanding the intricacies of concepts as complex as freedom and justice.

This level of abstraction must therefore be uniquely human. Still, a problem arises. We humans created the notions of freedom and justice and we pursue the experience of them. And yet as was discussed in the opening chapters, freedom and justice are rarely found in our world: At least they are not found in the true and original meaning of these terms. In fact, our use of time to order and arrange our lives very much shackles our freedom using abstract constraints, if not physical restraints. Therefore, it seems that to have created abstract concepts is not enough to master living by their meaning.

Interestingly, the fact that non-human higher animals don't get bored with repetitive tasks, tells us they have a different concept of time to us. Dolphins and chimps will repeat tasks endlessly for little more than a modest reward. They don't appear to be concerned about wasting time and will repeat tasks over and over for a food reward or a pat on the head, and will do so from within a prison cell (cage or enclosure). Provided these creatures are fed and regularly exercised they seem to be content. This is quite obviously not the case for us. Our understanding of past, present and future, i.e. our concept of time, and that time can be wasted, stands out as being unique to our species.

Time can move too slowly or too quickly depending on our expectations and level of engagement in a task, meaning we are both liberated and hamstrung by our experience of time. Also, to measure achievements, we set time based goals and then devote our energy to reaching them, which means our desire to achieve is, or is not satisfied according to how much time is consumed. One might argue the quality of the result is as important as how long it takes, but ultimately a task must be completed before we die or we cannot be satisfied with it.

But all this activity is based on a flawed premise: that a time-frame has relevance to our existence, or that how much we achieve financially within a time span matters in the slightest. That is, the natural world has no concept of time and so it is only relevant to we humans.

Thinking about time, it does seem our emotional drives, our primal survival drives, our ego and our unconscious thought processes can only create a sense of missing out if we are able to measure time. Measuring time and allocating tasks to time is a human concept and we understand its purpose, but we also fall victim to the artificial pressures it creates. All the while though, the only reality that really matters is to know we are alive and then we are not. Every moment in between has to be relished because it is never to be repeated.

As for the importance, or otherwise, of time to our existence, consider a plantation tree. The tree is ready for harvesting when it is a certain size. How long it takes to grow is irrelevant to anything other than our expectations. Trees grow at a rate determined by the sum of the energy put into them. They do not speed up to meet our schedules, nothing does, except to say that when we try to manipulate growth rates we usually create massive environmental implications and/or damage.

Time really is a messy and inefficient way to organise our lives. It was adopted primarily to allow us to value labour by working x number of hours for y dollars but has sadly resulted in a great deal of stress and rushing about.

This provides a second item to add to our list of what distinguishes us from the rest of the natural world.

1. The ability to **discern**: the ability to 'recognise' or 'find' meaning when presented with information that is difficult, complex or where an accurate meaning is obscured. This is an intellectual process where evolution is seeing our intellect slowly take over from our primal urges.

2. An awareness of **time** which leads to a sense of mortality. This is a purely intellectual process.

Children

The fear of arriving at the end of the short amount of time we have in our lives without having achieved our goals is a powerful driver of behaviour. Having children is no exception and is all but universal. In fact, it is probably one of the most cherished human goals. It is certainly widespread and not having children is not the norm. And obviously, unless we bear children our population will collapse.

How often is it said, 'We are building a future for our children?' or,' I'm trying to do the best by my kids.' This seems perfectly reasonable. However, the resources needed to provide for our growing population is rapidly undermining the future our children will experience and this is a conundrum we struggle with as a species.

We know overpopulation is an enormous issue, but it is an emotionally charged topic to discuss. Still we might ask, is it better to prevent excessive childbirth, or alternatively, risk seeing children suffering from the side effects of overpopulation? The point seems moot though because we are already allowing millions to die from food and water shortages, why not a few more? Perhaps when child malnutrition arrives in middle-class suburbia we will be more pragmatic about population control.

Then we can say a third human difference can be added to the list:

1. The ability to **discern**: the ability to 'recognise' or 'find' meaning when presented with information that is difficult, complex or where an accurate meaning is obscured. This is an intellectual process where evolution is seeing our intellect slowly take over from our primal urges.

2. An awareness of **time** which leads to a sense of mortality. This is an intellectual process.

3. A **biological** desire to reproduce or be productive. This is a primal biological drive.

Wilfulness

Our collective ability to impose our will on enormous numbers of people (often without remorse) is uniquely human.

In the home, parents seem compelled to impose their will on children. Children complain sometimes, and parents too often enter into a battle of wills with them. In fact, it takes a great deal of wisdom and personal restraint not to fall into conflict with a wilful or simply argumentative child. Noticeably, parents who listen first and demand later, usually end up with happier kids and relationships.

The main reason for wilfulness is that we tend to build our lives around a set of expectations as to how our existence will play out or how things will be in our lives. That is, for example, if we are not successful in some aspect of life our self-concept suffers. Wilfulness is the tool we use as we try to make the world fit our expectations of it.

Being right and imposing our self-righteousness on others, are the fundamental building blocks of politics, law, religion, parochialism, competitive sport, education and even a simple conversation. For instance, consider any past discussion with a friend, colleague or significant other. At some point in the conversation a difference of opinion may have occurred. It may be that the difference was minor to the point of insignificance, or alternatively, the issue may have been particularly important. Either way, the relevance is that we find it difficult to have a conversation without forming an opinion and then imposing it on others, or at least attempting to do so.

This is relevant because our will can be imposed with or without rational justification, with or without pragmatism, with or without wisdom, facts or reason. I.e. we can be driven by our ego. When the ego fires up our emotions, which in turn are typically magnified by financial considerations, the impact can be dire. Other creatures may seem wilful, but they are acting on instinct rather than stubbornness in the way we understand it.

Thus, our list of human difference includes a fourth item. The list now looks like this:

1. The ability to **discern**: the ability to recognise or find out when information is difficult or complex. This is an intellectual process where evolution is seeing our intellect slowly take over from our primal urges

2. An awareness of **time** which leads to a sense of mortality. This is an intellectual process.

3. A **biological** desire to reproduce or be productive. This is a primal biological drive.

4. Human **will**, or our drive to have our opinion succeed. This is a primal biological drive somewhat moderated by intellect.

Importantly, the list above includes the descriptions 'primal biological' drive and 'intellectual process'. The interaction of these two aspects of our humanness determines our reactions to events in the world around us. The question is, 'Should we react based on emotional urges, or rational and logical intellect?'

It seems obvious that which mode of response we choose will determine the quality of any interaction we have with others, and that consequently, our reaction determines our stress levels, our happiness, and how content with life we can be.

Allowing anger or frustration to dominate when our will is challenged is not particularly useful and is unlikely to end well. At the same time, we need not all aim to be Mr. Spock or some other unfeeling automaton. However, I do think we need to get our primal emotional urges under control and deploy more intellect. Pursuing that goal would lead to real progress for our species. It would be far more useful than ever changing our technologies just to ensnare others curiosity and make a few bucks.

It is worth taking a moment to consider that we have arrived at a set of differences between we humans and the non-human world we live in. At this point we can say:

Humans are an enigma. On the one hand we have the most highly-evolved brains of any organism on the planet. We are complex and social creatures capable of rational and logical decisions which can draw on history and our expectations for the future. On the other hand, we have a mind riddled with leftover primal biological drives and powerful emotions. We seek pleasure and comfort which flies in the face of what we know to be civilised behaviour. We fear our own mortality and so try to impose our will on the world around us regardless of who we endanger, even our children.

Our future really does depend on our ability to see the duality of what we are and manage it better, if for no other reason, than to be more content from day to day.

Perhaps what we need is a framework for change and a recipe for a revised outlook for humanity. A perspective which leaves our often myopic world view far behind and embraces the task of taking control of our emotional selves. 'Emotional' in this sense meaning the urges associated with greed, avarice, lust, competition for the sake of it, jealousy and so on.

Our unwavering will could do great good on planet Earth. That is, if we could just focus it on sustainability, compassion, tolerance and positive regard for all others and the environment, rather than the exploitation of resources and each other for profit. And, if this is too much to ask, if we can do no more than deploy our wilfulness to protect the natural world enough so that it can keep us alive, that would be a wondrous move in the right direction.

This vision is a far cry from what we have achieved since industrialisation just two hundred or so years ago though. As put by environmental lawyer James Speth (2008) in The Bridge at the End of the World, what we see as enormous progress has had an equally great cost. That is, the word progress implies a change for the better, but so often those changes bring about increased pollution, social crisis and resource depletion and so the change looks more like regression.

The objective of being a human, I suggest, might be the pursuit of a healthier, more content, genuinely sustainable way of living. This might well be our unifying commonality. It might be the uniquely human trait we can all agree to live by.

Where Does This Leave Us?

Being human can be defined by our unique ability to understand the past, present and future (**time**) and use this understanding to redirect our incredible **will** to create sustainability by **discerning** what is vital to life and what is optional to life without a **fear of missing out**.

We can achieve this by separating our **needs** from our **wants** and setting our expectations lower. We have the potential to apply our energy to deploying solutions which are intellectual by design and which adhere to the needs of our biological world and so, in turn, give us the best chance at survival.

The Way Home

Herein resides our amazing, exciting and fantastic opportunity for success. Not only can we look around us and understand how all creatures rely on each other for survival, but we can see where they have failed or succeeded and where our ancestors have failed or succeeded and learn from them. We can evaluate, plan, analyse, and then deploy our intellect in a way no other creature can. In other words, we can choose how we react to our primal urges.

Instead at present, we scurry about each day negotiating our personal involvement in the soulless economic maze of life. But, outside economics, we find the real world. This is where our food, water and air come from. It is our source of life and offers to engage us in all manner of meaningful and purposeful activities. For instance, the employment opportunities involved in undoing the damage done so far are all but endless!

Economic Rationalists

I sat with an economist and he listened to the perspective

presented in these pages so far. At one point I asked him, 'Are we not like laboratory rats in a maze. We run the maze and get the cheese only to remain trapped in the economic cage.' He replied, 'Provided we are happy living in a cage, what's the problem?' My answer was simple enough. 'Life in the cage will be good until the researcher finds another use for it and decides we are no longer welcome.' In other words, we know our economic systems cannot be trusted and are causing problems with our food and other necessity supplies. At the same time, we no longer can fend for ourselves in the real world because we gave up that skill long ago.

Therefore, now we face a very real fear of nature's demise, as well as, the threat of a crashed economic system and so we manipulate both as we try to stave off the inevitable.

It would be far better to reconnect with the natural world instead of butting heads with it. The real world has only so much to give and we are using it up faster than it can replenish itself. What happens when we hit the environmental end point? The economist said, 'Yes, but that won't happen before I die so why should I worry about it?' I waited for a laugh or smile after that comment, but sadly, he was serious. I looked at his son sitting across the room. He looked back and shook his head. We understood each other without words.

Our little group spoke for an hour or so longer and the economist gave two concessions. Firstly, he didn't say he loved his children and was trying to build a better future for them. He stopped short of that hypocrisy. Also, he accepted there needs to be changes to our life style if we are to avoid deeper climate problems.

Alternative Lifestyle

To suggest our global civilisation needs to find a more survivable way of life would seem self-evident, and what's more, despite the popular retort that a greener way of life implies a return to the Stone Age, that is clearly not going to happen. Nor is it necessary to give up all of life's luxuries to save our planet. However, the sustainable way forward will require us to redefine our priorities and actively apply our uniquely human attributes to the pursuit of a reductive philosophy with respect to consumption of resources across the board. In other words, consume less of everything, which is I admit, a major threat to the pinnacle of economic development, that is globalisation, which is supported by an enormous global logistics industry.

A second economist I spoke to on this topic, pointed out that globalisation is victimised by environmentalists. He said globalisation has brought about enormous benefits in the form of a raised standard of living. However, it was clear that all he could see was the economic benefits to upper class modern Western city dwellers. His comments did not mention over-population, exploitation in sweatshops, pollution caused by transportation of goods, glacier melts caused by greenhouse gases, children of low-paid workers dying of malnutrition and infection, or any other downside of globalisation.

Globalisation enables cities to grow and grow at the expense of the surrounding landscapes, and at the expense of developing nations which are exploited to feed resources into usually far away cities. These cities house and employ vast numbers of tax payers who, as previously stated, add nothing to the provision of the essentials for life.

This is not a criticism of anyone in particular. It is an observation of how we are forced to find work for people in office cubicles and factories because there is not enough work on the land due to mechanisation, which is itself driven by the massive consumption requirements of cities.

The standard of living globalisation and industrialisation have created, is available to far less than half the world's population and this situation enables the wealth pyramid to exist for the benefit of the privileged. Working class people occupy the bottom third of the wealth pyramid doing work which does not create food, water or shelter, but they do create tax revenue. Those taxes and profits end up in the pocket of the minority at the top of the pyramid. The people in between, the workers within striking distance of the wealthy elite, strive to move upward. A handful make it, but most don't and are forced to endure the conflict needed to tread water at their tier of the pyramid.

This aspect of modern civilisation utterly depends on conflict. In the workplace this conflict is given the more palatable label of 'competition for jobs'. Outside the workplace there is litigation in the courtroom and in developing nations there is overt physical violence against people whose land and or resources must be acquired or stolen to ensure profits are possible. For instance, the well documented twelve year legal battle over BHP's mine discharge damage to the Ok Tedi River which destroyed or damaged the livelihood of fifty thousand local people in Papua New Guinea.

Despite our knowledge of such disasters, it may seem the reverse is true, that modern societies are working to rid themselves of violence and that our laws are aimed at creating peace, but (police) force is being used to maintain that peace. In other words, the will of a few who make the laws is being *forced* upon the many. This can be expressed as *the freedoms of the few come at the expense of the freedoms of the many.* For more on this line of thought see Derek Jensen's (1999), End Game: The Problem with Civilisation.

This brings us to the human survival equation and it looks

like this:

$$\frac{\text{Fear and greed}}{\text{Will}} \quad >=< \quad \frac{\text{Intellect and wisdom}}{\text{Will}}$$

If we divide fear and greed by our wilfulness, is the result greater than, equal to, or less than our intellect and wisdom divided by our wilfulness? This is not so much a question of mathematics as it is about recognising the internal battle raging in each person who perhaps wants to be more environmentally friendly, but is financially entangled in the economic imperative and the baubles it lures us with.

Money is a bauble as are goods and services that don't directly keep us alive. We fear not having what economic activity provides and we fear not having money itself because we no longer have the skills or opportunity to gather food water and shelter for ourselves. Our freedom on that front has been stolen and now we fear the consequences of not playing the economic game...of actually trying to live outside the economic cage.

Environmental Fear vs Economic Fear

There has been a concerted campaign to associate fear of financial loss with green initiatives.

As a result, a common misperception is that green initiatives threaten economic security. However, it is economic activity itself which creates uncertainty and fear, and is the real threat. It should be obvious, green initiatives aim to overcome fear about the future by ensuring our resources are not exhausted.

The truth is, that if we were to change our economic systems towards sustainability, it is more likely a benefit would flow from that change. Firstly, we would gain a vibrant and healthy natural world with the capacity to support us long into the future. Also, we would create a brighter future for our children and their children: a future filled with opportunity in clean, green industries. We would also achieve economic stability as opposed to fearing the monumental and growing cost of environmental reclamation work.

As stated earlier, as of 2013, US$70 trillion was required to undo the environmental damage done to date. This is a figure our economies cannot afford to allow to rise. It is unimaginable where that number might land if we do further damage. One thing is certain, far greater loss is imminent if we persist with our present economic practices. This is what we should fear.

Also, it seems obvious most of us react poorly to our fears. Faced with a major challenge our ability to make rational decisions can falter and anger or frustration often follows. That reaction is difficult to avoid because our brains are hard wired by evolution to detect threats and respond to them with fight or flight. The more shocking the event we are confronted with, the greater is our anxiety reaction (Grohol, 2010).

This is a primal instinct and it is exploited by those who want to perpetuate our fossil-fuel based economic systems. The key to success here is not *whether* we react, it is *how* we react.

Advertising and marketing are used to ensure our fears about discomfort and financial loss remain at the forefront of our thinking and that we react poorly. To this end, jobs growth and the economy are persistently touted as being essential to life itself - they are said to be the safe haven. That's just more bollocks though! The safe haven is environmentalism not globalisation.

Persistently, we are told that green thinking is a threat to our modern gods, namely jobs, growth and the economy. To this I say bollocks also! These economic structures are the cause

---

of the problems we face, not the solution. It needs to be said again, 'These systems are predatory and can only survive if we accept there are more losers than winners and that profiteering is a civilised business practice.'

Can we change this situation? Is it possible to shift our thinking? Of course it is, provided we deploy a little discernment and put aside our unfounded fears.

Changing our Minds

What stops us from changing our minds? With respect to climate change issues there are two main predictors. The first is the impact of our ego and the second is fear.

According to a published research paper by Adam Corner (2012) titled Psychology: Science Literacy and Climate Views, it's not how intelligent we are, but what we come to believe which decides our allegiance to any topic. In fact, Corners' study showed highly educated experts tended to maintain their opinion on an issue once they had publicly stated their position regardless of any later information showing their position to be flawed. Conversely, less educated people were more likely to change their opinion but still resisted doing so.

Corner concluded that it is politically undesirable for experts to be seen to switch camps, implying an expectation exists stating that experts are supposedly infallible. However, on the issue of climate change it is evident many experts have in fact accepted a common stance.

To prove this point, Naomi Orsekes (2004) reviewed more than 900 articles with the words 'climate change' in the abstract (between 1993 and 2003) and found a 97% consensus. Based on this finding the vast majority of our scientific community is in agreement about the impact we humans are having. This suggests that at some point the sceptics amongst these researchers were convinced they needed to change their minds. Hence we can conclude the evidence must be overwhelming in order to overcome the usual tendency for we humans to want to defend our ego.

The other significant determinant of whether we will change our mind is fear of financial loss. Stock market volatility demonstrates financial decision fear in action. In fact, there is a market trader's tool quite literally called the fear and greed index! Beyond the stock market, in our modern Western economies we fear any perceived or real threat to our incomes. Add to this that green initiatives have been branded as a threat to jobs growth and the economy generally, and the obvious leap is that 'fear' and 'green initiatives' come together in a way that undermines our appetite for change.

I suggest though, the greatest source of fear in our world at present should be a fear of staying as we are, and that is, fatally entrenched in the economic paradigm of wealth and power which is destroying our natural world. The evidence is all around us as we see our natural world in a constant state of decline. Standing in the way of amazing human social progress on this front are the two foundations of the economic imperative – the wealth and power pyramids.

Chapter Twelve

Wealth and Power

George Monbiot, environmental columnist for The Guardian newspaper, sums up the theme of this chapter eloquently when he says: *'The demands of the ultra-rich have been dressed up as a sophisticated economic theory and applied regardless of the outcome. The complete failure of this world-scale experiment is no impediment to its repetition. This has nothing to do with economics. It has everything to do with power.'* (Monbiot, Jan 14, 2013).

The Power Elite

While there was a time in our past when it was useful to have the physically strongest leading the clan, today our societies are led by the economically and politically influential. These people have proved to be a greater threat than wild animals or opposing clan chiefs ever were in our past. These people have demonstrated their disregard for those below them and the natural world as they work to maintain power at any cost. The 'power elite' are those in our society whose political, industrial, military and economic positions provide the opportunity to effect national and global circumstances (Mills, 1957) and they do this with a claimed mandate from the voting and spending public.

The power elite are a product of the upward movement of wealth. Wealth is used to persuade the election process. In other words, money buys votes. The political elite are usually linked to the wider power elite and are all too often one and the same.

This is not a conspiracy though. Rather, members of the power elite are the new alphas. They rule because they are driven to do so and because the masses don't challenge them. In fact, they are able to rule because, as American Sociologist C Wright Mills said sixty years ago, we continue to vote for them and participate in their economic activities. We acquiesce because we see them as more capable than us and so they have a right to lead.

Alphas have been around since we roamed the landscape as nomadic hunter-gatherers searching for food and water. Today, spears, clubs and deep voices have been replaced with economic rhetoric, cash, capital, social policy and the smoothest talker. Those with the will and intellect to achieve high levels of influence rule as those with physical prowess once did.

However, I suggest it is an unfortunate waste of an opportunity to see such intellect and will applied to creating our social fabric in such a problematic manner. Fortunately, the masses are powerful because we *can* (even if we don't at present) choose not to vote for them and not purchase the goods and services from which they derive their power.

Perhaps the real challenge before us is to appreciate that those who have risen to positions of power and influence are likely to be the least desirable to lead our civilisation: Meaning, as James Speth points out, there is a need to deny leaders of industry the opportunity to become leaders of government.

The reason to oppose them, as proposed by psychologist Dr K Dutton (2012), is that the attributes which give rise to personal power lack a humanitarian element and operate independently of the individual holding the position. Or in other words, the job descriptions of the leadership positions within corporate structures demand a focus on profit and growth with little or no regard for any distraction from those goals or the people and environment affected by the methods they employ. The more desirable political and corporate leaders would be people who demonstrate a connectedness with, and an altruistic attitude toward, the natural world and all its occupants. The need to resolve the problem of vested interest between political position, the creation of public policy and the election process seems obvious and urgent.

Sadly to date, the lust for power and control demonstrated by the power elite has led humanity on a roller coaster of economic boom and bust, not to mention the collapse of many empires. The costs for humankind have been enormous. Inequity of access to basic food, water and shelter requirements abound (Food & Agriculture Organisation, 2005) and the environmental impact of overpopulation and industrialisation are clear. And yet, the power structures repeat decade after decade.

How has the power elite been so successful despite a massive increase in public access to knowledge and information in recent times? In all likelihood, they have simply been more motivated, fortunate, and often advantaged by birthright. In other words, if we removed the wealthy elite they would quickly be replaced from the ranks of their minions, meaning a restructure of the path to power is required.

Achilles Heel

Fortunately, or unfortunately depending on your viewpoint, the one and only source of power greater than the power elite is you and I, the masses who currently support them. We do so by repeatedly electing conservative governments, the representatives of which are motivated by self-preservation of their positions. They protect their positions by appealing to our wallets and bank accounts using job creation, growth and a strong economy as catch phrases. They are forced to do so, on one side by the power of those with wealth, and on the other by the demands of those without it. Clearly then, because those without wealth outnumber the rest, it is up to us to withdraw our support from the whims of the wealthy.

The truth is, many of us are unemployed, underemployed or work long hours for a relative handful of dollars, and often do so in mundane, uninspiring and life draining circumstances. But as stated earlier, there is one thing we have to our advantage. The upside is that the average person outnumbers the power elite by an enormous margin and if there is ever a coordinated move by the average person against the establishment, change will be rapid and pervasive.

We might ask why widespread change has not occurred already. The answer is reasonably straightforward. The vast majority of humanity operates more like a laboratory mouse in an exercise wheel than as intellectual beings endeavouring to escape the maze of economic life. Please don't be offended. The analogy is not a slight against humanity even though it is quite accurate. It's just that it is obvious we don't question what we don't like in a way that creates change. Perhaps that is because the power elite is what we aspire to be, or alternatively, we fear losing what benefits we already have. Then the answer to our life stress is to stop wanting to be them or have so much.

It's not possible for most of us to get to the top of the pyramid, so why strive for something unachievable? If we stop striving, we stop spending, if we stop spending, we stop stressing. This would be a much better modus operandi than the one we participate in at present. It has to be or our planet is doomed.

Regardless of how we describe the situation, it is observable that we endlessly chase a financial solution to the meaning of life question, not realising the economic wheel never ends: that with one regime removed from office, inevitably a new power elite rises from the ashes to fill the void and the process repeats. It would seem our consciousness is devoid of a perspective allowing us to look in on the cage of life and realise there is an outside or alternative world. Instead, we keep repeating the old structures. As evidence for this contention, we might consider the French Revolution after which it took only a short few years for the beheaded aristocracy to be replaced by a new power elite.

While we remain distracted by all the shiny toys and baubles mass production puts in front of us through economic activity, we are doomed to play the game and keep chasing the carrots and bread crumbs the power elite offer us. As stated earlier, they are who they are because those who lust for power have the drive to move to the top of the power pyramid. While those with humility and wisdom do not, by their nature, tend to seek such power. More is the pity. And it's a difficult reality to deal with. The very people who should be in power don't want to be.

The achievable path forward, is to understand the distractions and illusions which, by ensuring the upward flow of wealth in the pyramid, perpetuate our social order.

Regardless of how powerful a social system seems to be, it will change if its people refuse to play along. But to teach change, we need to be aware of and adopt a philosophy of contentment. Such values need to permeate our education systems and our media as well as our everyday activities.

The Wealth Pyramid

Possibly the most pervasive social institution across all human civilisations is the wealth pyramid. At the top of the pyramid sits a wealthy minority who control (via profits from the spending of the masses) how the vast majority of the population who just want to feel good will live from day to day.

Those below the top are driven by the human primal need to consume, and by the ego. Most people who pursue the illusion of personal power remain trapped in the lower levels of the pyramid. That is its design purpose after all. Only a few can make the climb or we will no longer have a pyramid. As evidence of this process consider the US class structure at present. There is a widening chasm between the rich and the poor and the middle class is disappearing. Will we see a revolution in America? It's a worrying possibility. It's a possibility which concerns the US military and so in recent times US forces have trained in crowd management across the continental US due to a fear of an uprising of the poorer population against the wealthy.

Under the heading of 'civil disturbance planning,' the US military is training troops and police to suppress democratic opposition in America. The master plan, developed by the Department of Defense (Civil Disturbance Plan 55-2), is code-named, 'Operation Garden Plot' and is summed up by activist Frank Morales as follows:

'Generally, the measures (in Garden Plot) *have sought to thwart the aims of social justice movements, embodying the concept that within the civilian body politic lurks an enemy that one day the military might have to fight, or at least be ordered to fight'* (Morales,

2013).

The extent of the defence mechanism surrounding the wealth pyramid need not exist as it does and the wealthy who manipulate our economics need not control our lives. The choices to be informed and be empowered by knowledge and to have the strength of our convictions are innate in each of us. This truly is what it means to be human: **to take up the challenge and prevail through will and intellect rather than bowing to primal urges which compel us to accumulate and hoard.**

The power elite and the wealth pyramid exist only because we are successfully lured by perceived value in goods and services which have no intrinsic value to life. Today, our task is to prevail over a set of illusions and distractions which operate in our society to justify the wealth pyramid.

Based on half-truths and assumptions, these distractions and illusions work to ensure our daily lives don't stray from the endless loop of acquiring income and using it to consume the products which keep the wealthy elite where they are and the rest of us where we are: at the lower end of the pyramid paying huge taxes.

How do we overcome these influences? We do so by critically examining how the social and economic illusions and distractions operate. With such an understanding we will be in a position to make changes by using our unique human trait of discernment.

Chapter Thirteen

Illusions and Distractions: A Primer

Distractions and Illusions operate to ensure our thoughts are preoccupied with economic matters. The reason is simple enough and is put nicely by Pulitzer prize winning journalist Chris Hedges (2010): *'To perpetuate the wealth and power pyramids, populations must be steered away from exploring history, social change and long term future planning.'*

The pursuit of what we see as our available choices in life, namely, family and personal interactions, education, employment, financial and personal status, entertainment and recreation, occupy the greater part of our daily routines.

As a result, all too quickly, the demands of life enmesh us (and each new generation) in a tangle of responsibility and routine which consumes so much presence of mind there is little left for contemplating life outside the economic maze or even that such a life is possible. This is where education fails us. Sadly, education is actively designed to convince us of the illusion that says financial entanglement (debt) is a normal and necessary part of life.

What are the Distractions?

Distractions are those ideals, activities and events which appear important but have little intrinsic value to life and ultimately keep our thinking away from questioning the need for the pursuit in the first place. The distractions include but are not limited to, personal power, success, status, affluence, possessions, title and competition.

Distractions also include the more tangible pursuits on offer such as excess food, illicit drugs, alcohol, addiction generally, relationship issues, non-essential retail therapy, and adrenalin sports. Additionally, they include any item or activity purchased or pursued which does not directly provide for basic survival needs and which are used in excess to make life bearable or more enjoyable. The key to the definition lies in the last few words, 'used in excess to make life bearable or more enjoyable.'

If products and services are consumed and personal relationships are formed, for the purpose of overcoming the pressures of life then the reason for their consumption is seriously flawed. The pursuit becomes little more than a distraction from the underlying affliction. The old cliché of prevention being better than cure is apt here.

It seems many people involve themselves in the distractions of our world to fill a dark hole in the human spirit, while others consume simply for the short-lived pleasure of doing so. Regardless of the motive, it would seem from the mountains of obsolete and failed products which arrive at waste disposal sites every day that these products do not succeed as cures for a troubled human spirit.

A cynic might suggest, interpersonal relationships and marriages (which have today become hugely commercialised) also often end up at the waste disposal site. And, many life taking illnesses (obesity, heart disease, diabetes etc) are symptoms of an economic system more interested in product sales than human welfare. Nevertheless, repeatedly chasing more of the same products and services, which ultimately bring little if any real or lasting satisfaction, fits the definition of a distraction.

That is, we tend to move from one good or service to another only because fashions change, our mood changes or an updated version of a product comes into our awareness. Far too often, goods and services are produced solely to make us feel good but ultimately fail to do so.

Perhaps it is better to understand why we don't feel good in the first place rather than adding to our trash piles by consuming more of the products and services which created our financial stress in the first place. For instance, food is intrinsically important to our survival, while a glass of wine is not. Similarly, a large, well appointed home may be a desire, but it is not essential to a healthy life. That's not to say we must go without wine or houses. The point is to define the nature and extent of the distractions we have to deal with.

What are the Illusions?

Illusions, which include the notions of freedom and democracy, justice and fairness, patriotism, nationalism, parochialism and how we deal with death, are wider in scope than distractions. While distractions include a component of choice to participate in their effect from day to day, illusions usually operate as social policy or cultural norm and so are difficult to avoid.

Illusions include anything which seeks to direct our lives using pretence as opposed to substance. Some examples are, the belief governments operate for the welfare of people; that the individual is powerless to effect change; that democracy guarantees freedom; that we must accept the pyramidal power structure of our society, or that we must participate in the economy or we will not survive.

Illusions operate to minimise any impetus to overcome them by maintaining an appearance of legitimacy, permanence, effectiveness and being reasonable and rational. This is achieved through promise and rhetoric, but usually there is questionable, if any, proof of delivery.

For instance, there is ample evidence of the fragility (or very existence) of democracy, the instability of economics, and the inequity of the wealth pyramid in our history books. Sure, these structures evolve over time giving the appearance they are changing and advancing to our benefit, but we see little useful or measurable difference in the outcomes from these structures from year to year, or for that matter from century to century.

Needs and Wants

A critical first step in gaining the upper hand over the illusions and distractions of our world is to clarify the difference between needs and wants. In the simplest terms, needs refer to air, water, food, shelter and a mate. These are things we humans cannot survive without. These have intrinsic value.

Wants are products and services designed to enhance convenience and pleasure - things we don't need, but sure feel good. Wants are usually something which has only a perceived value. Of course, there is some blurring and overlap and there is no intent to suggest products and services outside our survival needs should be altogether removed from our lives. It is suggested however, that over-consumption and/or our inability to say no to high levels of consumption are the direct cause of much financial trouble, general life stress, illness and unhappiness.

This uncomfortable existence can arise from working long hours to afford over-consumption, or it can be due to indebtedness which so often is associated with over-spending.

The important issue is the distinction between needs and wants. And that, that distinction is actively pushed to the rear of our daily lives by the allure of illusions and distractions. In this process, marketing and advertising, which are carefully designed to ensure our continued and increasing consumption, are the tools used by the wealth pyramid to perpetuate itself.

It would seem logical that if over-consumption of goods and services has created a host of economic, environmental and personal problems, then under consumption would see a reduction in the same problems. Unfortunately, our economic and scientific focus remains fixed on increased technological innovation and economic growth as a solution, rather than any reductionist stance.

The following pages define a host of distractions and illusions with the aim of empowering us to operate around, through and over them, rather than under their controlling influence.

To draw on an earlier analogy, we know rats placed in a maze, inside a cage which defines their world, escape the maze and appear content within the cage. I wonder if the rats would be so content if they became aware of the world outside their cage. We humans are vastly more intellectually capable than a rat and yet I suggest we scurry about in our life cage, not content, but at the same time rarely challenging the economic system which defines our experience of life. The real world is out there just waiting, if not begging, to be rediscovered.

Chapter Fourteen

The Illusions

Patriotism, Nationalism and Parochialism

A common expression of nationalism and patriotism is the singing of a nation's anthem. Anthems are typically an expression of a countries history and its people's efforts to build the nation, and they can rouse strong emotions. However, a less positive aspect to anthems is that they can incite and inflame divisive and supremacist parochialism. Parochialism in this context is particularly dangerous because when nationalism, patriotism and parochialism mix with a perceived threat to a nation, violence too often follows. At the very least dislike, distrust and racism are nourished.

This happens because fear, suspicion and pride combined with parochialism are too often used as manipulations designed to create ideologies of difference between people on opposite sides of a border or across cultural boundaries. International sports spectator violence is an obvious example of parochial patriotism at work. The same can be said for participating in an armed force for the purpose of persecuting people who are culturally different but represent no tactical or strategic threat.

Beyond these very public and overt examples of parochial patriotism, our so-called civilised societies display a more muted undertone of intolerance toward people whose only transgression is that they *are not like us.* Hence, we need to explore and better understand the source of that troublesome thinking if we are to weed it out of our social fabric.

A 2011 study by Tim Reeskens, published in the Psychological Science journal, included more than 40,000 respondents from 31 countries. The study identified two types of national pride. These were ethnic ancestry and civic nationalism. In short, civic nationalism is a fondness for a countries institutions and laws. This is usually more inclusive and social than ethnic ancestry which is described as belonging to a particular racial or religious background. Ethnic groups are more divisive because they tend to exclude those not like themselves, particularly in terms of beliefs and cultural identity.

Reeskens study found that love for ones nation typically elevates reports of well-being and happiness. However, civic nationalism had a far greater happiness rating than ethnic ancestry. This is because ethnic nationalists tend to be deeply entrenched in religious beliefs and their cultural history within a region. If these institutions come under threat all bets are off and conflict typically erupts. Conversely, civic nationalists are attracted to a nation's way of life more than its cultural roots. Civic nationalists are more likely to relocate if they perceive a different nation suits their lifestyle better.

The illusion to be identified, for either type of nationalism, is the belief that one nation or people are superior to another and that this is sufficient reason to exploit, dislike, hate, or enter into conflict with people from a different nation. It is better to say we are all citizens of Earth with equal rights to health, life and safety. Sadly though, these rights are all too often diminished or destroyed by parochialism.

By definition, parochialism is being of narrow scope or view and not considering wider issues and effects (Dictionary.com). Often, nothing more than rumour and myth underpin parochialism. Also, fragile egos which are drawn to bigotry are demonstrably parochial. As stated earlier, we see parochialism in crowd violence at sports events, and in racist comments generally, albeit these are quite innocuous compared to war and atrocity that are perpetrated over issues of ethnicity. However, war is quite removed from the everyday atrocity we participate in by consuming goods made available because we accept that others must endure the pitiful wages paid to produce them. This is the insidious parochialism of our time. This situation says we are happy to support the suffering of people only because their nation is less developed and therefore is somehow expected to endure the economic fallout of being less entitled to the comforts others enjoy at their expense.

Again, rousing a nation to economic, political or physical war by appealing to parochialism is something nations must avoid if they are to rightfully lay claim to being civilised. This is the essence of the illusion of parochial nationalism: that it is employed to rouse the emotions of the populace to take up arms to defend or enforce a set of values, which at the end of the day, have more to do with the whims of a nation's wealth and power elites, than of benefiting the wider community.

Patriotism, nationalism and parochialism are ego-based and emotive and are particularly difficult to avoid in daily life given the focus our economic world places on them, and given, our media operates to legitimise and reinforce such a focus.

Our unique defence against these illusions is our ability to discern. That is, to discern when we are over-reacting to our primal self-interest drive by participating in parochial nationalistic thinking. However, avoiding this is particularly difficult because we promote parochial nationalism simply by participating in an economic system which exploits other nations.

This is so because producing the stuff of our economies relies on exploiting resource-rich nations and the cheap labour of people within those, often less developed countries, whose people are forced to work to enable the lifestyles of wealthier nations. And to make things worse, when we send production to other nations to take advantage of cheaper labour, we also destroy industries in our own countries in the process. The whole situation is far too destructive and yet we accept it as part of our suite of democratic rights, as part of the economic system. Then it seems reasonable to say the system needs to change if we are to ever stop fearing those who look, speak or act differently to us.

The Democracy Illusion

To live in a democracy is to anticipate genuine freedom of choice, freedom of speech and a set of rights designed to protect a way of life. At least this is the popular rhetoric of political references to democracy.

However, by definition, democracy is a requirement for voters to have the right to vote for a representative assembly – a small group of people who will administer the will of the wider community – and that there will be the opportunity to vote for one of at least two political parties.

The definition mentions nothing of freedom, individual rights or a way of life. These rights *are* perhaps implicit and the implication is certainly leveraged in political rhetoric, but there is no rule or requirement to deliver freedom or rights. This suggests the popularised notion of democracy is more myth than reality. And if we consider that the member parties of most political duopolies are difficult to distinguish other than by party name and the colour of their banners, democratic choice really is an illusion.

Definitions of democracy by the following authorities on the subject are enlightening and add support to the argument:

Andrew Heywood: *'Rule by the people; democracy implies both popular participation and government in the public interest and can take a wide variety of forms.'* (Museum of Australian Democracy)

Dr John Hirst: *'A democracy is a society in which the citizens are sovereign and control the government.'* (Museum of Australian Democracy)

Joseph Schumpeter: *'The democratic method is that institutional arrangement for arriving at political decisions in which individuals acquire the power to decide by means of a competitive struggle for the people's vote.'* (Museum of Australian Democracy)

Considering the above definitions, we can say that a democracy that suits and benefits a small section of the community is by definition not democratic. That is today, virtually all democracies are influenced if not steered by 'the economy,' or in other words the status of the economic environment is more directive than the wishes of the voter. The following additional definitions of democracy support this argument.

Firstly:

*'The purpose of government is to enable the people of a nation to live in safety and happiness. **Government exists for the interests of the governed, not for the governors.***' (Thomas Jefferson, 1787).

And then there is this gem from Milton Freidman (1993):

*'...the result is a government system that is **no longer controlled by 'we, the people.'** Instead of Lincoln's government 'of the people, by the people and for the people, we now have a government 'of the people, by the bureaucrats, for the bureaucrats,' including the elected representatives who have become bureaucrats.'*

According to The Australian Collaboration (2012), a collaboration of national community organisations, government will ideally:

*'...be neither despotic nor over-bureaucratic. It should exist within a legal framework based on the rule of law and the protection of civil liberties. It should support civil society and its multiplicity of voices and activities. It should provide the economic framework and the essential infrastructure for public and private enterprise. It should be concerned with the well-being of all citizens. It should protect the physical environment and it should act to **alleviate the adverse impacts of the marketplace on individuals, groups and the environment**. These roles are often poorly understood and undervalued...'*

Clearly, all around our world government policy is failing to *'alleviate the adverse impacts of the marketplace on individuals, groups and the environment.'* This observation alone places a huge question mark over any claim that our governments are truly democratic.

Further, it seems even from this small selection of definitions from an all but endless list, that there is little agreement on what a democracy is. Moreover, the notion of individual voter involvement and determination in policy making are all but impossible to observe in day to day government operations.

Conversely, corporations operate by very specific rules and mission statements. Managers very much direct the actions of the corporation in line with its objectives. Corporations also spend a great deal of time, money, and effort lobbying governments and politicians to influence them in a direction beneficial to the business.

Like the corporate model, democracy needs to be defined because while no single definition exists and no mission statement has to be adhered to, no definitive set of rules can be applied. Without such governance, the democratic process will continue to be infiltrated by those who have the greatest motivation to do so, and I contend, that is exactly the intended outcome.

At present the most motivated group is almost exclusively the corporate sector, mainly because corporations have the financial capacity to fund personnel whose task it is to lobby governments. Wage slaves are excluded from this activity simply and effectively by the need to work, which again is in no way democratic.

Further, another definition of democracy suggests, *'Democracy is the basis for cooperative and collective action that may be required to solve or coordinate action regarding an issue'* (Coleman & Ferejohn, 1986).

All too often today though, action occurs without the cooperation or collective input of the community. More often at present, governments invoke action and then measure public reaction, only altering a decision if there is great disquiet. For example, recently in Western Australia the State Government set drum line traps to catch Great White Sharks. The public uproar at this move was loud. It drew world attention within a short time and the drum lines were removed.

However, the State Government applied to the Federal Government for the power to set the drum lines with less than one hour's consultation time. This effectively bypassed the opportunity for the public to participate. The drum lines went back in and sharks died despite public opposition. Is this democracy in action? If it is there are huge flaws in our understanding of what to expect from democracy.

Very often, a thin veil of legitimacy suffices as justification for government action. Usually, that veil consists of economic rhetoric about jobs, growth and the economy and omits environmental impact, social justice, or social equity of access to resources. In the shark example the rhetoric involved references to tourism and lost revenue.

The Illusion of Choice

Considering the previous topic, democracy is not so much about choice or freedom as it is about the perception of choice and an assumption of freedom.

In fact, as alluded to by journalist Chris Hedges (2012), in Empire of Illusion, defending democracy in itself is a very useful fall-back position for party leaders looking to justify going to war, or sanctioning another country which threatens a nation's security. We must defend democracy, freedom of choice and our lifestyle is the usual rhetoric.

These words are designed to inspire nationalism and patriotism and the strategy works particularly well, except for the unfortunate members of the military who have no choice but to die for their country when physical conflict erupts. And of course, we all pay the price of the war in our taxes. And, we have no real choice unless there is a pre-emptive anti Vietnam War style movement which stops wars before they cost a fortune. Sadly, these are few and far between.

Another worrying reality is emerging in our democratic societies. According to David Boyle, a fellow of the New Economics Foundation, rising house prices are and will continue to see the traditional middle classes unable to afford a home. Meaning today's children may well be forced to work two, three or four jobs to afford to pay rent with no prospect of home ownership.

This situation is a product of economic policies under our so-called democratic system of government, and it is these policies, which ensure the gap between the wealthy and the poor ever widens. Hence, our choice to obtain low cost housing has been effectively taken away.

Gradual changes to taxation law are a major driver in this social class canyon building exercise, and, the public is all but excluded from the decision making process. In fact, our capacity to make choices is constrained and steered within a narrow channel. Usually, that channel must create profits first and quality lifestyles as a last resort.

Do we have a choice other than to participate in the economic imperative? We do, but that path has been painted as dangerous and to be avoided. However, our capacity to demand change is no illusion. The real illusion is the fallacy that our dangerous economic activity can continue as it is without consequences.

The Equitable Taxation Illusion

Before constitutional government, in the time of kings and lords, taxes were unfairly and forcibly collected, often at sword point. Today, tax collection is enforced via written laws. The change from enforcement by the sword, to sanction via threat of imprisonment, was seen as a milestone in the emergence of our notion of democracy. Evidently we are expected to accept that being forced to pay tax by written law is more civilised than being forced at sword point. However, in both cases the tax payer is forced: the only difference being the lethality of the penalty for not paying.

Nevertheless, it is probably reasonable to say a prison term or a hefty fine is preferable to a sword thrust. Still, they are penalties to the same end. That is, the collection of currency into a coffer in which the hands of the wealthy are conspicuously present.

Today, those hands are represented by a process of tendering for government infrastructure projects, (as well as grants and salaries) the scope of which are often too large for small businesses or individuals to consider: the result being an ongoing movement of tax dollars from the public purse into corporate hands. The larger the project, the more centralised the funds become. In this sense taxation for infrastructure projects provides the illusion of benefiting the public, while the real financial benefit is heavily biased in favour of the businesses winning the tender process. Too many of these projects are non-essential and serve only to funnel public funds up the wealth pyramid.

It is said that taxation, in part, led to the fall of Rome, the rise of Islam, the signing of the Magna Carta (precursor to constitutional government) and the French revolution. Taxation is also seen as one cause of the American Civil War as it was the Eureka Stockade in the fledgling colony which would become Australia.

This suggests taxation plays a far more central role in our lives than most of us consider from day to day. As stated above, historically speaking, taxes have been collected at the whim of monarchs and religious leaders of the day, often with little or no regard for their effect on the population. Accounts of large storehouses being built in medieval times to store the tithe (usually paid in grain) collected from the peasant populations seem incredible. Today, even more enormous taxation reserves, albeit they are in the form of currency and gold bullion, raise no comment or opposition.

At present, in Australia, taxpayers are subject to at least one hundred and twenty-five different taxes. For US taxpayers, the list is ninety-seven taxes long, with corporate taxes making up just 7% of tax revenues in 2012 compared with 30% in 1950

(Snyder, 2012), meaning tax dollars are increasingly raised from average salary earners who can least afford to pay.

All of these taxes are compulsory and notably, attract little open resistance from the taxpayer.

Interestingly, the definition of a tax is a little slippery also.

Firstly, there is no direct and explicit link between the collection of taxes and the delivery of services (Australian Treasury, 2008) meaning service delivery does not necessarily follow tax collection. To quote the Australian Treasury directly: *'A core characteristic of a tax is that there is no clear and direct link between the payment of the tax and the provision of goods and services to the taxpayer. The funds governments raise via taxes may be used to provide goods or services to the community as a whole and this may provide a benefit to the taxpayer, but the payment will still be considered a tax if there is no direct relationship between the amount of the payment and the benefit to the taxpayer'.*

It seems the assumption that collecting taxes is carried out in order to provide goods, services, or infrastructure, is incorrect. While it is our individual complacency which allows this situation to exist, the fact remains we pay taxes under the illusion those taxes must be used for public welfare or benefit. The ultimate question becomes, 'what happens to the collected tax dollars which do not serve the purpose for which they are collected?' Typically they are used to pay for tendered projects.

How very convenient this is for those operating large enough corporations to qualify to tender.

Under a democratic taxation system, one might be forgiven for expecting the contribution to taxation across the population would be fair and equitable. This is not the case either. 'It is the very wealthy who pay the least tax' (Buffett, 2011). According to Warren Buffett, *'The 'mega-rich' pay about 15 percent in taxes, while the middle class falls into the 15 percent and 25 percent income tax brackets and then are hit with heavy payroll taxes to boot.'* While we might expect higher income earners to contribute larger amounts to the taxation system, our economies rely heavily on large numbers of low to middle-income earners as the tax paying backbone of economic activity. This hardly seems democratic, fair, or a display of social equity.

Taxation is just one example of the inequity built into our so called democratic system where traditional rhetoric suggests equal opportunity, equal access, choice, freedom and public welfare are paramount. Laws to enforce our participation are difficult to work around though, so it seems there really is little choice but to pay, which in itself is hardly democratic. But it is only through our apathy and quickness to acquiesce to so-called authority, that taxation is structured as it is.

Our democratic right is to call for change. Why don't we? If it's because we are too lazy to protest, then we should not complain about taxes or being caught in the economic grind - not at all!

The Taxation Iceberg

The story so far is only the tip of the taxation iceberg. Democratic US, British, and several other governments support the activities of individuals and corporations in the use of offshore tax havens. I.e. they support legal tax evasion which places an unfair burden on regular tax payers, but rarely if ever do we hear about this in our media.

First investigated as part of a strategy to track terrorist funding, seventy-three states and territories around our globe have been identified as providers of tax evasion facilities. Thirty of these tax havens have been identified as United Kingdom territories.

According to the Tax Justice Network's Matti Kohonen,

companies such as Ikea, Richard Branson's Virgin Group, Rupert Murdoch's News Corporation and a host of others enjoy the benefits of tax havens. At last estimate, US$11.3 trillion of private wealth was held in offshore tax havens. The global figure for resultant lost tax revenue stands at US$255 billion.

Clearly, it is not mum and dad wage earners who are benefiting from this situation. In Britain, taxes paid by individuals have more than doubled during 1989-2003 while taxes paid by corporations only increased by 2.8 percent. In fact, due to systematic tax evasion, the amount of corporate tax as a share of all collected taxes diminished during the 1990's. As a result, in the year 2003 individuals paid £109 billion in taxes while corporations paid £29 billion' (Tax Justice Network, no date).

The average income earner does not participate in offshore tax avoidance schemes and subsequently is taxed heavily as revenue offices attempt to meet the shortfall created by the corporations and individuals who do evade. These schemes could be dismantled, but for a lack of intent and will to do so within the ranks of those whose wealth is only possible if others are excluded from these schemes.

Dirty money in developing nations is also a primary driver of poverty. Dirty money is money gained by breaking laws and regulations, which includes tax law.

Matti Kohonen makes the point when he states, *'The drug economy is estimated to contribute US$60 billion, corruption 30 billion USD, while commercial sources contribute a total of 440 billion USD to tax evasion...we should turn away from thinking of corruption as a state inefficiency alone, but rather that it is rooted to the non-transparent structures of global financial markets.'* (Tax Justice Network, no date)

On this front, to be aware is to be empowered and how life proceeds is a matter of taking control via our vote and demanding change on such issues. Having control in itself relies upon taking up the right to challenge the social, political and economic illusions which are all around us. The fallacy of democratic process and the idea that taxation collection is in any way balanced and equitable, being two of those illusions.

Once again I say, the power to effect change is in our right to vote for that change. The right people to lead our nations are out there: our task is to fabricate a means to ensure they arrive in office and have our support.

That system must find people who do not operate from vested interest and who demonstrate the wisdom of altruism and selflessness. These people exist, but typically don't put their hand up to be politicians. If sporting bodies can find the very best athletes, surely we can come up with a means to find the very best politicians, and then, ensure they have the public support needed to create effective reform.

The Home Ownership Illusion

A great deal of time and energy is devoted to home ownership, but do homebuyers who are subject to finance really own their homes? In many cases the answer is, no.

The truth is, we can make payments for twenty years or more while living under the illusion the roof over our heads is ours. That's because firstly, under the terms of most mortgage contracts, a financial institution has the right to foreclose even if conditions of the contract are not broken, and secondly, the interest in the land is transferred to the lender until the debt is repaid. This means quite simply that the lender owns the property until the debt is cleared.

Of course, provided the loan terms are met, the mortgage *will be* discharged and the title returned to the home buyer. Until that time though, the borrower, or as we prefer to say 'the home owner', does not actually own the property. In essence, under this arrangement, a home owner is indebted to the holder of the mortgage.

Still, debt like this is popular because it gives 1) the impression of ownership 2) a sense of power 3) a look of prestige and 4) a feeling of success. Nevertheless, real freedom or even the quasi freedom democracy offers cannot exist under this arrangement. Real freedom would mean access to a home without debt or encumbrance. Instead we rely on credit and live with the illusion of ownership.

The Credit Illusion

Credit, or more accurately agreeing to a legally binding credit contract, is an overly optimistic term used to avoid speaking of indebtedness (debt) which is tantamount to slavery. Have no doubt, credit is debt. Debt contracts are legally binding. Debt in the form of credit gives the illusion of wealth. Credit is something we should always speak of for what it is – a contract under which we sell our potential to earn funds (wages) which we are forced to use to meet principle and interest payments. Hence the term, 'wage slaves'.

The reality of home finance is that when we take on housing debt we are beholden to the provider of the funds. The arrangement really is one step away from overt slavery. All we have changed is the wording in the contract, as well as, the standard of living of the wage slave. In effect, we have replaced ownership of the individual (slavery), with ownership of the individual's land, building and time (loan contract). In other words, when we work for the right of tenancy via a mortgage, our time is owned by the lender because the debt forces us to spend our time working to avoid the penalties which inevitably follow default on payments.

Further, I suggest democracies which regularly speak of freedom as a basic right of its citizens, but accept and support predatory debt arrangements, are displaying flagrant hypocrisy.

Obviously, wage earners are not technically owned today, but there is little difference if our lives and our time are controlled by others. If we are not free to live where and how we please, but rather do so to the design of others who own the right to decide how we live and how we use our time, are we not slaves?

Some would say we are free to choose whether we take on housing debt or not. As well, there is an asset (the home) which offsets our indebtedness (provided there is no GFC II). However, we have to ask, 'If not from a loan, from where does the purchase price of a home come?' The fact remains that the vast majority don't have a choice other than to apply for a loan because the price of a home is beyond a wage earners capacity to save. Could this situation be changed via legislation? Of course it could, but then that would mean a direct threat to the wealth pyramid would be created. Hence, it is unlikely to happen without a widespread, insistent and loud public voice.

Furthermore, where housing finance is provided, and the capacity of the consumer to pay is in doubt and this is known to the lender, we have a massive moral, ethical and civility problem. But we might say this is not how our housing finance sector operates. We might say there are regulations to protect buyers and many home owners profit from capital growth. Sure, we have rules and we know there are checks and balances, and some do make profits, but the fact that we have no choice between debt and not owning a home (due to the enormous purchase price), tells us the checking system has failed. Moreover, the vast number of people who lose money or their homes when market values fall attests to the failure of this system.

What has happened to our freedom to have a home without debt? What has happened is that our freedom has been sold to those whose wealth gives them an advantage. Moreover, the principles of democracy, freedom and justice have been sold off to free enterprise. Actually, that's completely wrong! The truth is that since their inception democracy and freedom have been little more than an illusion. These ideals were *invented* by free enterprise, and in return free enterprise offers wage slavery. And what's more, to clearly identify the slave masters of our world, we only need look at the wealth pyramid. In fact, this is probably the greatest illusion in our world, that the principles of freedom and democracy were ever anything but illusions created by those who own the factors of production i.e. the land, labour and capital needed to turn a profit.

As previously discussed, in the United States the illusion started when the Founding Fathers formed governments because they considered the average person incapable of sensible input into the running of communities. The Founding Fathers were wealthy businessmen and it is not difficult to see their real motive was to protect their personal positions. Little has changed since that time, other than the ever widening gap between the rich and the poor (via the disappearance of the middle class), and better and more convincing stories that ensure most of us do no more than grumble about our finances.

Functionally, the problem with debt is that the motives of those who provide it are represented in the binding contracts which show zero compassion for borrowers. I.e. the contract is designed to centralise wealth. To absolve their conscience about foreclosing, lenders hide behind contract law and the intent of the term 'buyer beware.' Morality and compassion are cast aside in such dealings between the so-called civilised expert lender and the not so informed borrower.

Buyer beware is not a proxy for morality, or a defence for casting it aside.

The chain of events in this situation starts with a contract which is a lawful binding of the individual. The contract defines the terms of payment. The terms of payment move wealth from the borrower to the lender. Wealth creates power. Power leads to influence over the construction of laws. The wealthy and powerful write the rules by which the rest are able to access debt. The less wealthy are permitted to live in housing provided we work for the wealthy. The link between borrower and wealthy land owner is masked by financial institutions, but it still exists and sounds strangely like slavery, only the look and feel of the whip have changed. That is, if we stop working soon we will have no place to live.

We may not be overtly whipped or otherwise abused, but I suggest homelessness in today's world is probably as difficult to deal with, if not more so. In fact, I would choose a whipping over losing my home without a second thought.

This suggests the threat of homelessness is certainly a powerful motivator. It also suggests we become homeless, not because we can't pay, but because laws prevent us choosing to live in anything but designed-to-be-excessive, overly luxurious and ridiculously expensive housing.

Rising house prices segregate communities into those who can afford debt and those who cannot. Education is the gatekeeper and filtration system to qualify for debt. Hence the great divide between the poverty stricken semi-educated and the educationally approved owners of capital and the other means of production.

A civilised society would move to dismantle this arrangement and by doing so would create real social justice, freedom and democracy. Evidently, we are not particularly civilised because we prefer to create social, economic and environmental misery for millions so that others can sip coffee on a balcony and I have heard it said on such balconies, 'I wonder what the poor are doing today?'

The Wealth Illusion

Given the pervasiveness of home loans and debt cards, it appears we are happy to live with the illusion that debt equates to wealth, affluence and ownership. However, none of this monetary activity accounts for the outstanding US$70 trillion in environmental debt we have not factored into global prosperity calculations. We also overlook the social cost and civil unrest created by economic activity, preferring to consider these issues as inconveniences. Conveniently, these costs, in the words of economic theory, are referred to as 'negative externalities'. However, these downsides are not external at all and cannot be marginalised in the way economic theory tells us to. In fact, by living in hope, we have to date trusted economic growth to provide a silver lining to the global environmental debt thundercloud. However, there are several problems with this strategy.

Firstly, our environment suffers greatly when we concrete over it and displace the biodiversity we depend on for life itself. Hope will not avert the consequences of this or the massive amount of financial debt in our world. This debt is now higher than pre GFC levels.

Secondly, there are usually many years between entering into our first home loan and clearing the debt. During this time we work, work, work and pray there is no market crash on the horizon which will erase any equity we have squirreled away.

Third, real estate growth is inflationary which pushes loans out of reach of those who need them most. The welfare cost to house these people grows and adds to our tax burden. Subsequently, our children are now faced with being these people.

Moreover, housing finance is a tool used by our economic system to ensure lower and middle class working people have access to the cash needed to fund consumerism. It does this by lending home owners part or all of the equity in the home, thus extending indebtedness to ensure the home owner's attendance at work for the foreseeable future. Increased consumer spending is then reported as economic growth, however, the value of that growth is exceeded by the cost of environmental loss.

The truth is consumers cannot become wealthy because, firstly, spending and being wealthy are mutually exclusive, and secondly, because we cannot have a wealth pyramid if everyone is wealthy. The wealth pyramid requires a wide base of taxpaying low-income workers. The end result of this situation is not so much for the benefit of society as it is designed to ensure ongoing centralisation of wealth into global, tax haven protected bank accounts.

Today, we are seeing a new social order emerging as the middle class evaporates leaving behind the very wealthy and the destitute. It is hard to believe eighty percent of Americans will experience incomes below the poverty line in their lifetimes, but this is the finding reported by CBS News on July 28 2013 in an article titled, '80 Percent of US Adults Face Near-Poverty, Unemployment, survey finds.'

The divide grows and grows which must eventually destabilise the wealth pyramid and so dire measures are taken to prop up the structure. For instance, and to reiterate an earlier point, recognising the danger of a social rebellion the US Military conducts crowd control drills in anticipation of internal protest over social inequity.

'*Current US military preparations for suppressing domestic civil disturbance, including the training of National Guard troops and police...have sought to thwart the aims of social justice movements, embodying the concept that within the civilian body politic lurks an enemy that one day the military might have to fight, or at least be ordered to fight.'* (Morales, 2013).

Why the heck do we accept this arrangement? Why do we accept it when it leads to financial meltdowns which cause so much suffering and creates so much risk?

As put by George Monbiot of the Guardian Newspaper: '*Housing bubbles in several countries, including Britain, could pop at any time. A report in September revealed that total world debt (public and private) has reached 212% of GDP. In 2008, when it helped to cause the last crash, it stood at 174%. The Telegraph notes that this threatens to cause, renewed financial crisis ... and eventual mass default. Shadow banking has gone berserk, stocks appear to be wildly overvalued and the Eurozone is bust again. Which will blow first?'* (Monbiot, Nov 19, 2014).

The last GFC crippled our economic system just a few years ago and already we are looking down the barrel of another: None of which matters at all if the end result is a ruined environment, meaning a house to live in is a non-issue if we cannot live.

Perhaps a different perspective will make the point more effectively. That is, the point that alternative lifestyles are possible, workable and can be pleasant.

Recently, while studying the impact of earthquakes as part of my son's geography class, we looked at events in the city of Bam, Iran, 2004. The project reviewed government policy on housing standards in Bam and the impact the policies had on the population before and after an earthquake struck. In stark contrast to the building codes imposed in most modern Western industrial cities, the Iranian government did not enforce building standards, nor did it accept responsibility for the citizens housing. As a result, the residents built their houses at their own cost and where they pleased, with no interference or assistance from the government. Accordingly, houses were built from local materials to meet the requirements of the people and were built at an affordable price.

The earthquake effectively levelled the city leaving the residents to fend for themselves, that is until the government stepped in and regulated.

The housing in Bam, post the earthquake was heavily regulated and became too expensive. Knowing they would not be able to make loan repayments to the government, the residents were distressed at the prospect of incurring long-term loans needed to rebuild under the new earthquake compliant rules. Some moved away, some endure the burden of debt. Few are happy.

Sadly, the new city buildings no longer have the same appeal to tourists, who were the lifeblood of the community. Today, Bam is modernised, indebted, and is as sterile to look at as any other modern city.

From a Western perspective, the government policy regarding housing in Bam prior to the earthquake seems strange. Most of us do not expect to be able to build wherever and whenever we please. Still, the building practices in Bam were neither right nor wrong. They were a choice and the people were happy. They were self-sufficient and enjoyed life. Housing in Bam was low cost, low maintenance and certainly did not require long-term financial commitments. In the end, debt was forced on the people of Bam due to criticism of government policy by outsiders trying to help after the quake.

When debt is all but forced on people as it was in Bam, we have to ask why? We have to ask, 'Who benefits from such debt arrangements', and also ask, 'What is their motive for providing debt facilities?' The answers to these three questions usually bring us to the profit-making imperative of our economic system which cares little for the welfare of people provided there is positive economic growth.

The Endless Growth Illusion

Our global economy imploded in 2008/9 when the GFC occurred. Many have offered explanations for why it happened, but few look back far enough to examine the root causes preferring to commentate on the market action of the event itself as it happens. The bottom line is the GFC was created because of an assumption that infinite growth from finite resources is, or was ever, possible. To appreciate how this illusion was built, we need to step back several decades.

Before the 1950's housing loans were very restrictive. Fifty per cent deposits were required and full repayment over as little as five years was demanded by banks, with harsh penalties applied in the event of default. By the 1970's, partial deregulation of the housing loan market saw deposit requirements fall dramatically. The lowering of deposits was to continue until eventually in the lead up to 2008/9 no deposit was required. During this time the term of a loan extended from a few years to the borrower's working lifetime.

But what drove these changes? Was it altruism? Did lenders have the interest of the consumer in mind or was the reason nothing more than the profit motive? We need to step back even further and understand more about the evolution of housing finance to answer these questions.

During and after the Great Depression of the 1930's, housing for less well-off people was of low quality and was in short supply. Add to this, a fall in corporate demand for finance after World War II and bank profit margins were severely threatened. At the same time, the demand for factory-made items was surging.

Over time, activities such as hand-sewing of clothes, bread-making and literally building one's own home were to disappear as mass production took hold. To pay for the factory-made items, which utilised the World War II inspired production lines, finance was needed to encourage spending.

So the scene was set after World War II for a housing explosion when returned servicemen were in the market for a home. New finance tools were created to make the building of homes and associated purchases of factory-made goods possible. Importantly, during this period businesses saw the opportunity to sell one of everything (fridges, washing machines etc) into each new home.

The scene was set for the biggest housing boom in world history. After a modest post war start, residential investment steadily increased for decades before rising exponentially as loan regulation was relaxed more and more. Eventually, in the lead up to the GFC, the world was literally living on credit, but the seemingly endless growth in home prices would prove to be a house of cards.

By 2005-2008, the market for housing loans in the United States became saturated. As a last gasp and to prop up the housing market, the finance industry handed out credit cards like they were candy at a birthday party. The credit limit on these cards was claimed as income on mortgage loan applications. Flipping houses was the only way to stay ahead of the debt bubble for the unemployed investor living on credit card limits. As the housing bubble expanded to breaking point, financial institutions sold off bundles of housing loans to unsuspecting overseas investors, ensuring the whole world was now under the guillotine.

The GFC of 2008/9 was the result of this outlandish behaviour and our economies have been reeling ever since. Overnight, mortgage securities sold to overseas investors became almost worthless and the whole world was set to pay for the mistakes of ruthless businesses. Financial institutions supposed to be too big to fail did just that and tax payer funds were used to bail them out.

Add to the availability of toxic loans, the endless marketing telling us it's okay to be in debt, or worse, that if we are not in debt we are not making money, and we have indeed neatly fitted the collar of debt to the metaphoric workhorse – the average wage slave.

A civilised society would move to overcome the problems housing prices create and ensure all people have access to basic housing. This may sound idealistic and if it does, I suggest that is because we don't hear such words very often. In stark contrast, we have heard the rhetoric of economics far too often to see the words of economists as odd. Our housing situation has crept up on us by hiding in plain sight as normalcy and this normalcy is spruiked by economists and our media.

Housing finance is simply another tool used to exploit our genetic predisposition to *want what we see* and *want what the other person has*. This is the basis of marketing and advertising: to create a sense of need by appealing to our desires and our fear of missing out. As Neil De Grasse Tyson points out, this urgency to get things done, or consume for the sake of it, is linked to our mortality. It is our primal fear of missing out in action, meaning we are driven to achieve our goals before we die. However, the science of genetics is said to be on the verge of making us live for hundreds of years, if not for ever. If this comes to pass it will be interesting to see what happens to our motivation to get things done. If we could live forever, what reason would we have to do anything, knowing that everything could be left until tomorrow?

Meanwhile back here in the real world, we have to ask, 'Can we not have a healthy conversation with friends without an expensive house?' We did so not long ago at a time when housing finance was uncommon, unthought-of and not considered a part of life. Is it really necessary to be surrounded by grossly expensive consumer goods paid for by environmental debt? Or, is this something we have come to expect only because it seems reasonable and feels right? Casual conversations around a coffee table in comfortable surroundings are certainly pleasant. Even so, often we have these conversations as we try to de-stress at the end of a busy working day. This raises the question, 'Were we to give up the coffee table, and balcony to put it on, and instead seek a quality conversation under the shade of a tree in a park, would we not be better off because we would not have to work so hard?'

The GFC was the end result of believing endless growth is possible and yet today the symptoms seen just before the GFC are repeating. It seems we have not seen through the 'endless growth' illusion.

Illusions Summary

The impossibility of infinite economic growth in a finite world would seem obvious and yet the economic imperative is as recalcitrant on this point today as it has ever been. If we are to prevent GFC II, and more importantly head off destructive climate change, it's time to heed the lessons of 2008/9 and the years leading up to that calamity.

Chapter Fifteen

Distractions

Distractions are more tangible than the illusions. Distractions appeal to our desires, capture our curiosity, engage our minds and occupy our daily focus. Even the mundane, such as finding the cheapest fuel when we need to fill up, is a distraction from engaging in and finding solutions to the broader structural illusions discussed in the previous chapter.

An old magazine comic strip from the 1990's defines a distraction nicely. The comic depicted several men chained to a dungeon wall. From left to right the men were in various stages of decay, suggesting each one had been there a little longer than the next.

The second in line said to the newcomer who had just been locked away from public contact, 'So, you invented a car that would do two hundred kilometres to the litre too eh?'

The price of fuel is not the issue, nor is vehicle economy. These are distractions.

The underlying problem is our willingness to burn fossil fuels when we know the damage the emissions are doing, and critically, that we continue to vote for the political and economic status quo instead of being the instigators of change. Economic distractions such as research into fuel economy, increasing productivity, reducing production costs and the like, fail to address the core problem of sustainability, but certainly appear to be worthwhile pursuits. Efficiency, productivity and cost reduction are the language of the political and economic status quo: of business as usual. It is these distractions, which are completely ineffective solutions to our global problems that we need to see through and then vigorously reject at the polling booth, in social media comment, or for that matter in any conversation we might have.

Too often, we find our days consumed with inane distractions that see us participating in maintaining the status quo rather than rejecting it. For instance, recently an acquaintance said she had been trying to negotiate a fifty percent contribution from a neighbour to repair a boundary fence between their respective properties.

For two years she had been writing and talking. Two years!

That a mundane task like this consumed a person's time and energy for so long attests to just how awry our priorities have become: how our lives are distracted by seemingly important issues. The more salient point being that the fencing material was never suited to the application in the first place. However, that fact has not stopped its production and winter after winter fences made of this material blow down. Like gosling's the people affected keep putting it back up when the product should be banned from existence or changed to make it stronger.

What is the background of this fencing material? The story is interesting and typical of so many products in our world.

Wittenoom, Western Australia 1930, asbestos is discovered.

A mine is established and by the 1950's the town is the largest in the Northwest region of the state. However, during 1966 the asbestos mine closed when the health risk associated with asbestos became known.

The town is now abandoned except for a few stalwarts who refuse to leave. Inexplicably though, asbestos was still imported into Australia, and through to the 1980's it was made into fencing sheets. Perth, the state capital, has millions of these toxic sheets separating residential properties. Contractors who remove this product to mitigate the health risk are required to hold a special license and use an approved disposal site. The sheets must be wrapped in plastic, sealed, and are eventually buried. All of which adds to the environmental impact of the product.

When asbestos could no longer be used for fences, the manufacturer switched materials and used compressed cement fibre to make a similar looking fencing product. These new sheets blow over in winter storms because they are weaker. Of course, replacing them year after year is hugely profitable. Apparently, this is an example of economic, social and technological progress! It seems absurd, but despite the known dangers of the product, it was not until 2004 that asbestos importation ceased in Western Australia.

All hail jobs, growth and the economy, at the expense of public health!

On another note, alcohol, sugar, fat, cigarettes, lead, salt, insecticides containing carcinogens, ozone depleting gases, fossil fuels, coal, nuclear power and so on, are sold regardless of the known risks. And like asbestos, we litigate for years to stop the use of such products which should never have been sold or at least they should have been withdrawn when the risks became known.

The litigation which ensues only adds to the distractions we take for granted.

The point is that 'distractions' pose as important, even essential aspects of our lives. The latest sports shoes, the latest whatever. It does not really matter what the product is we seem to want it just because it exists even if it is dangerous.

If life is at all stressful; if we are asking what the heck am I doing; or where is life taking us, the answers are likely to involve distractions. It really is time to apply our human distinctiveness and rid ourselves of the risky distractions that surround us.

Hunting

Recently, I debated the pros and cons of hunting with a young man from the country. The debate was a pleasant distraction.

He lives in the city today but originates from a farm where guns and the shooting of animals were a part of life.

He asked me this question: 'A celebrity recently paid $350,000 for the privilege to shoot a black rhino. Black Rhinos are endangered. Is this reasonable?'

My answer was an emphatic, 'No'.

'But the rhino was old and near its end. It was harassing and killing other rhinos and the gamekeeper would have shot the rhino himself. Does this make any difference?

'No,' I answered again.

'But the Rhino had been relocated several times. Wherever it went, it persisted with its aggressive behaviour. Is it not reasonable to shoot it? '

'No, it makes no difference.' I remained firm.

'The $350,000 paid by the celebrity was donated to the rhino park to help protect the other rhinos from poachers. Surely this makes sense, and as well the meat from the rhino fed a local village. It was not wasted.'

Despite the growing list of rationalisations, I would not

condone the shooting. Why?

There are three pertinent reasons:

Firstly, there are more humane ways to kill an animal than shooting it.

Secondly, connecting money and celebrities in this scenario legitimises our love affair with money, notoriety, guns and killing.

Third, the scenario reinforces the bond between money and privilege. It would be better to quietly euthanise the rhino. If the celebrity were truly altruistic, he would have given the money regardless. Anything else is just satisfying his desire to shoot an animal.

The subject changed slightly and the young man asked:

'If I go hunting kangaroos and shoot my evening meal instead of buying a steak from the butcher, is that okay?'

'No, it's not,' I replied, 'because if we all go out and individually kill an animal to eat, the carbon footprint is far greater than buying meat from the butcher. It is like saying it's cheaper to fly overseas in a large jet than it is to drive a hybrid car. That is, jet travel makes sense because of the economy of scale. But the logic is flawed. Of course flying is cheaper and uses less energy than driving individually, but we should stop doing either, that is assuming we are serious about protecting the biosphere.'

'But that's not likely to happen,' he said, 'we won't stop flying.'

'You're right, that *is* the problem. Until we stop worrying about where to find the cheapest airfare and start thinking about the damage jet exhausts do, we will make no progress. Getting back to the kangaroo shooting, it would be better to herd some kangaroos into a field and raise them as a meat source than shoot them one by one on individual hunting trips.

By farming them, we could avoid the unnecessary carbon footprint of the hunting trip. Think about this, beef in Western Australia is grown on rural properties, shipped to abattoirs, sent to distribution centres in the city and then transported back to the rural townships. This situation is madness, but it makes money for everyone along the way.

'But it would be cruel, keeping wild kangaroos in a paddock,' he said.

'Yes it would,' I agreed, 'but we do it to beef cattle. That seems right because we are accustomed to it.'

'Look,' I said, 'the bottom line is, we don't need meat at all. We can obtain the protein we need from non-animal sources. The methane expelled by beef cattle is enormously damaging and so we need to peg it back. Anyway, all of this is a distraction. Blood lust is not an excuse for killing anything. To hunt for food seems reasonable until we are honest with ourselves and accept most people enjoy the hunt and the kill rather than doing so to feed themselves. Regardless, hunting is not practical given our large population and what's more hunting has become a blood sport and killing for sport is ugly, which brings us to the real bottom line. It's not civilised, it's not the activity of morally advanced people, or the road to peaceful coexistence.

Also, there are too many of us for our old hunting and gathering ways to return, meaning, we either accept a lower population or our environment will eventually force the decision on us. Anything else is a Band-Aid designed to delay the inevitable.'

The young man was taken aback by that last comment.

'So you are saying there should be fewer people.'

'Yes, it's the only effective answer to resource depletion and pollution. And, by the way, if they hand out a human culling pill to every third person and you happen to get one, to make it easy, I will take yours.'

'Wow, really. You are advocating a culling of humans?'

'Well, given that is unlikely to happen, even if we are faced with a population collapse due to food shortages or environmental catastrophe, I guess not. The better option is to step up birth control and allow natural attrition to do the job. My ultimate fear, is that of living in a world of anarchy when we eventually incur the wrath of Mother Nature. The chaos could be caused by a food or drinkable water shortage, or it could be a virus outbreak. Whatever eventually causes a global panic, it will be gruesome to deal with. It may even be a revolt by the poverty stricken against the wealthy. Regardless, we are more likely to come out of it alive if we start with a lower population.

Our history shows we can't resist consuming and breeding, so eventually we will hit the wall. The Earth is only so big. Thinking that you can run off to the hills and hunt to stay alive in the event of a global calamity is a fantasy. Thousands will be trying to do the same thing, meaning you will soon have company.

You know, the real issue here is that we are distracted by such a conversation. The real problem is our global community preparedness to face the truth about our way of life. We want our cake and eat it too. No, that's too sanitised and nice. What we want is to be winners in the global power and wealth game; we want all the luxuries without the responsibilities. We want to stay in our personal little worlds of thought about life and not think wider. We want to be self-absorbed. I know I do, but I fight that desire every day, even so I don't think I am winning, which is why I don't think the rest of us have much chance. I am passionate about environmental issues, but I can't resist the distractions of our world. If I'm not immune, what chance does a person who is not interested have? Precisely none.

So yes, I will take the voluntary culling pill because it is the loudest statement I can make. The problem with doing so is that, if I and others like me do take the pill, that will leave the world with people who don't care and soon the problem will be worse.'

'So, you are saying, how to get people interested in protecting our world is the challenge? '

'Yep. That's the real issue sitting behind all the distractions our economic activity puts in front of us. How to engage the majority of our global population is the key. Find that answer and you may well save humanity.'

'Shit, that's all?' he said.

We left the shady tree in the park and went home to be distracted by television.

Chapter Sixteen

Consumer Goods

The Ultimate Distraction

Retail therapy is a term coined in a newspaper some thirty odd years ago. The article said: *'We've become a nation measuring out our lives in shopping bags and nursing our psychic ills through retail therapy.'* (Chicago Tribune, 1986).

Of course, this 'therapy' was popular long before 1986. Nevertheless, since that time consumerism has reached then unimagined levels. Moreover, the sentiment in the Tribune reflects an uncomfortable truth: people don't struggle with consumption, or how to resist it, we embrace it eagerly.

Research tells us Americans are not alone in their addiction to shopping. A European survey in 2001 concluded 33% of shoppers had *'a high level of addiction to rash or unnecessary consumption'*. This behaviour is now known to psychologists as oniomania. Furthermore, researchers at the University of Melbourne, Australia, have called for a formal classification called 'compulsive shopping disorder' to be included in the mental disorders bible – the Diagnostic and Statistical Manual or DSM.

According to psychotherapist Adam Szmerling, patients

'describe being in a trance-like state, or being in the moment and feeling a sense of exhilaration. Sometimes just feeling compelled and torn, being aware of what they're doing but not being able to fight it' (Lauder, 2016).

The real pity is that while we are distracted by spending and how to treat our addiction to it, debt is created, and in turn debt ties us to employment. Rather than avoiding debt, we work harder to accommodate more of it, all the while complaining about having to work. This is no accident. It is a necessary pathology if our economic system is to continue to grow. Sadly, this condition is spread and nourished in our kids from a tender age when we insist they attend schools which actively encourage participation in the wage game.

Having our freedom stolen by inculcation at a young age is the aetiology of the 'psychic ills' the Chicago Tribune referred to. As put by a good friend, *'Consumer goods are a massive infringement on our freedom, in that, the freedoms of some people to produce addictive junk products impinge on the freedom of others to live in the absence of such goods or advertising of those goods.'*

Obviously, not all consumer goods are problematic and we are not all addicted. Many are though, and it is the reasons for consuming them and the volumes we produce that we need to reconsider if we are to overcome the destructive and wasteful distraction they have become.

Planned Obsolescence

Poor quality products need no introduction. In fact, stories about failed products are endless in our communities and too often the warranties designed to protect us turn out to be worthless. Surely though, our science and technology is capable of solving the problem of high product failure rates, or, are the failures intentional? The latter is being investigated and there are government watchdogs allegedly looking into what is known as planned obsolescence, but the problem persists.

In a study of consumer reactions to poor product quality, Richard Ippolito (1992) concluded, *'Mass produced items have a conspicuously low price and equally conspicuous high failure rate and there is much community dissent about the latter.'*

Sadly, while we continue to accept the responsibility, stress, and cost of returning or replacing poor quality goods instead of refusing to pay for them, manufacturers will continue to take advantage of our complacency.

The time and energy involved in dealing with failed and short-lived consumer products, and for example, telephone help desks which take hours or even days to resolve simple accounting or technical issues, are an enormous distraction.

Low cost, mass produced goods appeal to our sense of *good value* but we trade our time replacing them, our time earning money to pay for them, and our time shopping for them, for ever increasing personal debt. To reiterate an earlier point, global debt in 2013 was running at 212% of GDP. As of January 2018 that figure has become 282%. It was 174% just before the GFC of 2008/9.

There really is no rationale for accepting the waste and short-lived, low-quality nature of consumer goods and the debt they create. These products serve only one ultimate purpose, to extract wages paid for labour from the employee back into the financial system, thus supporting the wealth and power pyramids and keeping taxpayers working.

Consumer goods, which do not meet our basic needs for survival and in particular entertainment-based products, are distractions designed to keep our thinking focused on the circular process of consumption and employment. Many of these goods are enjoyable, pleasant and convenient, and this is a difficult problem to address: hence the earlier contention that we base our lives on the, 'if it feels good, do it' idiom.

Perhaps a replacement base code might be, 'if it makes the planet feel good, do it.' This is a call to arms to be parochial and patriotic to the cause of human survival. It is a call to wave the flag that says we won't be distracted by trinkets which ultimately cause us great harm.

Do we need Money?

'Within the next generation the world's rulers will discover that infant conditioning and narco-hypnosis are more efficient as instruments of government than clubs and prisons. They will understand that lust for power can be just as completely satisfied by suggestive conditioning as it can be by flogging and kicking people into obedience.' The preceding thought can be attributed to English philosopher Aldous Huxley who wrote on the topic during 1949. Are his thoughts fantastic tales or can we find evidence supporting his predictions?

As George Monbiot (2015) reports, apparently Huxley *was* right. Note this excerpt from a June, 2015 Monbiot article discussing parents preparing their children for life: *'...they* (nursery consultants) *spoke of parents who have already decided that their six-month-old son will go to Cambridge then Deutsche Bank, or whose two-year-old daughter 'had a tutor for two afternoons a week (to keep on top of maths and literacy) as well as weekly phonics and reading classes, drama, piano, beginner French and swimming. They were considering adding Mandarin and Spanish. 'The little girl was so exhausted and on edge she was terrified of opening her mouth.'*

Or this passage which was intended for young adults, and I quote Monbiot directly,

'Last week a note from an analyst at Barclays Global Power and Utilities in New York was leaked. It addressed students about to

begin a summer internship and offered a glimpse of the toxic culture into which they are inducted. 'I wanted to introduce you to the 10 Power Commandments ... For nine weeks you will live and die by these ... We expect you to be the last ones to leave every night, no matter what ... I recommend bringing a pillow to the office – it makes sleeping under your desk a lot more comfortable ... the internship really is a 9-week commitment at the desk ... an intern asked our staffer for a weekend off for a family reunion – he was told he could go. He was also asked to hand in his blackberry and pack up his desk...'play time is over and it's time to buckle up.' (Monbiot, June 2015).

It seems Aldous Huxley was indeed correct about the manipulation and conditioning of future generations as is evidenced by George Monbiot when he reports: *'... the little girl was so exhausted and on edge she was terrified of opening her mouth.'* This child was just two years old! Surely there are laws to prevent such abuse! Sadly it seems there are not. Sadly also, I don't think this is an isolated example, as the following personal anecdote suggests.

While attending my second year of education, I was so frightened of my teacher who yelled at everything we did, I wet myself because I was too afraid to ask to go to the toilet. I was five years old. The stigma that followed was horrible to endure. That was fifty odd years ago, but it seems from the 2015 Monbiot examples above, the use of fear and threats to forcibly prepare children for employment persists.

Surely instead, we might create a world where employment as we know it has been replaced by working for the common welfare of people – without being forced to do so. This is after all the stated goal of economic activity: to improve the welfare of people, not to consign us to wage slavery. In fact, our world is changing on this front, but it is not through altruism. For instance, automation in its never ending quest to reduce the cost of production, is reducing the need for human labour. According to Yuval Noah Harari, in his book Homo Deus, the ultimate goal of capitalism is complete automation of the workplace and the evolution of a new kind of human. This new human will be genetically engineered to live longer, be smarter and less vulnerable to diseases. Further, futurist writers such as Calum Chace (The Economic Singularity) see a future where eighty percent unemployment is prevalent due to the machine age making human labour redundant. At that time, the problem will not be too much work stress, it will be boredom. What will we do if we live for one hundred and fifty years without work to occupy our minds? But that is only a predicted future and we need to remain focussed on the present.

So again I ask, 'If the goal of economic activity is human welfare why are so many people in our world still suffering what amounts to forced labour? Why are people stressed and angry? Why is there so much discontent? How is it possible so many people are not happy at a time when it is said we are enjoying the best lifestyles of any period in history? Why is our environment crumbling around us?'

The bottom line is the words spruiking the success of our economic endeavours are empty rhetoric. There is no intent to deliver on the promise of welfare for all. Economic activity is about the affluence of the privileged few who can, due to their wealth, lord over the rest and look down on them. This is the goal of capitalism – the ongoing centralisation of wealth using consumer goods and services (which includes resource stripping and exploitation of poorer nations in order to produce the goods) as the means to collect that wealth. This is happening to ensure the wealthy are able to believe they will be in a position to ride out any environmental disaster, but, who will be available to produce what they need? Money will not help if there is no labour source to employ.

Nevertheless, political rhetoric is replete with claims about the success of our modern Western way of life despite all the problems it brings. Then perhaps it's time to take a closer look at success itself.

Chapter Seventeen

The Sanctity of Success

Success

One can only imagine the feeling nomadic hunter gatherers must have experienced after successfully bringing down large game. Even though it's only a guess, it is highly likely that the hunters would have been quite euphoric, and very pleased to know their bellies would be full for at least a few days. Likewise, if they failed at the hunt sleeping on an empty stomach must have been a dreadful prospect and experience.

Equally impossible to know, is whether the winning feeling from Neolithic times is the same as, for example, closing an important business deal or receiving a high grade on a final exam. It might be impossible to prove, but in all likelihood, the sensations are probably very similar in both cases. However, there is one important distinction that should be fairly obvious. Today, typically the penalty for failure is not life threatening. In fact, it rarely even means going hungry.

Moreover, in our modern Western economic context success is an intellectual experience bound up with an expectation of increased wealth, status or position. The problem though, is that these days much of what we claim as success is in fact environmentally devastating. Were we to personally account for our individual share of the US$70 trillion in environmental debt the monetary cost of our success would rapidly look like failure. Of course, this is quite removed from our daily experience of life, which is after all why the seventy trillion dollar debt exists. If we were individually and personally responsible for this debt, I suggest more would have been done to prevent the huge bill arising in the first place.

This being the case, it is worth looking at a raft of outcomes from situations that are typically seen as success stories with a view to re-evaluating them.

Global Successes
1) Reduced infant mortality and death rate through improved medical knowledge and sanitation systems.

    <u>Result:</u> Overpopulation of the planet; rampant pollution and looming food supply shortages; water supply shortages and climate change threats.

2) Industrial Revolution accelerated new energy technologies and allowed mass production.

    <u>Result:</u> Associated global warming due to burning of fossil fuels; vast amounts of waste created; loss of habitat and loss of arable land and potable water.

3) Splitting the atom provided a revolutionary energy supply.

    <u>Result:</u> Problematic radioactive waste, nuclear weapons of mass destruction; contamination from nuclear accidents.

4) Large-scale commercial projects result in damning of rivers for water supplies; extraction of water from aquifers; broad acre farming and monoculture including large-scale trawling of fish stocks.

    <u>Result:</u> Loss of food fish species in our oceans; some rivers

no longer running to the ocean because of dams and irrigation; land degradation, erosion and lowering of water tables; loss of biodiversity and increased susceptibility to disease in food crops; large areas of land covered with concrete and road materials causing atmospheric heat to be increased.

As the above short list indicates, success is best measured in terms of how the financial, social and environmental benefits of what we do, compare to the financial, social and environmental costs. However, as individuals we might consider ourselves powerless to change such processes in our world. If that is so, we need to drill down to the level where individuals are able to see themselves as having an impact.

Personal Success
Attend tertiary education and secure lucrative employment.
Result: increased income and affluence including modern house and land package through the ability to take out an enormous mortgage and spend the rest of one's life making repayments. Being tied to fifty-plus hours a week at work and being on call for even more hours. Spending income on health and fitness services as there is little time left for recreational pursuits or stress management. Consuming medication and therapy for the stress the new job brings and dealing with the array of warranty claims which go with the low reliability products installed in the new home.

The above is a little cynical, and was presented with tongue in cheek, but I suggest the theme is not too far from the truth. The detail may change, the scenario may look and sound a little different from place to place, but at the end of the day many of us chase the financial dream but in doing so forsake a great deal along the way. And, if we do reach our financial goals, what then? Are we content to stop there? Of course not, at the end of a career we spend our time consuming more and more as we try to fill our retirement days from the vast array of entertainment choices that are purposefully designed to never quite satisfy our humanness. This is the reason why entertainers such as Neil De Grasse Tyson are so popular. The media content they deliver engages our intellect in a way no consumer good or service can. It satisfies our curiosity more so than unboxing some new digital device or other purchase ever could.

A Personal Note about Success

Toward the end of my Psychology degree, I was invited to a small awards ceremony for the very highest achieving students.

Because I was an award recipient, I was allowed to bring along two guests. At the time, and being a little naive, I invited two classmates to the event. As it turned out, my guests were supposed to be family or others from outside the university. There was quite a clamour when I walked in with my student friends as guests. After all, they were not the elite and were not invited. Reacting with much indignation to this realisation, I made it very clear that I would not tolerate discrimination against my friends in this way.

The atmosphere at the event became quite tense and what's more, to this day it is difficult to reconcile the blatant attitude of elitism demonstrated by the psychology faculty.

Nevertheless, and not long after the event, I was offered the opportunity to undertake the Honours stream. Despite several letters to the university advising that I would not be attending (because I preferred to be employed) I continued to be advised in writing as to when and where to attend the classes.

As time went by, more advices arrived stating that if I did not attend, I would not pass the course. Eventually, albeit several months later, the letters stopped coming. Curious about the process, I made enquiries and apparently no one had ever rejected an offer to undertake the Honours stream. Had I been a younger recent school leaver, I may have been intimidated by the university and felt obliged to give up the opportunity of paid employment to attend the Honours stream.

Such is the way of elitism, even in a faculty which supposedly had the human condition as its primary focus. The attitude of the School of Psychology raised three important questions:

• Why did the faculty react as they did?
• Who stood to benefit from the elitism they displayed?
and
• What underlying motive did my reaction oppose?

The answers are relatively simple in that profit, protecting and legitimising the power hierarchy, and maintaining a 'them and us' mentality (elitism) were the reasons.

Unfortunately, this is the artificial world of economics, power, control, high affluence, status and the like. It is how the status quo is maintained. The real world, the world of intrinsic value, the world of natural systems, communities, compassion, tolerance and equality is far more pleasant to look at and live within but it is disappearing fast both literally and figuratively.

Our opportunity then, is to take pleasure in creating a world free of the bond which comes with striving for socio-economic success and replace it with community and environmental success.

Our human spirit is so very capable of the changes and I

suggest it yearns for that life. This is clearly the source of our discontent with economic pursuits, they just don't provide a lasting source of satisfaction.

Instead, the human spirit has been kidnapped and held captive by the apparent rewards of aspiring to levels of success that are not sustainable, do not satisfy, and pose a massive threat to our prospects for survival.

Health Care Success

Death and dying are not especially inspiring topics to discuss. So much so that in modern Western societies there is a tendency to literally deny the inevitability of death. In fact, even though dying is a natural part of existence, today's (American) society is unique in the extent to which death is viewed as a taboo topic (Mental Help, 2012).

This taboo is partly due to the removal of illness, aging and death from the home and into care facilities and hospitals thus disconnecting families from the experience of death and dying. Don't be under any illusion though, these facilities compete in a market space like any other and their success is measured in dollars.

However, because of the emotions attached to ill health and death we tend not to question the cost, the business practices, or the intent of health care, or for that matter how health facilities are run. Even when there is a blatant and identifiable malpractice which attracts a media clamour for a short time, the care facilities mostly carry on with business as usual.

In fact, most discussions surrounding the provision of health care are about the sanctity of human life, or in a completely disconnected manner, are about the improvement of health care. Rarely do we hear an honest discussion about cutting the provision of services to those who can't, due to a terminal condition (which includes old age), be helped. The result is that providing health care is typically treated as a fait accompli rather than exploring whether there are significantly harmful consequences.

It is well documented, and perhaps common sense, that population growth on planet Earth closely mirrors advances in medicine (Ehrlich & Ehrlich 1990). But, I ask, 'Is it in our best interest to always deploy these advances?' It may sound callous, to imply people should die when health care is available, but death is a reality for all of us sooner or later and denial in itself is not a healthy life strategy. What's more, we allow millions of people to die from over-population driven causes every day, meaning we really are being two-faced and self-righteous on this issue. That is, often only the wealthy can afford specialised health care.

On a personal note, and to explain my perspective somewhat, consider this: At the age of sixteen I underwent a relatively simple appendectomy at a small local hospital. While on the operating table my heart stopped and after resuscitation I was rushed to the intensive care ward of a large metro hospital.

During the operation at the local facility, I vaguely recall being aware of a sense of drowning and gasping for air and catching a brief glimpse of the operating theatre as I drifted in and out of consciousness. When I finally awoke in the intensive care ward many hours later, my family was very relieved to hear me speak because the doctors had told them I was likely to have incurred serious brain damage.

Without the medical knowledge used at the time, I would certainly have died from a ruptured appendix. Had I died, there would be two fewer people in this world because my son would not have been born. I often reflect on which would have been the best outcome for planet Earth.

My family may have been sad if I had died, but it's not sadness that drives us to keep people alive at a time when nature is trying to keep our global population sustainable. Rather, our belief in the sanctity of human life presumes we have a greater right to life than nature recognises. In fact, the Hippocratic Oath is based on a belief that all human life is more important than the rest of the natural world. This is a central issue we need to spend some time debating publicly. It is also imperative that we accept the nexus of our global environmental problems come down to seven plus billion being an unsustainable population.

Population Growth Success

I suggest our sanctimonious attitude with respect to human life is a concept that's become maladaptive and dangerous. For instance, threats to human life (by nature) are dealt with via an attitude of shoot first and ask questions later. Typically, no expense is spared in hunting down any non-human perpetrator accused of taking a human life. What we don't want to accept is that nature is simply trying to keep our human numbers in check.

According to Rev Robert Fleischman, in a 1989 article titled *The Value of Human Life*, the source of our supremacist attitudes towards human life resides in religious rhetoric and the morality of the Christian belief in the absolute value of human life from conception until death. From its historically distant beginnings, this idea has pervaded the Christian world and found its way into the rest of society.

Seeing ourselves as superior and separate is very convenient because it enables the economic growth model, which relies on population growth, to survive.

It is a preposterous belief though because we cannot escape

our reliance on everything from micro-organisms to the apex predators and the habitats that support them, which instead of protecting we destroy to make way for more of us. This is not a circle of life relationship. It is a spiral into environmental death.

Beyond religious belief, our fear of death and our refusal to address deaths role in the natural order originates in our distant past: meaning we have always been affected by sorrow at the loss of a loved one, and have always tried to avoid losing people we care about. The question to ponder though is this, 'How do we deal with our obsession with medical intervention and the cost of those interventions to our environment, to our economies, and to the sustainability of our population?

With a medically-assisted aging population profile across most Western nations, there are more and more aged persons to care for and proportionately less income-aged taxpayers to fund the cost of institutional medical attention. One has to wonder where the line should be drawn. Is it kinder to prolong the life of someone who is suffering pain and personal humiliation, or to allow life to end naturally by withdrawing medical care? While this may sound odd, consider the treatment options open to doctors for patients close to death from terminal disease. A point can come where the patient is suffering greatly and doctors will, and I quote two instances I have personally witnessed, 'stop giving fluids'. This decision effectively kills the patient through dehydration. It would seem far more sensible to allow the patient to choose a more comfortable end much sooner.

Another medical anecdote: When I was thirteen, my father was hit by a car while he was on a pedestrian crossing. At the time of the accident he was placed on a ventilator, but he did not regain consciousness and the ventilator was turned off after nine days.

Several days after his death, we were informed his brain injuries were so severe that he never had any chance of survival. I wonder to this day, why the doctors prolonged the inevitable for nine days. Perhaps it was because they were giving us time to come to grips with the tragedy. More likely, it was the Hippocratic Oath operating. Looking back, it would certainly have been better for our family if we had been told the truth earlier. This would have avoided us building our hopes only to have them shattered at the end.

During the time we spent visiting the hospital, I was under the impression my father would one day wake up and say, 'Hello' and the ordeal would be over. When the doctors said my father was not coming home, I was emotionally numbed and stayed that way for several years. Hence today, I have a very different perspective on death and dying and perhaps my view is a little distorted compared to others given what happened. Nevertheless, I see medical procedures, medications, death and dying are hugely profitable and so treatments for terminally ill patients will carry on and the tax payer will ultimately foot the bill.

My views may be abrasive and seem cynical, but having lived through the emotional torment of losing a parent, nowadays I see death as part of life. After all, it is inevitable for all of us sooner or later. And of course, I too want to protect my loved ones and see them lead a healthy life for as long as possible. Even so, I still question the quality of life that is on offer under the effects of life-sustaining medication in circumstances such as very old age when the mind is no longer aware of the world around it.

To the extent health care is essential to our modern lives there are obvious reasons for it. However, like everything else in our world, we need to take a pragmatic look at how many resources we can sustainably put into ever more costly medical innovation. And importantly, who stands to benefit from its use. In other words, we fall back on the profit motive to explain much of the activity in the medical world. For instance, where does the Hippocratic Oath shift from a position of benevolence to one of economic convenience?

As with all arguments in this book, the above is intended to provoke thought and consideration of the manner in which the profit motive underlies and drives the provision of all (including medical) services. When the profit motive manipulates by appealing to our love for family and friends and uses our emotional attachments as a means to justify service provision, I suggest there is a need for a critical eye. This is not to say the ill or injured should be sacrificed. Rather, the contention is that we could adopt realistic and sustainable limits for health and indeed all industries.

Allowing ourselves to be distracted by the Hippocratic Oath and archaic religious fervour such as a belief in the sanctity of human life, at all costs, is particularly dangerous. I understand and accept the amazingly powerful emotional drive to keep loved ones alive and healthy, but at the same time, we risk everybody on this planet when we artificially extend life spans.

Educational Success

According to Dr. Michael Peterson (2009), of the Whole School Consortium, education serves one of two purposes: *'...schools are expected to (1) create a pool of workers with at least minimum competence and attitudes from which businesses can select employees; and (2) provide a way of sorting workers in rank order of ability, eliminating those from the pool who do not have the perceived capacity to function as employees.*

The goal for businesses, of course, is to have a large pool of potentially qualified candidates with requisite skills that far exceeds the availability of jobs. This allows the business to select the best candidate, and critically, the resulting competition for jobs drives wages lower, thus decreasing costs and increasing profits.

Further, Peterson contends: '*...few school districts actually state that their prime mission is to serve as a personnel department for business and industry. However, functionally many schools make this clear by engaging in practices designed to ensure such outcomes.*' '*...as schools are evaluated based on very narrow criteria (e.g. tests of math, basic literacy skills and science), the curriculum of many schools is narrowed, de-emphasising social studies, the arts, physical education and even, on occasion, eliminating recess for elementary children.*'

If we ask: 'can our current education practices create competitive workers and, at the same time, establish a sense of community and sustainability,' the answer is no. This is because grading and test scores are contrary to the notion of self-determination and community-mindedness. Instead, and sadly, today's education encourages competitive thinking focused obsessively on wealth creation.

Alfie Kohn (2014), author and education lecturer, makes a compelling case that two traditional features of schooling, grades and homework, '*...are not only unnecessary but actually undermine students' interest in learning.*'

Research consistently finds that giving students letter or number grades leads them to think less deeply, avoid challenging tasks and become less enthusiastic about whatever they are learning – and that's true for those who get A's as well as D's.

Similarly Kohn states, '*making children work what amounts to a second shift after having spent all day in school, not only proves frustrating, but also turns learning into a chore. Surprisingly, claims that homework enhances understanding or promotes better work habits are contradicted by both research and experience'.*

Also according to Alfie Kohn, *'A plague has been sweeping through American schools, wiping out the most innovative instruction and beating down some of the best teachers and administrators.*

Ironically, that plague has been unleashed in the name of improving schools. Invoking such terms as 'tougher standards,' 'accountability,' and 'raising the bar,' people with little understanding of how children learn have imposed a heavy-handed, top-down, test-driven version of school reform that is lowering the quality of education in this country.

It has taken some educators and parents a while to realise that the rhetoric of 'standards' is turning schools into giant test-prep centres, effectively closing off intellectual inquiry and undermining enthusiasm for learning (and teaching). It has taken even longer to realize that this is not a fact of life, like the weather -- that is, a reality to be coped with -- but rather a political movement that must be opposed.'

Education too often creates disinterest and when we are disinterested, in anything but financial wealth, we are unlikely to unite to pursue a common cause - even one as important as a survivable environment. Hence, education, as it stands today creates workers who by design are distracted, isolated, insular and most importantly, accept being indebted. The latter necessitates being highly competitive and too often leads to conflict. Thus, a huge question mark can be placed over the real or perceived success of education.

Rather than move to repair this situation, education grade systems have become legislation, thus ensuring educators are unable to teach anything but economic doctrine and employment readiness.

Given high-level affluence itself poses the greatest limitation on achieving a sustainable planetary population size

(McCluney, 2004) education designed to enable affluence is a serious problem. In fact, those who design its content are complicit in destroying our environment. The questionable success, which is affluence enabled by education, is a powerful motivator, but I suggest that's only because education conditions our youthful years to seeing financial success as the most important endeavour in life. The truth is, and this is supported by the declining state of our natural world, that education as it stands is a self-serving cannibalistic process.

If the premise that education provides the means to understand social and environmental issues is truly defensible, why are our scholars and world leaders, who speak of human welfare so often, allowing the problems we face to continue? I suspect the reason is their thinking is so deeply entrenched in the economic ideology and elitism taught at prestigious schools, that they actually believe their actions to date are in fact appropriate and are indeed for the benefit of humankind. In other words, they have lost sight of the real world and are now trapped by their allegiances and the politics of their positions.

To reiterate an earlier point: In a 2012 study by Adam Corner, of highly educated and less educated persons, it was found less educated people were more open to changing their view on a subject than those with higher education and professional status. Corner found that once a professional person took a public stance on a topic, they were very reluctant to alter that position. It seems from the study, people with less education are more likely to shift to an informed decision than professionals in the field. This is a sad indictment of education: that high-level education (at prestigious universities) is able to promote pride and ego over discernment.

In fact, according to Pulitzer Prize winning journalist Chris

Hedges (2009), education at the highest levels has the specific intent of nourishing the power elite and actively insulating students from contact with those outside the institution.

At the same time, education per se remains the key to the future. We need to teach our children about our mistakes and how to avoid them.

Unfortunately, if our science is correct, we don't have the luxury of time to wait for a new generation to pass through a changed education system. It is up to the current generation to think outside the agenda of the school system and economic ideology: To put our existing knowledge to work on solutions which are immediate and progressive, regardless of wealth or status.

At present, education is the process of taking excited, creative young humans and transforming them into unquestioning worker drones who are lured by the promise of financial wealth and (at best dubious) economic security. Global economics depends on this being the case because it can't afford the next generation to see the futility of chasing wealth before they are fully committed to employment by debt and financial entanglement.

What chance do children in education have, of building a balanced world-view, if we insist on hiding from them the real issues facing our society? While education itself remains just another business with a clear agenda to support an ailing economic system, there is little faith to be placed in its direction.

According to David Adams (2009), Coordinator of the Culture of Peace News Network, the Town Hall (voting) is the path to overcoming humanity's readiness to turn to conflict. Unless our vote changes education systems so that they teach the path to sustainable coexistence with our natural world from a very young age, each generation of students is likely to follow the path of our ancestors and take up arms, literally or figuratively.

Part Three

Denial

Chapter Eighteen

Defending our Investment

Denial is perhaps one of the most common ego defence strategies used if and when we are confronted by an accusation. Often, there is an element of our thinking compelling us to defend our stance whether we are right or wrong. Children are masters of this art. Facts do not seem to matter to a child. Even when caught red-handed they will often deny their culpability. This suggests the reaction is an automated ego-defence mechanism rather than something we learn.

Accordingly, adults too, readily adopt denial statements to protect one's ego. Let's explore a few examples of ego defence comments that are often heard when discussing environmental protection.

Denial Statement
I understand what you are saying; that we need to change, but what about our jobs and building a future for our children?

Response: There is a very bleak future in persisting with environmentally destructive economic activity. It makes far more sense to work with nature than to go head to head with it. If we really are concerned about jobs for our children, sustainable, environmentally friendly employment is the only survivable option.

The reason we hear so much negativity about sustainable industries is because making the changes to them challenges the position of the power elite and their dominance of the wealth pyramid. Hence they spread rumour and misdirection and it is effective because what they say defends our egos.

Denial Statement
I can't see the effects of global warming so why should I be concerned about it?

Response: Climate change is long-term and cumulative, meaning the symptoms do not grab our attention, but it is happening every day. Like sunburn, the pain of climate change comes after the damage is done.

Denial Statement
I am already environmentally-minded. I recycle and use low energy light bulbs.

Response: Unfortunately, recycling the by-products of mass production has little impact on carbon production or resource use. In fact, recycling uses additional fossil fuel energy and so creates more carbon. The only meaningful statistic is the one that demonstrates a reduction in CO_2 in our atmosphere. This necessitates a per-capita reduction in fossil fuel derived energy consumption. It means reducing large-scale burning of coal, oil and gas and more importantly scaling back the beef industry. The latter being a massive producer of methane which is the worst greenhouse gas.

The cost to clean up just the carbon we have already released is far higher than the cost to change to renewable energy sources. As stated more than once already, the environmental clean-up cost has been conservatively estimated at US$70 trillion. This does not include the cost increase between 2013 when the figure was calculated and when we eventually make the changes.

Denial Statement
We need a strong economy to allow us the opportunity to protect the environment.

Response: Perhaps this type of comment (made by political candidate Elani Evangel, 2012) could be re-written as the well-known cliché which recommends closing the gate after the horses have escaped. To suggest the causes of environmental degradation should be ramped up in order to allow it to undo its own damage defies logic or common sense.

The strongest economy is the one which stands the test of time. Renewable energy industries are just that, renewable.

Denial Statement
How do we change our current economic system without risking economic collapse?

Response: Our current economic system generates its own likelihood of failure because economic activity today is polluting our natural world and so is undermining its own foundation. As pointed out by political historian and economist Gar Alperovitz in his 2005 book America Beyond Capitalism, civilisation and empire collapse are historically imminent in our world, meaning change is occurring all the time. Will managed and planned change to our economic system cause collapse? Absolutely not. Will continuing as we have been in our recent history place us at extreme risk? Absolutely yes.

Change is a fact of life. It is all around us every day - we should manage it in a way that is sustainable.

Denial Statement
When will the imminent environmental collapse occur? When should I make the changes you are suggesting?

Response: This is a strange question given the science behind the need for change has been available for at least forty years if not longer. The answer is: the sooner, the better. To use an analogy, why would we wait for an oncoming car to hit before trying to step aside? We cannot know precisely when our environment might force our hand and, to the extent we typically only react to immediate threats, we are likely to choose significant economic collapse at some time in the future over initiating small steps now. However, if our unique ability to discern and understand the past, present and future are put to work for us, we have the opportunity to redirect our technological advantage. Then managed change can take place without dire consequences.

Denial Statement
What would an alternative government do that the present one is not doing? Why should I vote for change if the alternative political party is likely to be just another clone of what we have today?

Response: On the surface, the question seems reasonable. That is, regarding the way they function, most political parties are likely to be similar as they will have to operate within the expectations of government. What is important is to realise a vote for the status quo is saying, 'I am happy with the way my country is run today. I accept all the inequities of my situation; I accept the rules and processes that are the cause of the threat to our children's future. I can't see a better way to live life and would prefer that our society continued towards trouble rather than changing to something better.'

The real question here should be: 'Are we really happy with our circumstances given the dangerous activity of corporations or the distractions and the illusions which have been so effective in determining the course of our lives up to now?' Why not try someone else?

Denial Statement
What do you propose as an alternative? I want to know how it would work.

Response: Moving to a sustainable economic system does not mean moving into the nearest cave or igloo and hunting with spears. What it does require is improved management of resources, reduced production of non-essentials by making products last longer through better manufacturing techniques, and higher energy production efficiency (Speth, 2008). And, of course, personal restraint which means buying less stuff.

Clearly, there is far more detail to this topic. That work has been done by others such as James Speth and Jacques Van Parijs (1995). Both references are available in the bibliography. The aim here is to look at denial and understand we have an opportunity to alter our thinking. We have the opportunity to be actively aware that we can seek an alternative lifestyle and much of the fear of doing so has been created for us and has no basis in fact.

Denial Statement
Technology will provide the answers to the environmental issues, why should I worry?

Response: In short, our history tells us, as does our climate science, it is unbridled technological development which has brought us to the environmental situation we are faced with today. As we try to produce energy for billions of people we are killing the planet. Unmanaged research and development has been a double-edged sword and we desperately need to constrain our deployment of technology.

Denial Statement
Changing our social structure will mean my personal comfort will be threatened. Everything I have worked for may have to be given up.

Response: This statement is perhaps actually saying: 'I fear and/or do not want to accept change which will mean letting go of what I know is problematic for the environment, but makes me very comfortable.' The response to this is two simple questions which have a powerful message: Can the environment survive without the economy which provides these comforts? Certainly, yes. Can that same economy survive without the environment it is currently destroying? Certainly, no.

It seems a simple enough equation: protect our environment and in doing so protect our economy and our survival, or keep polluting and be ready for the consequences which are likely to include wide-spread population collapse.

Denial Statement
I don't think you have thought this through very well. There are problems with your ideas about a sustainable economy.

Response: As and when required, nations will spend multi-billion or even trillion dollar budgets to wage war. Also, space programs are funded to go to the moon or send probes to Mars or Saturn. If a corporation is challenged on an environmental issue, or by a class action, it is able to fund a multi-million dollar legal defence. On the political front, the Eurozone bailed out Greece. In other words, if we want to change our economic system to protect our planet, we will find the means to do so.

Summing up Denial

Denial is an emotive word. Moreover, being told we are in denial is not pleasant and certainly falls into the category of criticism which is more likely to offend than bring about a useful discussion. However, it does seem the criticism is warranted. I have to wonder if we really want our children to look back and say, as the environmental lawyer James Speth put it in The Bridge at the End of the World, Capitalism, the Environment and Crossing from Crisis to Sustainability, '*Why the bleep did our parents not do something before it was too late.*'

Unfortunately, based on our history to date, the answer would appear to be yes. Yes we do want to wait and see, and we are willing to take the risk of being wrong and take the risk of being chastised by our children.

The words of Albert Einstein really do ring true and are worth repeating here: 'We can't solve problems by using the same kind of thinking we used when we created them.' (Harris, 1995).

Still, these words are only relevant if we accept there is a problem to deal with and are prepared to re-evaluate our notion of what feels good versus what is good for us. It is time to leave denial behind, prioritise the protection of what is left of our environment, and speak out rather than turning a blind eye. In other words, let's stop denying there is a problem.

Chapter Nineteen

Dealing with Denial

Powerlessness

The belief that the individual is powerless to change the design of our social fabric is widespread. But is it valid? It's not, provided we are prepared to go against the prevailing crowd on polling day, and, personally campaign on social media pages and in our everyday conversations. In other words, it is up to each of us to be proactive in every way possible if we want to see change occur. Politicians will listen to our vote, and to the informal social sentiment of the electorate, before anything else. If the electorate is pro economic development, so will be our politicians.

Even though we are bombarded with messages telling us to be part of the winning team and that only losers vote for parties unlikely to be elected, quite the reverse is true. Votes are the lifeblood of politics and we still have the right to cast our vote without fearing the sword or for that matter any other recrimination.

Obviously today, instead of the sword, economic ideology and rhetoric is deployed to sway our thinking. Sadly, it is very effective, even sadder is that it is effective because it appeals to that part of us which wants more comfort, convenience and pleasure despite knowing the dangers these things bring about.

The profit motive and fear of economic hardship are used to coerce entire populations to vote for the status quo. That is, for more of the same dubious governance that has led us into our present environmental, social and economic circumstances.

Powerlessness is a myth of our times. Our vote is enormously influential and every individual vote is important, as are our purchasing choices. Still, the repeated re-election of conservative, business influenced governments, suggests the majority of us have allowed ourselves to be convinced by their rhetoric. Their words certainly appeal to our self-interest and yet our self-interest to stay alive and have a safe environment should be telling us not to listen to the foxes we have elected into the henhouse.

Scepticism

Scepticism, as it is used by the fossil fuel industry to argue against human-caused global warming, relies on our ego, our feel-good-proclivity, and the idiom, 'I will believe it when I see it.' In other words, one can fall back on the erroneous thought that the effects of climate change are not forcing our hand yet. However, as stated earlier, climate change is like sunburn, the effects come after the damage is done.

The sceptics tell us whatever they think we want to hear and have no concern for fact or consequence other than delaying action on greenhouse gas emissions. They help us to feel powerless by creating doubt and spend millions doing it. Doubt creates an aura of difficulty around the issues we need to deal with, and, because we want to avoid more difficulty in our lives we avoid participation in those issues. This is mission accomplished for the fossil fuel industry. An uninterested public is exactly what they want.

Why we Should be Sceptical

Being sceptical of any issue is important to the extent that questioning assumptions explores options rather than taking anything for granted. Researchers use scepticism to test their theories as they seek to enhance knowledge. The peer-review process of science is also based on healthy scepticism. The scientific method attempts to disprove a theory and if it cannot be disproved it is more likely to be correct. Conversely, if a theory cannot be tested, it is seen as worthless.

Healthy scepticism is not the practice of fossil fuel industry sponsored rhetoric though.

These sceptics have just one aim and that is to discredit climate science with the intent of creating inaction in the wider community. They work to create a sense of powerlessness by creating doubt. Given this situation, it becomes our individual responsibility to ensure fact dominates our thinking. Of course, it is particularly difficult to do this when the facts are at odds with our desires for pleasure, convenience or apathy for that matter.

Even though the climate change sceptics present out of context (and erroneous) data, their publications provide sufficient doubt to enable many people to overlook directly observable climate effects and deny the logical conclusion that climate change is occurring due to human activity.

For example, it is argued by some sceptics, that volcanic emissions of CO_2 are largely responsible for the current level of CO_2 in our atmosphere, not human activity. However, studies by Schumacher et al (2011), confirm a molecular signature is present to identify the source of CO_2 molecules in our atmosphere. This allows a direct identification of how and when CO_2 in the atmosphere was produced.

Using this knowledge Schumacher et al, showed CO_2 from

and since the Industrial Revolution *is* warming our planet – the source of the CO_2 is not volcanoes or other natural sources.

Scepticism, as it applies to the global warming debate, relies on our human tendency to want to believe that which is convenient to believe, thus eroding our incentive to change how we live from day to day, or for that matter, to take responsibility for our actions.

In fact, we strive to maintain the status quo in the face of even the most irrefutable evidence, preferring to say, 'What difference can one person make?' In doing this we are falling back on our perceived powerlessness to effect change.

The message about change then, is that we have the responsibility to sift through information by using our ability to discern and our understanding of time, history and emotional responses, so as to arrive at the best decisions for a sustainable future. It can only be to our advantage to avoid being lured by convenient half-truths designed to give us a back door escape from dealing with critical issues.

If we are to embrace change, and let's face it we deal with change every day, let us perhaps start by making people who publish alleged scientific but intentionally misrepresented research, accountable for what they state in those publications. We seem to respond very well to any threat to our financial position which means a penalty for false or misleading publication makes perfect sense.

What to Change?

Environmental Lawyer James Speth, captures the essence of what we need to change when he suggests, '...*we seek fulfilment, but settle for abundance. Prisoners of plenty, we have freedom to consume, instead of the freedom to find our place in the world.*'

How to repair the situation we find ourselves in can be divided into three categories:

1. Personnel changes
2. Corporate changes and
3. Empowering governments to enact changes.

In as much as we are all members of society, creating change relies on overcoming our susceptibility to the economic illusions and distractions created by those who profit excessively at our expense. We can do this by applying our ability to discern rather than reacting emotionally to shiny new toys, and by overcoming our use of denial. We can shift responsibility from the external (blaming others, or circumstances) to the internal (ourselves and what we do). In other words, 'the buck stops' with each of us. Accepting responsibility can be difficult meaning we will, almost certainly (and, in my view, unfortunately), require legislation and penalties to force us to change. The other choice is to use extreme ownership and simply get on with it before governments make laws we may regret or the environment forces our hand.

Personnel Change

It is easy to criticise governments and politicians for our plight and to do so from the comfort of our living rooms. But politicians per se have a tough job. And, of course, they will protect their self-interest just as everyone else is inclined to do. Thus, they need our individual support to get the job done without the fear of being ousted as soon as they speak of change.

If we accept that we live in a democracy, then we (the people) give politicians a mandate to act on our behalf. In other words, the ultimate responsibility for government actions rests with us, the voting public. And yet there is widespread distrust and suspicion of politics in general. This suggests there is a need to select the right people for the job and build trust in our leadership. We do this by participating in the process of selecting them. Why? Because our complacency in the past has allowed the foxes (the people who only have their self-interest at heart) to rewrite the foundations of democracy.

Let's define what we mean by foxes. A study by psychologist Kevin Dutton (2012), revealed alarming similarities between criminals, politicians and world leaders. The significant difference between the groups was whether or not members of each group were willing to break the law as part of their endeavour.

According to Dutton, *'Traits that are common among psychopathic serial killers - a grandiose sense of self-worth, persuasiveness, superficial charm, ruthlessness, lack of remorse and the manipulation of others - are also shared by politicians and world leaders.'*

Dutton's research explains how some politicians and corporate leaders are able to negatively affect many people's lives without themselves suffering debilitating remorse and how they can, when questioned on a past event, offer up memory loss as an explanation stating, I have no recollection of that event. Or something like, 'at the time that was correct, but now the situation has changed.' I suspect if a school student offered up this type of self-defence for poor performance, such an excuse would very quickly be dismissed by educators.

Currently, there is little formal qualification or screening required to enter political office with far more for corporate leadership. Certainly, there is no requirement to demonstrate an outlook favourable to sustainability, empathy, morality or civility when entering politics. In fact, the harsh world of political survival demands a very robust self-confidence (perhaps to the point of appearing out of touch with voters?). On the other hand, private sector recruitment agencies are known to employ a battery of psychological testing designed to isolate a desired personality profile. Selection processes are rigorous and unapologetic. The right person for the job is sought out and performance targets decide how long the person remains in the position. Those targets are invariably economic.

How we address this situation requires a rethink of corporate law.

Corporate Change

At present, corporations (in the USA) share several basic constructs, as set out by Environmental Lawyer James Speth and summarised below.

1) Shareholders may technically own a corporation, but do not manage day to day operations, meaning owners who do not participate in the management of their business are at the mercy of those whom they appoint to do so.

2) Limited liability protects the corporation's stakeholders. Hence, shareholders may lose their initial investment, but cannot be brought to account for the corporation's activities. Corporations are protected by constitutions and corporate laws, meaning in many cases corporations hold the rights of individual persons.

3) The principle of 'best interests' states that directors and managers will act in the best interests of the corporation, meaning action to maximise profit is required. The requirement to act in the best interests of profits reduces the ability to enact social responsibility. Externalising of costs is the prime directive and any action deemed to improve the profit bottom line is protected by legal process. These constructs serve to protect the corporation and its executives and shareholders from action taken against questionable corporate activity.

Suggested changes to corporate law offered by Speth and designed to increase accountability include:

- Increased government powers to penalise corporations acting irresponsibly.
- Empowering communities to expel unwanted corporate activity.
- Restructuring limited liability to include shareholders and directors.
- Removing corporate funding from the election process and mandating public funding.
- Increased monitoring and control of the use of shareholder funds in campaigns to lobby government support.
- Revoke the capacity for a corporation to be protected by a status of person-hood.

Obviously, the ultimate challenge resides in making these changes a reality. At the same time and equally obvious, is that active support for our political leaders is the key to making these changes happen. This has been argued throughout, that as individuals our opportunity to create change resides in our opinion expressed when we vote. James Speth again provides support for this contention when he says '...*the main driving force in corporate greening... is government action, actual and anticipated, domestic and foreign.*'

In light of the manner in which our fears operate to cloud our judgement and there are illusions and distractions working to dissuade us from demanding change, our one simple, effortless and private opportunity to effect change is our vote. There is no attempt to suggest or prescribe any specific party support. Albeit that support can only be of benefit if given to a party or candidate willing to stand for real change in the context of the discussion so far.

Throughout, it has repeatedly been stated there is resistance, denial and rejection of change caused by fear, misinformation and misdirection. Not to mention the attraction of the toys (unnecessary consumer goods) of this world. Our needs and wants have become perceived as one and the same and the outcome of this – consumption of goods and services - is a major factor driving climate change.

Individual Input

Throughout this book, the argument has been leading to a point where we might come to appreciate we are in our current circumstances because our evolution has made us who we are.

Our exciting next evolutionary step then, is to overcome the last remnants of our primal urges and realise our potential as enlightened, compassionate, friendly, caring people who do not need our egos stroked by the baubles of mass production. Rather, we might fall in love with the natural world which offers so much more and does so free of charge.

But the question still remains, how do we redistribute the wealth inequity we see in our world?' Well, suppose for a moment, personal fortunes (above an agreed upper threshold) were redistributed at the end of one's life. That is, we restructure inheritance laws and look to redistribute wealth upon death as suggested by Philippe Van Parijs in his 1995 book Real Freedom for All. This notion will likely raise blood pressure and anxiety if not outright anger from those who hold onto the world's wealth but it needs to be done nonetheless.

Redistribution of wealth upon death offers a means to satisfy the human desire to accumulate, and display success, and even display an active superiority complex, but at the same time ensure eventual redistribution and fairness. After death, when an individual can no longer be affected by circumstance, emotion or intellect, wealth (above an agreed threshold) accumulated over a lifetime would become available for the common good. A charitable donation if you like. The mechanism is not important – the outcome is.

Like going to the moon or creating a new tax, we can work out the detail very quickly once we decide to do so. The important issue is to start considering if we can bring ourselves to do it.

Taking the argument one step further, we might ask whether the right of inheritance complies with the notion and laws of equal opportunity. That is, a child born into inherited wealth clearly has an unequal opportunity over one who is not. Also, social mobility suggests one is free to move up the social ladder, but equal opportunity suggests downward movement should also be possible. As discussed in an article in The Economist (2013), entitled 'Repairing the Rungs on the Ladder,' inheritance denies the opportunity for downward movement, thus we can conclude inheritance actually restricts social mobility.

That argument aside, and regardless of the moral and legal implications, and it is clear there would be considerable debate, the accumulation of large portions of available wealth by a very few people is mostly made possible by inheritance rights. Even partially redistributing this centralised capital would provide substantially improved social equity and would bolster our reputation of civility by addressing the problem of poverty in our world. It would also churn cash within our economies making them more stable and reliable.

According to a study by Stutz & Mintzer (2006) in which well-being and affluence were compared, there is an inverse relationship between affluence (above the poverty line) and measures of well-being, meaning more wealth does not lead to higher reported happiness. There were several reasons for this which support the overall argument for wealth distribution and consumption restraint presented throughout these pages.

Firstly, rising affluence does not inherently satisfy, but rather it fuels the drive-for-more as we seek ever new highs. In this process, our ego strives to be separate and superior and consumer goods are seen as a means to achieve the ego driven higher status. For example, being able to afford a motor vehicle once demonstrated personal success. Today, having a motor vehicle is not sufficient because having a vehicle is common. Today, status via vehicle ownership is only available if the vehicle is considered substantially more valuable than the norm. This circular and inflationary process places enormous financial stress on the consumer to work more, earn more and subsequently, spend more.

Secondly, Stutz and Mintzer (2006) also demonstrated the process of endless goal resetting as being detrimental to well-being. As one goal becomes the social norm, new goals are set to ever higher standards. Again, the life pressure of attaining these goals diminishes reported well-being. This cycle of achievement and goal resetting sees baseline affluence targets also continuously rising.

Third, measures of dietary health follow a similar, but opposite trend. As affluence increases, obesity rises. The causes are interesting and overeating alone does not explain the increase in obesity. Obesity is a result of a process of affluence reducing available exercise time and healthy food preparation time, as well as, increased pressure to perform, plus increased working hours. Reduced food preparation time increases junk food intake, which means higher, fat, salt and sugar intake. At the same time, increased stress leads to increased spending as a therapy. In turn, increased spending requires increased working hours and individual health suffers accordingly.

The Stutz and Mintzer study included thirty OECD countries and arrived at a needs-based income figure of just US $22,000 (2006). Affluence beyond this point provided only marginal increases in well-being ratings as indicated by life expectancy, time spent in waged labour, environmental health, personal health, income equality and happiness.

The environmental impact of overconsumption is apparent and the health effects have been documented. However, there remains the issue of how to provide a means to escape overconsumption and the endless affluence goal-setting loop, in a practical and achievable manner.

Chapter Twenty

An Alternative Lifestyle

T o the extent that individuals are the fabric of corporations, governments and society as a whole, individuals
are the source of change to a healthier happier world. To
assist our decision making Stutz and Mintzer offer the following framework for alternative work practices that would
alleviate much of the stress in our lives and our impact on the
environment. The list is not definitive or complete. It is a
suggested starting point for discussion and should be considered in light of James Speths' changes to corporate law set out
in the previous chapter.

1. A shorter working week for individuals. Twenty, thirty
    or forty rather than sixty-plus hours, for example, would
    mean more time to enjoy the benefits of income. Also, re-
    duced working hours for individuals, or in other words
    job sharing, would increase the opportunity for the un-
    employed to fill the labour demand associated with
    shorter working weeks, thus reducing unemployment.
    The cycle of work-to-spend-to-work would be broken,
    meaning the habit of spending to de-stress from work
    pressures would be unwound.
2. With a shorter working week, health issues would be

addressed, firstly by a reduction in fast-food consumption, and secondly, via increased exercise due to increased time being available for both food preparation and exercise.

3. Fewer working hours would mean better productivity. Labour shortages would then drive up wages without extra hours. Reduced economic growth would occur due to labour shortages and/or interruptions, thus reducing carbon emissions.

4. Reduced health system costs would be seen as a result of lowered stress, more exercise and less money to spend on junk foods. There would be less need to spend on junk food because there would be more time to prepare food in a relaxed environment.

5. Crime rates would reduce due to increased employment and reduction of the affluence gap between the disadvantaged and the affluent. Disrupting the cycle of work-and-spend would disrupt over-consumption and over-production.

6. Less work would mean more family time rather than more spending time, hence a subsequent slowing of economic growth and its associated environmental costs.

7. Fewer working hours could be combined with a higher minimum wage and increased social spending to balance the ledger.

Again, this is an incomplete list designed as a start point for development of a more comprehensive approach. However, it is based on available published research on the subject.

Also, it is worth saying again, how readily our kind is able to fund popular projects and achieve amazing results such as putting a man on the moon. Why would we think it any less achievable to alter our economic system as one step in saving our planet? Actually, it's probably better to say we would be saving ourselves!

Back to the Future

At the start of this book, it was argued we have not progressed past blood sacrifice and false god worship. Historically, shamans, witch doctors, priests and chieftains all used manipulation of beliefs to control their followers. Looking at our world today, little change can be seen given many people now worship the econo-god and its unholy trinity - growth, jobs and the economy.

We kill innocent millions of soldiers to 'defend' democracy, but really this is the rich defending their wealth as has always been the case. Also, we speak of being 'more civilised' but really all this means is we are technologically different. And, we cannot legitimately claim technological 'progress' when our technologies are destroying our world. Progress implies being better, but clearly more and more pollution caused by ever changing technologies is not 'better'.

The truly amazing thing is that, as a population, we are more educated today than ever and yet we remain collared and blinkered wage slaves. Theoretically, education should make us less susceptible to manipulation and yet here we are still worshipping Gods and idols – all bow to the ministers of jobs, growth and the economy. It seems we are afflicted by a compulsion to believe in something or someone outside ourselves to find meaning in life. What underpins this eagerness to believe? Or, more importantly, why do we accept the presence of distractions and illusions which set out to deceive us?

According to Andrew Newberg MD (2006), in his publication, Why we Believe What we Believe, a 'belief' is a means to satisfy a hard-wired human need to understand: when understanding is conflicted by contradictory information, stress results. Then it follows that attaching meaning to a belief whether it is flawed or not, is a pain-avoidance or stress reduction strategy. This fits neatly with the contention that primal drives operate to intercept our intellectual capacity to discern. That is, we are driven by a base code which says, 'If it feels good do it' and even if it only promises to feel good later, do it anyway. In fact, in some instances it seems even if there is no reward, we still do it and then convince ourselves what we do must feel good. For instance, my first drink of beer told me I hated the taste of the stuff. However, like many others, I still drink it!

Nevertheless, it is being educated that allows our intellect to overcome the 'feel good' base code we are afflicted with. As discussed repeatedly, the problem issue is the content and delivery of our education and media at present. Learning to consume more than we need (which is what our education system teaches at present) is hardly valuable in environmental terms. Nor will it reduce our stress levels.

While no scientific evidence supports the existence of any God, many remain faithful to religion because it provides an escape from the pain associated with doubt. That is not to say faith and belief are intrinsically wrong or bad - far from it. On the upside, belief in a cause is a powerful driver and can achieve a lot when used pragmatically. If our need to believe is so powerful, why do we not place our faith in the church of the natural world and worship the environment? After all, it is surely the only observable and reliable faith that will give us life year, after year, after year.

It would seem we humans worship unobservable gods because we can fabricate whatever belief system around that god we need to suit our self-interest at the time. However, these structures (churches etc) are composed of ordinary people with ordinary susceptibility to temptation, and yet we place massive trust in them – usually at our own peril. We go to war and commit unbelievable atrocities in the name of our gods. We make laws to punish crime in civilian life, but throw those laws out the door when we go to war, usually at the first sign of a threat to our sovereignty, politics, religion, or economy. Blatant law breaking is one thing, but the more insidious crime is manipulation of a populations beliefs and the practice is rampant today.

The most prolific perpetrators are those who hold positions of power and control over our media and its content. We have seen also, that growth of economies relies on an unwavering increase in population. To ensure this growth, a belief in the sanctity of human life over all other existence is perpetuated in our media and education. Finding comfort in the belief humanity has the right to exist, regardless of the cost, seems somehow to comfort us as it resolves the inner conflict of needing to feel superior. Population size is our ultimate enemy though. Were the population of the Earth just 1.5 billion, we would be hard pressed to create sufficient environmental damage to have any significant impact. The multiplier effect of seven billion people should be self-explanatory.

Population

Population research demonstrates the maximum supportable population of planet Earth varies depending on the level of affluence of the population. Ross McCluneys' 2004 paper titled, How Many People Should the Earth Support, reports that given an average global affluence equivalent to middle-class Western societies, the maximum sustainable population is two billion, through to around forty billion if we accept North

African living standards.

Currently, there are about seven billion of us, which is in the red zone for sustainability assuming we continue to aspire to a high standard of living for all. Interestingly, if Earth's CO_2 production were around 25% of what it is today, or about the amount 1.5 billion humans would produce, then our global warming problems would not be occurring.

What would it take to reduce our population to 1.5 billion? The first option is simply to stand by and wait because the environment is likely to create the change on our behalf. Alternatively, there is the option to manage our population back to sustainable numbers.

Natural attrition and a program of birth control would be effective and are certainly more attractive than catastrophic population crash due to global food and water shortages, or dramatically rising sea levels. Given that medical technology has enabled our population explosion, it may well be the medical technology of contraception, which will see us survive the future.

Whatever the approach, we are little different from a pond of breeding fish, in that, we breed and breed regardless of the fact that sooner or later we will overpopulate and all but a few of us will die out due to a lack of environment to support us. And the process will start all over again, assuming there are two fish left. Again, we ask the question, 'What the heck is life all about?' It seems, despite all our self-proclaimed difference to the rest of the natural world, we are demonstrating that ultimately we have a far less useful approach to surviving than most other species in that we find it impossible to self-regulate. The opportunity and capacity exists, but the question is, do we have the will to deploy our inherent skills?

Chapter Twenty One

Toward New Values

James Speth cites US Presidential science adviser John Gibbons, who puts the need for a new goal for humanity this way: *'If we don't change direction, we'll end up where we're headed. And right now, we're headed for a ruined planet.'*

Working toward a new society may well cross the boundary of what appears possible. Oceanographer, Dr Bob Ballard made the point when he said words to the effect of, the momentum of human society may well be too great for any significant change to occur.

However, considering human society has undergone unbelievable change since our meagre beginnings as nomadic hunter-gatherers, and our societies continue to change every day, change is the norm and is certainly nothing to fear. We have faced plagues and famine, wars, the threat of nuclear holocaust and near extinction events, yet here we are. Then it is clear the potential for change to protect us from global warming is present if not active. Also, many of the solutions are close at hand. We just have to decide to implement them which is perhaps what Dr Ballard was referring to. That is, are we capable of changing direction?

To facilitate the needed change, the hunt for personal power and national power needs to be reconsidered. Also, the manner in which we settle disputes is destructive and costly on all fronts and shows little if any maturity or wisdom.

For instance, not so long ago war was waged in Iraq. Putting aside all the well-documented reasons for going to war, consider another option. Instead of dropping bombs and waging war, we send plane-loads of metaphoric chocolates and blankets. In other words, we send goodwill to the people of Iraq - not bullets or exploitation. In return, we ask only for a fair share of their resources and offer equal value in return for what we want. I have to wonder if the people of Iraq would consider that a radical idea!

Also, rather than accepting the unfounded justifications for conflict offered up by the warmongers of the day, we open a dialogue and offer friendship, peace and cooperation. Now, let's assume that this approach ultimately fails. What has it cost us compared to what actually transpired? I suggest it's very little.

What is the cost of chocolates and blankets compared to civilians and soldiers' lives? It's hard to imagine any nation on Earth, faced with impending military invasion not wanting a peaceful solution. Yes, the politics behind the Iraq wars were complicated and the situation was probably irretrievable by the time the war began. And, I also accept the actions of a very small number of real extremists need to be dealt with. But it is also conceivable that had there been no prior unjust interference, the outcome may well have been very different. Chocolates and blankets are a metaphor for a peaceful and cooperative approach based on respect, which is a far cry from false accusations of hiding weapons of mass destruction.

The time for conquest by war is over. Our planet can no longer sustain the impact of our modern technologies of battle.

Throughout, this book has looked at social institutions, politics and corporate operations and has made some suggestions for change. Those changes have (purposely) been from a slightly left, or unconventional, perspective. That's because the main problem with trying to implement changes to mainstream thinking is that the changes are often consumed by the very process they are attempting to affect. To achieve change, there is usually a long and energy-consuming process of consultation and often a watering-down of original intent which is aimed at maintaining the status quo. The catch-cry is, for goodness sake, let's talk about change, but my god don't actually do anything. Many initiatives do not survive this watering down process. Hence, what we start with must be as radical as possible.

To be fair, on the surface our social institutions do appear to manage some change over time. Still, too many questions remain unanswered and too many problems remain unresolved.

Are the fundamental beliefs which underpin our social institutions any more advantageous to our survival today than they were a hundred years ago? Some mainstream thinkers would argue in the affirmative. The observable evidence tells another story.

The overwhelming body of evidence tells us we are seeing change for the sake of change, rather than improvement lending itself to systemic or fundamental differences. Future change initiatives will require a new level of mature thinking.

Mature Thought

Being capable of mature thought is perhaps one of our greatest hopes but at present is one of our most underutilised skills. Is this a bold statement? That is, is it too offensive to suggest most do not employ mature thinking on a day to day basis, or is it a logical conclusion given the state of our world? Perhaps a definition will help soothe any irritation. Mature thinking is a demonstrable ability to consider and accept the validity of contradictory ideas simultaneously, as well as, being able to see the merits (or otherwise) of ideas without falling into confusion and indecision, or anger. Thought without confusion is made possible when emotional reactions are cast aside, as much as is humanly possible.

Personal maturity is the ability to change direction, opinion, or attitude without a sense of loss, or a sense of letting go of personal investment of energy, or having wasted time arriving at a point of view. At the same time, we must acknowledge a sense of loss, or having wasted time, are powerful drivers of emotional reactions for we humans. This is where mature thought comes to the fore.

In practical terms, mature thinkers do not become emotionally attached to beliefs. Rather, they remain flexible and reflective and are free to choose to change at any time. In proverbial terms, we can say, it does not matter how far down the wrong road you have travelled, it is never too late to turn back.

Also, many of us believe there must be one right answer to any issue, which, of course, is rarely the case particularly when facing more complex issues. Nothing is as simple as black and white for emotionally charged creatures like us.

Nevertheless, mature thinkers will typically question and seek understanding that is beyond the face value of an event or information encountered and see an array of options. This is good news because having options to choose from reduces stress and leads to discussion. Instilling mature thinking then might be the aim of our education system if humanity is to survive itself in the future.

The task of acquiring mature thinking is not in itself particularly difficult. Regardless, there has to be a will to do so: a will driven by a discerning choice which is free of fear and a sense of missing out, and which uses an appreciation of how short the time left to make these changes truly is.

And so, we have come full circle.

The human differences identified at the start, those differences which have worked against us to create our current circumstances, are the same differences which will allow us to succeed, albeit by adding a fifth human difference, namely, mature thought. This rounds out our set of human differences to the rest of the natural world and it offers a path to a bright future. Mature thought would help us see past profits and short term self-interest.

Now our list of human uniqueness (in no particular order) reads as follows:

1. **Mature thought**: an intellectual capacity to let go of past practices without suffering debilitating emotional reactions - to see the value in questioning and rejecting the distractions and illusions created by our economic activity, and appreciating the difference between intrinsic and perceived value which clouds our judgement between human needs and human wants.

2. The ability to **discern**: the ability to 'recognise' or 'find' meaning when presented with information that is difficult, complex or where an accurate meaning is obscured. This is an intellectual process where evolution is seeing our intellect slowly take over from our primal urges.

3. An awareness of **time** which leads to a sense of mortality. This is an intellectual process.

4. A **biological** desire to reproduce or be productive. This is a primal biological drive.

5. Human **will**, or our drive to have our opinion succeed.

This is a primal biological drive somewhat moderated by intellect.

The brightest future for humanity lies in separating beneficial science from that which depletes, degrades, or otherwise damages our natural world and in turn creates volatile economics and degrades our life experience and our survival prospects. Deploying our human attributes is the path to success on this front, but with the caveat that time is short.

Is it reasonable to say there is an urgency to re-assess our priorities as a species, society and as individuals? That is, that a reassessment would be best undertaken with respect to the finite nature of nature itself and then move as quickly as possible to embrace anything resembling sustainability. Is our purpose as sentient beings to self-destruct or to evolve our societies into something better than we have now? In order to find out what our ultimate purpose is, we need time. Not just a few hours or days, but hundreds and thousands of years because this is the time scale of evolution. To have this time we need to protect our natural world so that it continues to provide for us.

Given what climate science and the damage from pollution is telling us, it is clear enough that there is no time for further meaningless chatter. We already know what we are doing threatens our survival. We do not require more information on this front. What we require is to find a mature line of thought, as well as leaders who are capable of mature action. And, leaders who will pursue a program of change which relentlessly removes any facet of our existence which poses a threat to our long-term survival. In this, they will need support from you and I, the voting public.

Above all else, I suggest we seek out facts over convenient half-truths and relish the joy of living simply, rather than living to consume. If we do this, the rest will take care of itself.

Chapter Twenty Two

Closing

To finish, I want to leave you with two stories which capture a sense of the new thinking needed to break out of old habits.

The First Story:

Once upon a time there was a rich and powerful king. He commanded a kingdom, vast and wealthy. In the kingdom were all manner of people, undergoing all manner of activities, all of which were devoted to the king.

In the kingdom, there were priests and they worshipped their God. They called themselves Christians and practiced Christianity.

The commandments were simple and numbered only ten.

Happy lives would result from following the rules.

One day one of the local workers came to the temple of worship and saw money changers working their magic amongst the priests and pilgrims.

When the man questioned the Christian values that were on display and threw out the money changers from the temple, the response was simple enough. After passing judgement, they nailed him to a cross calling him a heretic and left him there to die.

His name was Jesus.

These are the same Christian values espoused in our democratic politics today. This is not a slur against Christianity, faith or belief though. The story speaks for itself: we have a long history of placing personal agendas ahead of the common good.

The story of Jesus and how that man was treated now seem antiquated and relegated to a distant past.

Still, it is not difficult to find examples in our more recent history of similar treatment of revolutionary people. Nelson Mandela spent most of his life in prison for speaking his mind, before eventually leading his nation.

The Second Story:

During the 1970's, a television current affairs program in Western Australia set up a challenge. A squad of Army personnel and a group of local Aboriginals were set the task of travelling across the outback from a town to a remote location. The distance was not exceptionally far but covered harsh terrain. Both parties were given the destination and they all set-off.

It was not long before the Army personnel lost sight of the Aboriginals. Thinking the Aboriginal group must know a shorter route, the army moved faster and in a straight line by compass.

This route took them through a nasty swamp, across ridges and through valleys. One of the soldiers had to be airlifted out with heat stroke, but the others eventually made it to the destination, albeit they were exhausted.

For some time, no one could find the group of Aboriginals.

Now, you have to remember the object of the exercise was

to see if local native knowledge was better than maps and compasses for navigating the Australian outback. Eventually, the group of Aboriginals was located resting, swimming and fishing at a nearby Billabong (water hole).

When asked why they did not go to the destination, they replied, 'We are still on our way.' They were quite serious. They simply did not see the point in putting themselves through the hardship of a forced march.

What is the point to this story? The Australian Aboriginals have a history of some sixty thousand years of sustainable living, and yet here we are facing environmental catastrophe after less the three hundred years of white settlement in Australia. It does seem our way of life is less survivable than our predecessors.

A Final Word!

We have seen how our day-to-day life is influenced by the evolutionary aspect of our mind which seeks to consume and operates with self-interest at heart. Knowing this, is it reasonable to say that, in our modern era, a time when we claim to be civilised, we might expect to operate more from intellect rather than instinct.

In my view, that transition goes a long way towards answering the question, 'What the heck is life all about?' It seems we are a complex mix of instinctual evolutionary leftovers and emerging intellectual adaptations. Of course, it is difficult for us to override our instinctual drives from day to day. After all, these drives are innately part of who we are.

Perhaps, at some point in the distant future (should we survive that long) evolution (or genetic modification) will remove, or at least diminish, our primal urges.

Until then the best we can do is be aware, be informed, and

apply our capacity to discern and our capacity to apply wisdom to the task of defending ourselves from our own evolutionary heritage.

We no longer need to hunt the occasional deer or gather nuts and berries.

We don't need to hunt and gather consumer goods and affluence in the manner we do today either.

Being surrounded by distractions and illusions of our own making means it is particularly difficult not to consume, but we should, I think, try.

Perhaps, then, we might choose to surround ourselves with (and I speak metaphorically) fruits and vegetables rather than chocolate, salt and fat. But now I am repeating myself, and we can't have that because I might start sounding like the economic paradigm.

Thank you for reading.

The End.

Bibliography

Adams, D, 2002, The American Peace Movements. Global Movement for a Culture of Peace.
http://www.culture-of-peace.info/apm/title-page.html

Alex, D, 2014, World War II Statistics.
https://www.secondworldwarhistory.com/world-war-2-statistics.asp

Alperovitz, G, 2005, America Beyond Capitalism: Reclaiming our wealth, our liberty and our democracy.
John Wiley and Sons, Inc., Hoboken, New Jersey.

Ancient greece.com, Socrates.
http://www.ancientgreece.com/s/people/Socrates/

Anderson, A, 2014, Many Animals can think Abstractly. The Scientific American, May 1 2014.
https://www.scientificamerican.com/article/many-animals-can-think-abstractly/

Annenberg Foundation, 2013, Bio Diversity Decline. Online Text Book.
http:/www.learner.org

Asia Times Online August 13, 1999.
http://www.atimes.com/oceania/AH13Ah01.htm

Atherton, J, 2011, Learning and Teaching: Behaviorism
http://www.learningandteaching.info/learning/behaviour.htm

Australian Collaboration, 2012, Role-government-FactSheet.pdf
http://www.australiancollaboration.com.au

Australian Conservation Council 2010, Wetlands: underpinning a robust rural economy. A briefing paper on the economic benefits of Australian wetlands. Hattah Lakes case study.

Australian Treasury, 2011, Architecture of Australia's Tax and Transfer System
http://www.taxreview.treasury.gov.au/content/Paper.aspx-?doc=html/publications /papers/ report/section_2-03.htm

Bacchus, S, Alabama 2013
http://bachus.house.gov/index.php?option=com_content&view=arti-cle&i d=106&Itemid=97

Beeder, S, 1996, Valuing the Environment Engineering World, December 1996, pp.12-14.

Baker, T, 2002, Embracing Risk. University of Chicago Press.
Becker, E, 1973,
The Denial of Death. New York. The Free Press.

Berwin, B, 2014, USA: Judge rules against Arch Coal mine expansion due to impact on climate change. Business & Human Rights Resource Centre.

Bordo M.D. 1981, The Classical Gold Standard: Some Lessons for Today, Federal Reserve Bank of St. Louis Review 64(5) (May), 2-17. (1984).

Bourton, J 2009, Logging 'caused Nazca collapse.'
http://news.bbc.co.uk/earth/hi/earth_news/newsid_8334000/8 334257. Stm

Bowles, S, Edwards, R and Roosevelt, F, 2005, Understanding Capitalism 3rd Edition.

Buffett,W, 2011. Sunday, August 14th, Warren Buffett says the super-rich pay lower tax rates than others. New York Times.

CATO Institute, 2002: How Washington Funded the Taliban, by Ted Carpenter
https://www.cato.org/publications/commentary/how-washington-funded-taliban

CBS News, July 28, 2013. 80 Percent of US Adults Face Near-Poverty, Unemployment, survey finds.
ttps://www.cbsnews.com/news/80-percent-of-us-adults-face-near-poverty-unemployment-survey-finds/

CGER 1996 University of Iowa Center for Global and Regional Environmental Research.
http://www.cgrer.uiowa.edu/education/ssep/sealevel.html

Cherry, K, 2012, Theories of Personality.
https://www.verywell.com/defensemechanisms-2795960#step3

Chace, C. (2016), The Economic Singularity: Artificial Intelligence and the Death of Capitalism. Three C's.

Chicago Tribune, 1986, Mary T Schmich. A Stopwatch on Shopping. December 24 edition.

Cleary, T 2005, Translator of The Art of War by Sun Tzu Mass Market Paperback – January 11,2005.

Coleman J & Ferejohn J 1986, Democracy and Social Choice: Symposium Paper Chicago Journals Vol 97, No 1.

Cook, J, et al, (2013), Consensus on consensus: a synthesis of consensus estimates on human-caused global warming. Environmental Research Letters, Volume 8, Number 2.

Corning, P, Ph.D. 2000, Biological Adaptation in Human Societies
Journal of Bioeconomics 2:41-86 (2000)

Corner, A, 2012, Psychology: Science Literacy and Climate Views
Nature Climate Change 2 710-711 September 2012.

Dangerfield, W, 2007, The Mystery of Easter Island
http://www.smithsonianmag.com/people-places/
The_Mystery_of_Easter_Island.html

Dawkins, R, 1976, The Selfish Gene, Oxford University Press.

Dumhoff, G, 2006, Who Rules America, Quoted in JG 2008, The
Bridge at the End of the World, Capitalism, the Environment and
Crossing from Crisis to Sustainability.

Dutton, K, 2012, What Psychopaths each Us about How to
Succeed The Scientific American, Vol 307, issue 4, 18 Sept.
http://www.scientificamerican.Com/article/what-psychopaths-
teach-us-about-how-to-succeed/

Economist ,The, 2013, Repairing the rungs on the ladder
http://www.economist.Com/news/leaders/21571417-how-
prevent-virtuous-meri-tocracyentrenching-itself-top-repairing-
rungs

Ehnert, I, 2008, Sustainable Human Resource Management: A
conceptual and exploratory analysis from a paradox perspective.
Physica Verlag. A Springer Company.

Ehrlich, P. and Ehrlich, A, 1990, The Population Bomb. The
Electronic Journal of Sustainable Development (2009) 1(3).

Elliot, S, 2008, What is Ego? Coherence Newsletter. July 2008.
http://www.coherence.com

Fleischmann Rev. Robert R, 1989, The Value of Human Life. http://www.christianliferesources.com/article/the-value-of-human-life-359

FAO Food and Agriculture Org of the United Nations 2005, Some 36 countries Worldwide face serious food shortages, says FAO report. http://www.fao.org/Newsroom/en/news/2005/90082/

Free Dictionary www.thefreedictionary.com/progress

Freidman M, 1993, Why Government is the Problem. Essays in Public Policy, no. 39. Stanford, California: Hoover Institution Press, 1993.

Fritscher, L, 2011, Cognitive Theory- Phobia's http://phobias.about.com/od/glossary/g/cognitivethedef.htm

Gill, N, S, 2012, Reasons for the Fall of Rome http://ancienthistory.about.com/od/fallofrome/tp/022509Fallof RomeReasons.htm

Global Policy Forum, 2005-14, US and British Support for Hussein Regime http://www.globalpolicy.org/iraq-conflict-the-historical-background-/us-and-british-support-for-huss-regime.html

Greening Australia 2012, Corporate Responsibility. http://www.greeningaustralia.org.au/our-projects/corporate-responsibility

Grohol, J, 2012, What's the Purpose of the Fight or Flight Response? http://psychcentral.com/blog/archives/2012/12/04/whats-the-purpose-of-the-fight-orflight-response/

Griskevicius, V Cantú, S and van Vugt, M, 2012, The Evolutionary Bases for Sustainable Behavior: Implications for Marketing, Policy and Social Entrepreneurship, Journal of Public Policy & Marketing Vol 31(1) 115-128

Harari, Y, N, (2015), Homo Deus: A Brief History of Tomorrow. Signal Books.

Harris, K,1995, Collected Quotes from Albert Einstein
http://rescompstanford.edu/~cheshire/EinsteinQuotes.html

Hansen, K 2010, Carbon Dioxide Controls Earth's Temperature NASA Earth Science News Team.
http://www.nasa.gov/topics/earth/features/CO2temperature.html

Happer, W, 2011, Will increased carbon dioxide levels actually benefit the planet?
http://hockeyschtick.blogspot.com.au/2011/08/prof-will-happer-will-increased-carbon.html

Hedges, C, 2011, Empire of Illusion: The end of literacy and the triumph of spectacle. Nation Books, New York.

Hickman, K, 2014, World War I: The Christmas Truce of 1914
http://militaryhistory.about.com/od/worldwari/p/xmastruce.htm

Huxley, A, 1949, 1984 vs. Brave New World.
http://www.lettersofnot.com/2012/03/1984-v-brave-new-world.html

Ioannou & Serafeim, 2010, What Drives Corporate Social Performance? International Evidence from Social, Environmental and Governance Scores. Working Paper Harvard Business School 11-016

Ippolito, R, 1992, Consumer Reaction to Measures of Poor Quality: Evidence from the Mutual Fund Industry. Journal of Law and Economics Vol. 35, No. 1 (Apr., 1992), pp. 45-70.

Jackson, G, 1971, Blood in My Eye, https://archive.org/stream/GeorgeJacksonBloodInMyEye_20151 2/George%20Jackson%20-%20Blood-in-My-Eye_djvu.txt

James, W, 1887 What is Instinct? Reproduced in The Mead Project. http://www.brocku.ca/MeadProject/James/James_1887.html

Jeanes I, 1996, Forecast and Solution: Grappling With the Nuclear, a Trilogy for Everyone. Pocahontas Press.

Keen S, 2011, Debunking Economics: The Naked Emperor dethroned? Zed Books. London. New York.

Kennedy, P, 1987, The Rise and Fall of the Great Powers: Economic Change and Military Conflict From 1500 to 200

Kohn, A, 2003-9. Rescuing our Schools from Tougher Standards. http://www.alfiekohn.org/stdtest.htm#nul

Layton, J, 2005, Fight or Flight. http://science.howstuffworks.com/life/fear2.h

Lauder, J, 2016, 19 year-old uni student Maddy couldn't tell you the last thing she bought. ABC Radio, Tripple J, The Hack. http://www.abc.net.au/triplej/programs/hack/fashion-addiction-onionmania/7430164

Lauder, J, 2016. Oniomania: when shopping becomes an addiction. TripleJ Hack.May 20. http://www.abc.net.au/triplej/programs/hack/fashion-addiction-onionmania/7430164

Leitenberg, M, 2006, Deaths in Wars and Conflicts in the 20th Century Cornell University Peace Studies Program Occasional Paper #29, 3rd ed.

Lovell, T, The Fall Of The Soviet Union: Whys And Wherefores
http://www.coldwar.org/articles/90s/links.asp

Makan, A, 2013, Shale gas boom now visible from space Financial Times January 27.
http://www.ft.com/cms/s/0/d2d2e83c-6721-11e2-a805-00144feab49a.Html#axzz36fvEKPZP

Mason, P, (2015), Postcapitalism: A guide to our Future. Allan Lane Publishing.

McCluney, R, 2004, How Many People Should the Earth Support?
http://www.ecofuture.org/pop/rpts/mccluney_maxpop.html

Mental Help, 2007, Patricelli, K: Death and Dying Introduction.
https://www.mentalhelp.net/articles/death-and-dying-introduction/

Mills, C, 1957 The Power Elite.
New York: Harper.

Monbiot, G, 2013, Bang Goes the Theory, January 14, 2013
www.monbiot.com

Monbiot, G, 2014, A Gunpowder Plot Against Democracy, November 7, 2014
www.monbiot.com

Monbiot, G, 2014, The Insatiable God, November 19, 2014
www.monbiot.com

Monbiot, G, 2015, Work-Force, June 09, 2015
www.monbiot.com

Morales, F, 2013, US Has been preparing to turn America into a military dictatorship.
http://whatreallyhappened.com/WRHARTICLES/suppression.ht
ml

Museum of Australian Democracy, No Date, Defining Democracy
http:moadoph.gov.au/democracy/defining-democracy

Newberg, A, 2006, Why We Believe What We Believe. Free Press.
New York.

Erwin, S, I. Top Five Threats to National Security in the Coming
Decade.

National Defense Magazine Nov 2012,
http://digital.nationaldefensemagazine.org/publication/?i=4342
15#{"issue_id":434215,"page":32}

New World Encyclopedia: Aztec Civilization.
http://www.newworldencyclopedia.org/entry/Aztec_Civilization

Oreskes N, 2004, The Scientific Consensus on Climate Change
Science, December 2004: Vol. 306no. 5702p. 1686.

Peace Pledge Union, 2014, War and Peace. What's it all about?
http://www.ppu.org.uk/learn/infodocs/st_war_peace.html

Peterson, M, Dr. 2009, The Purpose of Schools.
Whole School Consortium,
http://www.wholeschooling.net/WS/ WSPrncples/WS%200%
20purpose% 20schls.html

Radford, T, 2001: Scientists Warn of Sixth Great Extinction of Life
Guardian UK 29 Nov 2001

Reeskens, T, Wright. M, 2011, Subjective Well-Being and National Satisfaction: Taking Seriously the "Proud of What?" Question. *Psychological Science*, 2011; 22 (11): 1460 DOI: 10.1177/0956797611419673

Rockmore T, 2011, Before and After 9/11: A Philosophical Examination of Globalization, Terror and History. Bloomsbury Academic; 1 edition (April 21,2011).

Rosenman, R, Fort, R, Budd, W, 1988, Perceptions, fear and economic loss: an Application of prospect theory to environmental decision making. Kluwer Academic Publishers, Dordrecht. Policy Sciences 21:327-350.

Schumacher, M, R. A. Werner, H. A. J, Meijer, H. G, Jansen, W. A, Brand, H,Geilmann and R. E. M. Neubert, 2011: Oxygen isotopic signature of CO2 from combustion processes. Received: 21 July 2008 – Published in Atmos. Chem. Phys. Discuss.: 5 November 2008. Revised: 2 February 2011 – Accepted: 5 February 2011 – Published: 16 February 2011. http://www.atmos-chem-physnet/11/1473/2011/acp-11-1473-2011.pdf

Skeptical Science 2012, Climategate-CRU-emails-hacked http://www.skepticalscience.com/Climategate-CRU-emails-hacked.htm

Speth, J,G, 2008, The Bridge at the End of the World, Capitalism, the Environment and Crossing from Crisis to Sustainability.

Srini 2010, What is Ego? http://jnanagni.com/2010/07/what-is-ego

Snyder, M, 20120, 24 Outrageous facts about taxes in the United States that will blow your mind. http://theeconomiccollapseblog.com/archives/24-outrageous-facts-about-taxes-inthe-united-states-that-will-blow-your-mind

Stutz, J and Erica Mintzer: Tellus Institute June 2006, The Affluence Paradox: More Money Is Not Making Us Happier. A review of
statistical evidence.

The Tax Justice Network, Matti Khonenen, How tax havens cause
poverty and undermine welfare states.
http://peopleandplanet.org/ dl/taxhappens.pdf

Tolle, E, 2011, The Power of Now. Hodder Paperback.

Thomas, P, Nain, Z, 2004, Who Owns the Media?: Global Trends
and Local Resistance. Zed Books Ltd, New York.

United Nations Food and Agriculture Organization 2010, The
State of Food Insecurity in the World (2012)
http://www.fao.org/hunger/en/

Van Parijs, P, 1995, Real Freedom for All: What (if anything) can
justify capitalism? Oxford University Press.

Veblem, T, 2005, The Vested Interests And the Common Man.
Cosimo Classics; abridged edition (May 15, 2005).

White, L, 2011, Early Warning Signs,
http://www.charteredaccountants.com.au/News-
Media/Charter/ Charter- articles/Economy/2011-03-Early-
WarningSigns.aspx).

Wikipedia, Ok Tedi Mine,
http://en.wikipedia.org/wiki/Ok_Tedi_Mine

World Bank 2013, Make Climate Change a Priority,
http://www.worldbank.org/en/news/opinion/2013/01/25/ope
d_-_make_climatechangeapriority

Being Human: A Question of Survival

World Health Organization, 2014: 7 million deaths in 2012 due to air pollution Western Pacific Region, the world's worst for air pollution, http://www.wprwho.int/china/mediacentre/releases/2014/20140325/ en/

Yale University 2012, Psychology: Science literacy and climate views. Nature Climate Change 2, 710–711, 2012.

Yale University, 2002, I'll see it when I believe it - A simple model of cognitive consistency. Cowles Foundation Discussion Paper No. 1352, http://cowles.econ.yale.edu/P/cd/d13b/d1352.pdf

Yen, H, 2013, 80 Percent Of U.S. Adults Face Near-Poverty, Unemployment: Survey. Huffington Post. Cited in http://www.huffingtonpost.com/2013/07/28poverty-unemployment-rates_n_3666594.html Also cited in: Global Entertainment Media, A Critical Introduction, Lee Artz 2015,John Wiley and Sons.

Ylvisaker, M, 2006 What Are Concrete And Abstract Thinking? http://www.projectlearnet.org/tutorials/concrete_vs_abstract_thinking.html

Zen Gardner, 2014, Patriotism vs. Nationalism – The Deliberately Blurred Line. http://www.zengardner.com/patriotism-vs-nationalism-the-deliberatelyblurred-line/ http://smokereality.blogspot.com.au/2012/07/patriotism-vs-nationalism-deliberately.html?m=0

Zimmer, K 2008, How Smart is the Octopus? http://www.slate.com/articles/health_and_science/science/2008/06/how_smart_is_the_octopus.html

306

www.ingramcontent.com/pod-product-compliance
Lightning Source LLC
Chambersburg PA
CBHW020604270326
41927CB00005B/171